JACQUES CŒUR

MERCHANT PRINCE OF THE
MIDDLE AGES

JACQUES CŒUR.

JACQUES CŒUR

MERCHANT PRINCE OF THE MIDDLE AGES

BY
ALBERT BOARDMAN KERR

ILLUSTRATED

CHARLES SCRIBNER'S SONS
NEW YORK · LONDON
1927

TO
R. K.

"There is
One great society alone on earth:
The noble living and the noble dead."
—WORDSWORTH: *The Prelude*, Book VI.

PREFACE

IF books were as scarce as in Jacques Cœur's lifetime there might be no need to apologize for the issuance of a new volume. Nowadays, however, when the great invention which made its appearance with his death produces so vast an annual supply of printed matter, a word of explanation is, perhaps, due the reading public for adding to the perplexities of its choice. It is only natural that historians should seek to preserve the record of a life so heroic as that of Jacques Cœur. The memory and example of lives such as his, wherever lived, belong to the common heritage of mankind. Yet, cosmopolite that he was, the epic story of this great Frenchman is but little known beyond his native land. The only previous attempt to narrate the tale in English was made eighty years ago, when the facts regarding it still were meagre and obscure.

No writer can approach this subject without a deep realization of his obligation to Pierre Clément, whose *Jacques Cœur et Charles VII*, published in 1866, must ever remain the base upon which all subsequent monuments to this memory are reared. I gratefully acknowledge my debt also to Mademoiselle Guiraud, whose scholarly and painstaking researches in the notarial registers and archives of Montpellier, the results of which are embodied in her work, *Recherches et conclusions nouvelles sur le prétendu rôle de Jacques*

Cœur, have added much to our knowledge of the great merchant's business life and the commercial methods of his time; to M. Valet de Viriville, whose life of *Charles VII* has greatly aided me in constructing the background of my story; to M. Albert Malet for assistance obtained from his invaluable small text-book, *l'Histoire du Moyen Age*; and to the numerous other authors on whom I have leaned in the preparation of my book and whose aid I have tried to acknowledge in my notes.

I have not been willing to accept so much without endeavoring myself to contribute in some small degree to the common fund of information on the subject. As a result of the chivalrous co-operation of Monseigneur Angelo Mercati, the Prefect of the archives of the Vatican, I have been enabled to refer to bulls of Popes Eugenius IV and Nicholas V which have not heretofore been available for such purpose. The kindness of Professor Edouard Chichizola, of the City Library of Genoa, has brought to light certain letters of the Doge Janus Campo Fregoso in his negotiations with Jacques Cœur which are of historical interest. Then, too, I trust that my reading of Pope Nicholas V's proclamation in the Argentier's favor may give a new significance to this document.

For the frontispiece portrait of Jacques Cœur, I have departed from my original intention of reproducing Grignon's plate of 1653, referred to in the text, and, instead, have employed an engraving of a comparatively modern painting by J. Boilly which appeared in a work entitled *I Benefattori dell' Umanità*, Florence, 1860, an Italian translation of an earlier

French compilation published by *La Société Montyon et Franklin*. Although bearing an unmistakable resemblance to Grignon's celebrated plate, the portrait which I have selected, it seems to me, gives the great French merchant a mien more in keeping with his bold and resolute character.

It only remains to express my gratitude for courtesies and help to M. Billoud, of the Municipal Library of Marseilles, to M. Pierre Virenque, of the Municipal Library of Montpellier, and to M. R. Lanoue, a subordinate in the Municipal Library of Bourges.

ALBERT BOARDMAN KERR.

VILLA UNICORN,
GOLFE-JUAN (A. M.), FRANCE,
April 20, 1927.

CONTENTS

PART ONE—EARLY LIFE

PART TWO—THE MERCHANT PRINCE

PART THREE—KING'S MINISTER

PART FOUR—PROSPERITY

PART FIVE—ADVERSITY

CONTENTS xiii

CHAPTER   PAGE

XXVI. TRIAL. TORTURE. JUDGMENT 234

XXVII. IMPRISONMENT CONTINUED. ADMINISTRATION OF ESTATE 244

XXVIII. ESCAPE 251

XXIX. AT ROME. REAL REASON FOR HIS DOWNFALL 259

XXX. THE CRUSADE. DEATH 270

EPILOGUE 276

NOTES 285

APPENDIX 307

INDEX 319

ILLUSTRATIONS

JACQUES CŒUR

MERCHANT PRINCE OF THE MIDDLE AGES

PART I

EARLY LIFE

"They that go down to the sea in ships, that do business in great waters." (Psalms 107: 23.)

CHAPTER I

YOUTH. TRAINING

In the closing years of the fourteenth century, while Europe reeled from the shock of its crushing defeat by the Turk at the battle of Nicopolis, there was begun at Bourges, in the heart of France, a life, the marvels of which continue to hold interest and sympathy after the lapse of five hundred years. For the Western nations the menace of the Crescent was, for the time, to be obscured; but the career, thus begun, was to be strongly influenced throughout its course by the "Moon of Mahomet."

Like the Maid of Orleans, with whose name his is often joined as her successor in the story of the liberation of France, Jacques Cœur had a modest origin. His father, Pierre Cœur, a rich merchant furrier, coming from the near-by town of Saint Pourçain, had established himself at Bourges shortly before the birth of his son Jacques. (1).* The move was both wise and fortunate. Then one of the flourishing commercial cities of the kingdom, Bourges enjoyed the patronage of John, Duke of Berry, who played so well the rôle of Mæcenas as richly to deserve his surname of "the Magnificent." Son and brother of preceding kings and uncle of the existing one, he kept up a royal state, erected buildings, imposing and beautiful, and patronized the fine arts.

* The numbers in parentheses refer to the notes beginning on page 287 of this volume.

3

It was in a house near the ducal palace, in a street doubtless frequented by its rich clientele, that Pierre Cœur set up his shop and established the home where his son Jacques was born. (2). The father could not then have foreseen that his adopted city was shortly to become the capital of patriotic France, and, as in the time of Julius Cæsar, was again to furnish the last refuge to the Gallic national cause.

Nothing is known of the boyhood of Jacques; if, like the young Hercules, his struggles commenced in the cradle, we have no record of them.

Of the other children of Pierre Cœur we have certain knowledge of but two: Nicholas, who took holy orders, became canon of the Sainte Chapelle at Bourges, and afterward Bishop of Luçon, and a sister, who married Jean Bochetel, the King's secretary, who later served the Dauphin Louis in a similar capacity. (3). Of the mother or of the order of birth of the children there can be only surmise.

Tradition and the testimony of several contemporary chroniclers, whose main interests are in the splendor of courts and the pomp and circumstance of war, have attributed to the family Cœur an origin much too lowly. (4). That it was in comfortable, even affluent, circumstances can be gathered from the quarter in which it lived.

Their near neighbor, a document of the times informs us, was Lambert Leodépart, a former officer of Duke John's household, whose father-in-law was, or had been, the Director of the Mint. Both houses still remain and, outside of Italy, compare favorably with the better class of bourgeois dwellings of the period

—for example, with the London residence of Sir Richard (Dick) Whittington, England's celebrated early
merchant, then Lord Mayor of that city. (5).

Learning in its higher branches was at this time, as
we know, largely restricted to the Church and all teach-
ing was in its care. Its instruction was given mainly
in Latin, and, owing to the scarcity of books, was chiefly
oral. (6). Printing, that great legacy which, in dying,
the Middle Ages have left us, had not yet begun to un-
lock the minds of the masses. Half a century was to
pass before Gutenberg's fingers were to frame in type
those majestic words of the Bible, so prophetic of the
work in hand: "Let there be light; and there was
light."

None the less the era which succeeded that of Dante,
Petrarch, and Boccaccio in Italy, was contemporaneous
with that of Chaucer in England and Froissart and
the author of the immortal *Imitation of Christ* on the
continent, and was about to burst forth in the full
glory of the Renaissance, was not a period of utter
darkness even for the man of lowly estate.

The records of the Archbishopric of Rouen just after
the English occupation of that city, show 5,229 pupils
as having attended its schools within an eight-year
period. (7). That the people at large were not without a considerable measure of educational opportunity
is proven by the great number of them who at this
period began to fill high places in the land. Jean Gerson, then serving as Chancellor of the great University
of Paris with its throngs of students—among whom later
was to be found Jacques Cœur's eldest son—the Chan-
cellors of France Robert le Maçon and Guillaume des

Ursins, the Secretary of the King Étienne Chevalier, the Procurer-General Jean Dauvet, and many others in high public station during Charles VII's reign, were all "sons of the people."

All contemporary chroniclers praise Jacques Cœur's genius; one alone, Thomas Basin, describes him as "unlettered" (*sine litteris*). If this assertion meant to imply that he had no scholastic attainments, the entire history of his later life refutes it. We need only recall the great honor and friendship accorded him by the learned Pope Nicholas V—the scholarly Pontiff who reorganized and enlarged the Vatican Library and gathered around him the most celebrated humanists of the age—were there not more direct denial in the examples which have come down to us of Jacques Cœur's able correspondence in both French and Latin. (8).

Nor is Basin's statement much more credible if it be taken to imply that Jacques Cœur had not received, in his early years, any systematic schooling. Bourges was a cathedral town which was even then "*plus célèbre et digne de gloire perpétuelle*" because of "*toute manière de discipline très ornée, érigée de long-temps*," both under the system of instruction presided over by its Archbishop, and that maintained by the canons of the Church of Saint Ursins, who had been confirmed by ancient papal bulls "*au droict et coustume qu'ils avoient de tenir escoles publicques et faire exercise de litérature.*" (9).

These were free schools, open to all. If the child is in any degree father of the man, the progenitor of that bold and complex genius who, by his industry alone, became the renowned merchant, manufacturer, and ship-owner, the able banker, the great finance minister and ambassador, the soldier, sailor, patron of the arts Jacques Cœur—such a youth, we may be sure, did not neglect any of the opportunities, educational or otherwise, which were open to him.

It is of record that letters of tonsure were granted him prior to his marriage, thus giving him the status of a *clerc* and rendering him justiciable only before ecclesiastical tribunals. True, this was a privilege then often sought without spiritual aims. It was popular with merchants and other laymen leading adventurous lives, who desired, in the dangers and uncertainties of the times, to gain what shelter from the harsh enforcements of secular law was to be found in the right to invoke the more merciful forum of the Church. Benefit of clergy was, however, not granted to the ignorant. Possession of letters of tonsure then, as the holding of a modern diploma does now, presupposed the successful issue of some sort of educational test. (10). In Jacques Cœur's case, the probabilities are that, like his brother Nicholas, and afterward two of his own sons, he sought at first to prepare himself for holy orders but was early turned aside and drawn into the business of his father's shop.

There is some authority for the belief that he served the long apprenticeship necessary to learn the art of the goldsmith, the craft then the most esteemed, and beginning to assume the additional functions of banking. In the Middle Ages, as we know, every one was not free to open a shop or factory, or to direct it in the making of whatever merchandise he pleased. No

one could manage a workshop who had not learned
all the details of the craft and proven that he knew
them; no one could fabricate except according to the
special rules laid down by the guilds for each trade.
And so Jacques Cœur's later extensive dealings in the
products of the goldsmith's art lead, naturally, to the
view that the trade was one which he had acquired in
his youth.

The boyhood of the young Jacques, as, indeed, his
entire life, was spent amidst stirring scenes and exciting events. France was then engaged in the last
and longest period of continuous warfare in her desperate and prolonged struggle to expel the English from her
national soil, called the Hundred Years War. Beginning with the destruction of her fleet in the harbor of
Ecluse in 1340, rendering her powerless to carry a
vigorous offensive to the shores of England, followed,
as a result of the overwhelming defeat at Crécy, by
the fall of Calais, whereby her adversary obtained a
convenient port on the French coast for the debarka-
tion of hostile troops, the war had been marked by a
series of terrible reverses to the arms of France. Blow
had followed blow and disaster been heaped on disaster. After Crécy had come the still more crushing
defeat of Poitiers. The wise reign of Charles V had
been all too short an interval. The country was now
given over to the rule of the poor, imbecile Charles VI
under whom the government and defense of the realm
broke down completely. The Kingdom was not so
much one country obeying its sovereign as a loose knot
of vassal states, with different interests, following
greedy and selfish chiefs. While the King's relatives,

the powerful Dukes of Burgundy and Orleans, contended for the regency and disputed the possession of
Paris and the custody and control of the mad monarch,
in a civil war, marked by an unexampled record of assassination and fratricidal strife, too bitter to permit
care for the public weal, came again the foreign enemy
with mien more terrible than ever. Henry V, "the
lion of England," seizing the opportunity created by
French dissensions, recommenced the war in alliance
with the Duke of Burgundy, and dealt the patriotic
party a stupendous blow at Agincourt. (11).

The French people, meanwhile, were reduced to the
utmost depths of misery, "the pity that was of the
kingdom of France," as Jeanne d'Arc was shortly to
call it. Everywhere were murder, revenge, robbery,
pillage, burning of towns, slaughter of peaceful people,
wretchedness, and despair. Trade was at a standstill,
fields had run wild, wolves and starvation were at the
gates of the cities.

The evils of the times are vividly portrayed by Alan
Chartier, contemporary author and poet, in an elo-
quent and pathetic invective, reminiscent of Cicero,
which he places in the mouth of a peasant, speaking
in the name of the entire French people: "Labor has
lost its reward, commerce can find no safe road. All
is in prey which sword and steel cannot defend. Have
I any prospect in life except to do as those have done
whom plunder of me has enriched, those who prefer
booty to the honor of war? What do I call war? It
is not war which holds this kingdom in its grasp; it is
private robbery, an abandoned larceny, violence under
the guise of campaigns, and rapine, which the lack of

proper justice and suitable ordinance has made lawful. A call to arms is issued and the standards are raised against the enemy; but the exploits are all against me, to the destruction of my poor substance and miserable life. Look upon, O Mother [France], and take note of my most sad affliction and you will know that no refuge is left me. The fields no longer give me home and no more have I the wherewithal to cultivate them to gain my daily bread. Other hands hold all that strength of wall and depth of moat do not encompass." (12).

The present was indeed dark and the future uncertain. Yet at this time a young shepherdess is growing up in a remote part of France adjoining the Duke of Burgundy's country, giving ear to mystic voices, and a young merchant is laying the foundation of his commercial training in the sheltered city of Bourges, "from the one of whom Charles VII is to borrow the sword and from the other the funds" which are to bring ultimate deliverance to France.

CHAPTER II

BOURGES. MARRIAGE

WHILE Jacques Cœur was in his early twenties there happened in Bourges an event of great moment both to himself and to the kingdom. Word ran through the city that the Dauphin, Charles of France, then a youth of fifteen, the successor as Duke of Berry and heir of his great-uncle John, was at the northern gate, seeking the refuge of his ducal capital. On the side of the Orleanist or Armagnac party in the civil war then raging, Charles was arrayed against that of his cousin John the Fearless, Duke of Burgundy, to whom his mother, Isabelle of Bavaria, had given her support; his standard was the sole symbol of defense against the foreign enemy, shortly to become Burgundy's ally. Rescued with difficulty by Tanguy (or Tanneguy) Duchâtel from the unavailing shelter of the Bastille, during the frightful scenes attending the capture of Paris by the rival party, he was now falling back upon the protection of the city which has ever formed the natural base of French resistance in times of threat to the national destiny.

> "Bourges, cité par deça des Itales
> Est des Gaules l'une des principales.
> Son fonds est mis par nature en defense
> Droit au milieu de l'Empire de France.
> Bien equippé et garni de remparts
> D'eau, de fosses et murs de quatre pars" (13),

it had become, and for a score of years was to continue as, the real capital of the kingdom, henceforth the centre of those operations which were ultimately to lead to national liberation. The citizens of Bourges rallied loyally to the cause headed by the boy Prince who, in view of the complete ruin of the mental faculties of his father the King, and the control of the royal person by the Duke of Burgundy, proclaimed himself the Regent of the Kingdom pending such "*détention et maladie.*" Meanwhile the course of the war with England was going badly for France. The fall of Rouen after one of the bravest defenses in history, placed Henry V in complete possession of Normandy. Thus, all northern France above the river Loire belonged to the enemy, whether Burgundian or English, the duty of reconquering which devolved upon the youthful Regent, all too weakly endowed by nature for the task.

In the midst of these stirring public incidents Jacques Cœur was engaged in bringing to an issue an important event in his own personal life history. Propinquity, in the case of the neighboring families, Cœur and de Léodépart, was not without its results. It proved an excellent matchmaker and about the year 1422 Jacques Cœur was married to Macée de Léodépart, daughter of the Provost of Bourges, thus allying himself to one of the notable families of the city. (14). We do not know where the ceremony uniting the young couple was celebrated. We should like to believe that it was held in the magnificent Bourges cathedral, one of the chief glories of France, of which their eldest son was one day to be the Archbishop.

CATHEDRAL OF BOURGES.

Biographers of Jacques Cœur, on what seems to be all too slender authority, have described Macée as a spend-thrift, much given to love of luxury and her toilette. Shortly after her death a judicial inquiry was held as to the whereabouts of the family plate and furnishings, seeking to subject it to an unjust confiscation by the Crown. At this hearing Guillot Trépant, an old steward of the Cœur household, testified, with reference to Macée, that "she was in the habit of spending and dissipating all that she could lay her hands on, and for this reason the said Cœur (her husband) did leave but as little as possible in his house." Is this tribute quite as naïve as, on its face, it seems? The old servant had just admitted, under searching cross-examination, hav-ing aided his mistress to whisk away from the grasp-ing fingers of the royal officers, certain gold goblets, very precious—an ably managed enterprise, of sympa-thy with which even her son, the good Archbishop, was suspected. Who cannot see, in the worthy Guillot's testimony, the ruse of a faithful servitor to evade a more embarrassing explanation of the bareness in which the King's bailiffs found the Cœur palace, of whose seizure the family had ample warning? At most, his story represents below-stairs gossip. All things are rela-tive, and what the worthy Guillot would see as idle prodigality would probably appear to those more used to large affairs as merely the necessary outlay required to maintain the station in life of a great man, widely renowned as a rich merchant, a rival of the Médicis, a minister of the King whose court had then become one of the most brilliant in the world. (15).

As for the other side of the picture, we know that

Macée died while her husband was a prisoner in the midst of malevolent enemies, with the fear of his torture and death ever present. Is it too much to believe that the continual state of dread overcame her and that she fell, a victim to her wifely devotion?

Several years before Jacques Cœur's marriage good news had spread among the townsfolk of Bourges. A truce, so the rumor ran, was about to be arranged between the warring French factions, leaving them free to unite for national defense against the foreign foe, then rapidly turning Normandy into an English province. Some preliminary parleys to this end had already been held and a meeting-place for the conference agreed upon. Early in August, 1419, Charles and his escort, headed by that intrepid old warrior Tanguy Duchâtel, rode amidst cheers through the northern gate, "*la Porte Gordaine*," on their way to the ill-fated rendezvous with the Duke of Burgundy on the bridge of Montereau, carrying with them the good wishes for peace of the citizens of Bourges and the hopes of the patriot cause. The tragic result of this meeting is known to all; John the Fearless, one of the few survivors of the appalling massacre of European prisoners by the infidel Turk, after Nicopolis, was slain by his Christian countrymen with ferocity equal to that of the Ottomans. So dramatic and fraught with such dire political results was his assassination, as to recall that of Julius Cæsar in ancient Rome. The later deed differed from the earlier in that it was probably not premeditated; it resembled it in that many individuals so mingled their cruel strokes as to make it difficult for historians, as for contemporary inquirers, to identify the author of the first blow. Popular tradition of the time ascribed it to Tanguy Duchâtel. Certainly he was capable of it and bitterly enough inclined toward the Burgundian Prince; John the Fearless, some eleven years before, had caused the murder of the Duke of Orleans, Tanguy's chieftain, and thereby lit the fires of civil war. Far easier is it to name those clearly innocent of the crime: the young Dauphin, who at the first assault had run horror-stricken from the scene, and Barbazin, his knight "*sans reproche*," who alone of Charles's party is known to have uttered disapproval of the deed. (16).

One hundred years later Francis I is said to have visited the mortuary chapel of the Dukes of Burgundy and to have viewed the remains of John the Fearless. Himself an expert in the effects of strokes at arms, he expressed his surprise at the size of the gash in the skull. "Sire," said the Carthusian monk who accompanied him, "it was through that hole that the English entered France." (17).

With Philip the Good, the murdered Duke's son, the call of vengeance stifled the last murmurs of patriotism, ever faint when contending with the louder promptings of Burgundian pride. Under the cloak of filial duty he turned his arms against his country in open alliance and common cause with Henry V of England. With his Burgundian ally, Henry occupied Paris, and carrying in his train the mad ruler of France and the captive King of Scots, stalked through the land, reducing at his leisure the remaining French strongholds. Thus he compelled the Treaty of Troyes, in 1420, whereby he gained in marriage the hand of the

Princess Catherine, the Dauphin's sister, and he and his heirs were appointed to be Kings of France—as well as England—in succession to the weak-minded and then moribund Charles VI.

Meanwhile, Charles the Regent, disavowed and made a pretender by the treaty, like Shakespeare's banished Duke, maintained a shabby court in the city of Bourges in the centre of what had formerly been the realm of France.

CHAPTER III

ONE HUNDRED YEARS WAR. ROYAL FAVORITES

As we know, Henry of Monmouth was never to inherit the French throne, that contingency for which he had so carefully provided in the unjust treaty which he had compelled. His death preceded by less than two months that of his pathetic father-in-law, the ill-starred Charles VI. Over the latter's bier, at St. Denis, the ancient burial-place of French kings, the former's son, then a babe in arms, was proclaimed by the herald as Henry VI, "King of France and England," for whom, in the governance of the latter kingdom, the infant's uncle, the Duke of Bedford, acted as Regent, holding his court at Rouen.

The news of his father's death found the Dauphin in his favorite castle of Mehun-sur-Yèvre, near Bourges. From thence he rode in procession to this city and there inaugurated his reign as Charles VII at a fête held in its proud cathedral. (18). His kingdom was but a sorry remnant of the domain handed down to him by his royal ancestors. Neither Paris nor Rheims were included within it. The English held all the region north of the Loire, and Guienne besides; he, only the country to the south of the river, exclusive of that province; hence his mock title of the "King of Bourges" given him by his enemies.

Charles hoped at first to reconquer his kingdom with the aid of foreign troops. He renewed France's ancient alliance with Scotland and called to him Archi-

bald, the Earl of Douglas, whom he rewarded by making Duke of Touraine, and John Stuart, the Earl of
Buchan, to whom he gave the high honor of Constable
of France. He also engaged the service of Castillian
and Genoese mercenaries. After some initial successes,
his troops, largely in consequence of their lack of uni-
son, suffered a stunning defeat at the battle of Ver-
neuil. The Scots, led by Buchan and the Douglas in
strong force, were almost wiped out, their leaders slain,
and the English, headed by the Duke of Bedford, returned in triumph to Paris to celebrate their greatest
victory since Agincourt. Henceforth, and until the
advent of Jeanne d'Arc, the superiority of the English
became more preponderating and the cause of French
patriotism took panic before the imminence and extremity of its peril. (19). Never since Clovis forged
the kingdom from the scraps of the Gallic Roman province have its fortunes touched so low an ebb. Hostile
waves of Hunnish and Arab invasion were incapable
of sustaining permanent occupation. The Normans
came as marauding settlers. Even the latest German
onset found France united for defense. But the dis-
ordered, reduced, and well-nigh hopeless state of the
country which immediately preceded the unfurling of
the banner of the Maid of Orleans must always rank
as the most perilous and critical period of French
history.

A vacant throne has ever been a danger to a mo-
narchical state; an insecurely occupied one, a peril only
lesser in degree. A vacant mind enthroned can be no
better than an empty royal seat, and immaturity or
weakness in its occupant is an evil but relatively smaller.

The history of times under a ruler such as was Charles
VII, as of those under his imbecile father, must therefore largely be a record of the broils of proud and turbulent nobles and the intrigues of contriving courtiers,
seeking power through the royal person. Sometimes
the strings which move the kingly marionette are
silken ones.

Charles VII, however, cannot be dismissed as merely
a puppet king. Biographers justly credit him with
sporadic acts of wise statesmanship and with continuous though irresolute purpose for the liberation of
his kingdom. The contemporary chronicler, Chastellain, says of him that he was "fickle, inconstant, suspicious, and envious." Valet de Viriville, his modern
historian, thinks that the hereditary malady of the
father left its traces in the son. History will always
remember his indifference to the fate of Jeanne d'Arc,
and the ingratitude with which he repaid Jacques
Cœur. He was justly called "Charles, the Well-
Served"; he could have been as truly styled "Charles,
the Ungrateful." He was, withal, throughout his life,
so ruled by favorites of both sexes, that no proper understanding can be had of his motives or actions at
any given time, without turning aside the arras for a
glimpse of the constantly shifting power behind the
throne.

Like being wife to Bluebeard, the position had its
dangers. The first objects of royal regard, Tanguy
Duchâtel and President Louvet, were soon dismissed,
sacrifices to the Duke of Brittany, whose friendship it
was useful to obtain. The next in order, de Giac and
de Beaulieu, were removed in ways more summary,

the former, neatly sewn in a sack, dropped in a convenient river; the latter set upon and slain by armed assailants. Behind these removals was the hand of the stern and martial Constable de Richemont, the patriotic though cruel brother of the Duke of Brittany, who desired thus to untrammel the King for the noble task of reconquest to which Providence had appointed him.

At the time of Jeanne d'Arc's appearance at court, the ruling favorite was Georges de la Tremouille; his sinister influence upon her mission is well known. Selfish, false, able, but above all artful in retaining his power, for six years he was the real King of France. The fierce though petty quarrel between his partisans and those of the Constable diverted the latter from the conduct of the war against the English. Not until after the death of the Maid was the doughty and determined de Richemont enabled to resort to his favorite remedy for this desperate disease by having la Tremouille set upon, wounded, and frightened from the court, the comparative mildness of the treatment being a variance from the prescription.

During his enjoyment of royal favor la Tremouille succeeded in inspiring the King with a strong aversion for the Constable. The latter strove vainly to unhorse the favorite; the matter came to clash of arms. In league with the Duke of Bourbon and a certain Count de Pardiac, during an absence of Charles VII and his cherished companion at Loches, the troops of the Constable entered the city of Bourges by the Bourbonnais gate and occupied the Mint and other public establishments of the monarchy. The "Leaguers," as they were

MACÉE DE LEODÉPART.
Wife of Jacques Cœur.

called, were well received by the burghers, to whom
la Tremouille was ever odious. The citadel of Bourges
—its ancient great tower stanchly defended by its
loyalist garrison—held out bravely against the Leaguers until the arrival of the royal forces, which, led
by the King and la Tremouille in person, raised the
siege and made themselves masters of the town. The
King remitted Bourbon and de Pardiac, but excluded
from pardon the Constable, then on his way to the
scene of action. (20). The latter was compelled to seek
the seclusion of his ancestral estate and had been banished the court for some months when Jeanne d'Arc
was acclaimed the savior of Orleans. Ever ready to
lend his sword to any rally of the patriot cause, de
Richemont brought his sturdy arm and strong forces
to Jeanne in time to aid in her great victory at Patay,
and persuaded her to sue the King for his return to
leadership and power. (21).

To explain the historical vindictiveness of la Tremouille and de Chartres against the Maid we need not
seek to quiet our curiosity with the mystery-play ideal
of Vice always opposed to Virtue; these traits are often
political allies, as we know. The true reason for the
antagonism of these courtiers was far more definite.
All unconsciously Jeanne had taken sides in a bitter life-
and-death struggle between two rival factions of the
court. That de Richemont had made the cause his own
was reason only too ample for la Tremouille to intrench
himself against her. Well did he know, with the re-
lentless Constable as her patron, what her success
would mean to the royal favorite. The people hailed
her as a deliverer, therefore it was necessary to dis-

semble. But henceforth in his heart and in that of his confederate, Reginald de Chartres, until her martyrdom at Rouen, there never ceased to exist the fixed purpose to frustrate at every step of its progress the mission of the Maid.

After his marriage and the birth of his eldest son Jean in 1423, we next hear of Jacques Cœur as being one of the directors of the Mint at Bourges; he was there at the time it was taken by the Leaguers in 1428. Unfortunately, owing to the loss by fire of so many of the early records of that city, we have no certain indications as to how he employed the interval. During it his sons Henri and Ravant were born; his son Geoffrey and his daughter Perrette probably shortly afterward. (22). We may picture him during this period as a busy merchant, devoted to his family, laying the foundation for that fortune and training which was one day to prove so serviceable to his country.

CHAPTER IV

THE BOURGES MINT. PUBLIC FINANCES

AMONG the refugees who sought the court of the Dauphin, after the fall of Rouen in 1418, was one, Ravant Ladenois (sometimes called le Danois), a merchant who had enjoyed considerable prestige in the Norman capital. The terms granted the brave Rouennais by Henry V were, for the times, liberal, even magnanimous; their leader he caused to be hanged, but all others who would render him homage were set at liberty. Many of the nobles refused the conditions, preferring to suffer confiscation of their goods rather than to become subjects of the English King. This patriotic stand was taken as well by the merchant Ladenois, an action for one of his calling, in itself remarkable, almost heroic. (23). Merchants of those days did not, as a rule, follow the wars as did the feudal chieftains whose trade was war, and who feared no end so much as that of dying in their beds—"like a beast," as they expressed it. Ladenois, it would seem, quickly re-established his fortunes in his new surroundings. We find him later a sufficiently great personage to lead ten or twelve mounted men-at-arms to the coronation of the King at Rheims and the campaign connected with that historic event. Two years before this service he had been granted by Charles VII the privilege of minting that sovereign's money in the cities of Bourges, Orleans, Poitiers, Saint Pourçain, and Chinon. As we recall, all currency at this period

23

consisted of coins of gold, silver, or baser metals; "blest paper" money, "last and best supply," had not yet loaned corruption "lighter wings to fly," but was awaiting the advent of its forerunner and boon companion-to-be, the printing-press. (24). Any merchant or other person could take bullion to the mints and have it made into coin. As in other forms of milling, the miller charged a toll for his service and this deduction in excess of the actual cost of minting, known as seigniorage, was a perquisite of the sovereign whose image the species bore—an expedient for increasing his immediate revenues at the expense of his future fame. The practice of debasing the coinage, giving it a face value higher than that of the metal employed, an evil nearly as old as money itself, was then already of ancient origin in the kingdom of France. Philip the Fair had been justly accused of it by Dante, his contemporary, who speaks of the woe that sovereign was "bringing upon the Seine by falsifying the coin." (25). John the Good, in one year, 1351, effected eighteen changes in the value of his issues. Charles V alone, of French rulers of the epoch, seems to have omitted the fault; Charles VI had excused his resort to it by proclaiming it to be necessary to resist "his adversary of England and to frustrate his damnable enterprise." (26).

In the times of Ravant Ladenois the evil had reached an extreme stage. Public office was not then conceived of as a public trust; nearly every function of government was farmed out; the tenant's only duty was to render unto Cæsar the lion's share of the tillage yield. The Mint—more analogous to a mill operated on share account between miller and proprietor—exacted heavy tolls. Their real enormity was concealed from the merchants and people generally by secret and changing orders of the King or his ministers fixing the seigniorage at rates different from those proclaimed by public ordinance. The share of the tolls which fell to the directors of the mint, although highly profitable, was but a fraction of that appropriated by the monarch who contributed to the enterprise the false passports which, stamped upon the face of the coins, gave them their currency. "The many were the dupes of the few who conducted the machine of these speculations." In an era in which the King could do no wrong, which believed in divine right of an absolute monarch as an article of faith, we need not be surprised to find that the post of the Prince's confederate in this game was one highly esteemed and carrying with it especial privileges and honors, including exemption from taxes and military service and the right to be judged by a special court established for the purpose. On the other hand, the rôle was a perilous one, in contravention, as we have seen, of public statutes, under protection of verbal instructions easily to be disavowed by the royal accomplice.

Ravant Ladenois associated with him, in each of the cities covered by his franchise, agents or partners with whom he shared the profits, giving them, as he testified, sometimes a third, sometimes a quarter. In Bourges he had for his associates "Pierre and Étienne Godard and Jacques Cœur." The enterprise came to grief. The partners were accused of coining money of less weight and value than that prescribed in the public

ordinances, and on confession of their act and the payment of a fine of 1,000 livres, were granted letters of
remission or pardon dated December 6, 1429. Ravant
Ladenois, in his statement in open court, explained
that the King "had made them pay him such large
sums out of the benefits derived from the minting of
the money that it would have ruined them had they
not found salvation by the subtle means of abasing
the proportion of silver in the alloy or in reducing the
weights." Jacques Cœur contented himself with the
statement that "if he had made money of less weight,
it was the fault of the King's officers." (27). In ap-
praising the value of the admissions made in the letters
of remission, it is necessary for us to keep in mind the
nature of these royal instruments. They were the exact
reverse of any modern judicial procedure of which we
know, in that they were not a grace, extended after
conviction, but an indulgence granted as a result of a
bargain before prosecution.

By a form of procedure somewhat analogous to that
of the Church, the King only pardoned what was ac-
knowledged in the prayer for forgiveness; hence the
avowals in these documents, like the charges under
modern indictments, were exceedingly broad. They
were, indeed, a form of self-indictment in which the
accused had a motive for arraigning against himself
every conceivable charge which could reasonably be
brought against him. It is not to be contended that
false crimes were likely to be avowed under such a
system. What is probably true, however, is that it
often rendered unnecessary any defense of the moral
quality of the action which sometimes constitutes all

of the difference between guilt and innocence. In any view of the matter it does not seem that Jacques Cœur, whose rôle in it was but a secondary one, can be severely censured for not being beyond his generation in virtue. "Every age and every nation," says Macaulay, "has certain characteristic vices which prevail almost universally, which scarcely any person scruples to avow, and which even rigid moralists but faintly censure. Succeeding generations change the fashion of their morals, with the fashion of their hats and their coaches; take some other kind of wickedness under their patronage, and wonder at the depravity of their ancestors." (28).

Nor can a generation with a financial history such as ours very severely condemn Charles VII or his ministers for having stooped, in times of great emergency and public peril, to measures to which, since his day, in like extremity, resort has been so freely had. At the time of which we speak, which is that of Jeanne d'Arc's earlier campaigns, the royal coffers were empty and the exhaustion of the royal credit almost complete. The King was hard put to it for funds to carry on the war, even to supply the royal family and the court. Many allusions to his indigence are made by the chroniclers and poets of the time. We are told, for example, that for his marriage ceremony with Marie of Anjou the palace halls were garnished with the tapestries of the castle of Blois, loaned for the occasion by his cousin, the Duke of Orleans, then a captive in England; that he had recourse to the chapter of the cathedral of Bourges for supplies furnished on credit to the royal table; that he borrowed from a money-

lending merchant of Geneva, even from his cook, and
that at the time of his historic interview with Jeanne
d'Arc at the castle of Chinon there were but four écus
in the royal treasury. (29).

An amusing tale, of contemporary origin, illustra-
tive of the state of the royal credit at this time, is told
by M. Leber in his "*Essai sur l'appréciation de la fortune privée au moyen âge.*" He relates that one day,
while the King was at Bourges, a local shoemaker,
having called at the palace with a pair of shoes to be
fitted to the royal feet, and having already tried on
one, on learning that his sovereign had no cash,
promptly unlaced it and departed with his merchandise.

The English, also, began to feel the financial burden
of continuous warfare and were forced to accept a loan
from Pope Martin V, pledging as security therefor the
expected ransoms to be received from the French
prisoners taken at Agincourt—an incident which throws
a curious side-light on the morals of the age, that the
welfare of the Church should not scruple to be thus
identified with the distresses of its children. (30).

The French ruler's straitened financial state was
the cause of much of the apparent lack of object and
purpose in the movements of his soldiers in their
earlier campaigns. It was to be some time yet before
Charles VII was to have permanently established
troops at his command. Regular armies must be regularly paid, and their establishment presupposes ordered
public resources, far beyond those which the young
King found available in the troubled years of his rule
which preceded and immediately followed the advent

of Jeanne d'Arc. For the moment he must accept the service of irregulars—an almost *opéra bouffe* soldiery whose leaders, though brave, were ineffective and fought, raided, pillaged, ran away, were captured, ransomed, and released to commence again the somewhat futile cycle. Their commissions were, in some degree, akin to those of the privateers of more modern eras, to whom, in times of war, have been granted letters of marque and reprisal to prey upon the enemy; they were independent contractors who, in lieu of pay, received tacit permission to forage, even to pillage—their own country.

Indeed, not the least of the marvels of the battles under the standard of the Maid of Orleans is that, in the condition of Charles VII's credit then existing, it was at all possible to subsist armies relatively as large as those which fought under her leadership. The Duke of Alençon testified with regard to the proposed expedition for the relief of Orleans: "But money was lacking. To get it and pay for the supplies I returned to the King. I apprised him of the fact that the supplies were ready, that there remained [to furnish] the wherewithal to pay for them, and the soldiers. The King sent some men who delivered the necessary sums, so that both men and provisions were ready to move on Orleans and try to raise the siege."

One of the more recent of Jeanne d'Arc's historians cites this incident with the following comment: ". . . It sounds simple enough as Alençon tells it, but the King's treasury was empty. . . . There must have been a general levying and borrowing at Tours and Poitiers and Bourges and other good towns. It is something of a mystery, and Alençon offers no hint of a solution." (31).

This was but eight months before the judgment imposing a fine against Ravant Ladenois and his partners for cheapening the King's money. In view of the exhaustion of the royal funds and credit, the needy sovereign's well-known practice with regard to his coinage at this period, the direct testimony of Ladenois and Jacques Cœur quoted above, who can doubt the rôle that the mint of Bourges played in the financing of the historic relief of Orleans?

We know, at least, where the sympathies of its head director lay. Ravant Ladenois, although, like his partners, exempt from military service, was one of Jeanne d'Arc's lieutenants on the coronation campaign; he helped her actively with men, probably with money. Jacques Cœur was not only the latter's partner, he was also his friend, as the name given to the former's third son goes to show; Ravant is too rare a given name to lead to any other conclusion than that Ladenois was the child's godfather.

Whether Jacques Cœur was one of the twelve cavalrymen furnished by the latter on this occasion, we can only conjecture. That he was at all times a strong partisan of the Maid of Orleans is indicated by his close and lifelong associations with her companions at arms, most of whom later resorted to him for loans of money or purchases on credit; during the interval of her campaigns the young heroine had spent three pleasant weeks in Bourges as the guest of another officer of the finances, the Receiver-General la Touroulde. (32).

Was it a mere coincidence that her patent of nobility was signed at the same time and place—during a visit of the King, in December, 1429, at his castle of Mehun-sur-Yèvre—as the letters of remission to the partners of the Bourges mint, or were the two cases regarded as having some common bond? With the authorities available, the question can only be speculative. But, as to an era in which public prosecutions were so often started from motives far removed from love of abstract justice, it is perhaps a justifiable suspicion that Jacques Cœur may have owed this earlier encounter with the law to his zeal for the side he had espoused, and that the sinister forces which wrought so badly for Jeanne d'Arc, brought to grief, as well, the early public service of the subject of this memoir.

CHAPTER V

THE HOLY LAND. SHIPWRECK. PIRATES

THE next we hear of Jacques Cœur is as a merchant in the Orient, about September 1 of the year 1432.

The narrative which records his presence there is in itself of great interest. A certain Bertrand de la Brocquière, Lord of Vieux-Château, "Counsellor and First Esquire-Carver" to Philip the Good, Duke of Burgundy, has left us the story of the travels made in that year to the Holy Land by a small company of young and venturesome Burgundian nobles, himself included, following the customs of the times with regard to such pilgrimages. (33). Bertrand relates that the party went by sea from Venice to the Palestine port of Jaffa, thence by land to "the holy city of Jerusalem where our Lord Jesus Christ suffered death for us. After performing the usual [local] pilgrimages, we made those to the mountain where Jesus fasted forty days; to the Jordan where he was baptized; to the church of Saint John near to that river; to that of Saint Martha and Saint Mary Magdalen, where our Lord raised Lazarus from the dead; to Bethlehem where he was born; to the birthplace of Saint John Baptist; to the house of Zachariah; and lastly to the Holy Cross, where the tree grew that formed the real cross, after which we returned to Jerusalem."

Sir Bertrand tells us: "Jerusalem is situated in a mountainous and strong country, and is at this day a considerable town, although it appears to have been

32

much more so in former times. It is under the dominion of the Sultan to the shame and grief of Christendom. Among the free Christians, there are but two
cordeliers who inhabit the holy sepulchre, and even
they are harassed by the Saracens; I can speak of it
from my own knowledge, having been witness of it for
two months."

The Sultan to whom our traveller refers, was the
ruler of Egypt; it was to be nearly a hundred years
before the grievous yoke of the Turk descended on the
Arab Kingdom and its Palestine and Syrian depen-
dencies.

At Acre, which is described as "a handsome port,
deep and well enclosed," the Burgundian pilgrims encountered some Venetian merchants who told them
that a galley from the Mediterranean port of Narbonne, under charter to certain French merchants,
was expected at Beirut, and Sir Bertrand's comrades
being desirous of taking that opportunity of returning to France, the party took the road to that place.
As for the Esquire-Carver himself, he had formed the
bold design of returning overland from Jerusalem to
France, that which, since the rise of Islam, no Christian could do without encountering almost insur-
mountable dangers and difficulties.

". . . Solely occupied with my grand journey, I
employed the time we staid in this town [Beirut] in
seeking information concerning it; and to this end addressed myself to a Genoese merchant, called Jacques
Pervézin. He advised me to go to Damascus, assuring
me that I should find there merchants from Venice,
Catalonia, Florence, Genoa, and elsewhere, whose

counsels might guide me. He even gave me a letter of recommendation to a countryman of his, named Ottobon Escot. (34).

"Being resolved to consult Escot before I proceeded farther, I proposed to Sir Sanson [de Lalain, one of his party] to go and see Damascus, without however telling him anything of my project. He accepted my proposal with pleasure and we set out under the conduct of a Moucre. I have before said that the Moucres in Syria are the people whose trade is conducting travellers, and hiring out to them asses and mules.

"On quitting Baruth [Beirut], we had to traverse some high mountains to a long plain, called the valley of Noah, because it is said that Noah there built the ark. . . .

"It is two days' journey from Baruth to Damascus. The Mohammedans have established a particular custom for Christians all through Syria, in not permitting them to enter the towns on horseback. None, that are known to be such, dare do it, and, in consequence, our Moucre made Sir Sanson and myself dismount before we entered any town. . . .

"Damascus may contain, as I have heard, 100,000 souls. The town is rich, commercial, and, after Cairo, is the most considerable of all in the possession of the Sultan. . . .

"It was in 1400 destroyed and reduced to ashes by Tamerlane. Vestiges of this disaster now remain; and toward the gate of Saint Paul there is a whole quarter that has never been rebuilt. There is a khan in the town, appropriated as a deposit and place of safety to merchants and their goods. . . .

"The Christians are hated at Damascus. Every evening the merchants are shut up in their houses by persons appointed for this purpose, and who on the morrow come to open their gates when it may please them.

"I found there many Genoese, Venetian, Calabrian, Florentine, and French merchants. The last were come thither to purchase several articles, and particularly spiceries, with the intention of taking them to Baruth, and embarking them on board the galley expected from Narbonne. *Among them was Jacques Cœur, who has since acted a great part in France,* and was Treasurer to the King. He told us the galley was then at Alexandria, and that probably Sir Andrew and his three companions [all of the Burgundian party] would embark on board at Baruth.

"I was shewn the place, without the walls of Damascus, where Saint Paul had a vision; was struck blind and thrown from his horse. He caused himself to be conducted to Damascus, where he was baptized; but the place of his baptism is now a mosque. . . .

"Having seen Damascus, Sir Sanson and myself returned to Baruth, where we found Sir André [Toulongeon], Pierre de Vaudrei, Geoffroi de Toisi and Jean de la Rae, who had come thither, as Jacques Cœur had told us. The galley arrived from Alexandria two or three days afterward. . . .

"The evening before the embarkation, I took Sir André de Toulongeon aside, and having made him promise that he would not make any opposition to what I was about to reveal to him, I informed him of my design to return home overland. In consequence of his promise, he did not attempt to hinder me, but represented all the dangers I should have to encounter, and the risk I should run of being forced to deny my faith to Jesus Christ. I must own that his representations were well founded; and of all the perils he had menaced me with, there was not one I did not experience, except denying my religion. He engaged his companions to talk with me also on the subject; but what they urged was vain; I suffered them to set sail, and remained at Baruth."

And here we, too, must take our leave of the lone Burgundian knight. The thread of our story follows the ship which he watched fade away toward the setting sun and the homeland of France. We will wish him Godspeed on this venturesome journey, and we are relieved to find him depicted in the illuminated miniature which precedes the ancient manuscript relation of his travels, safely arrived, on his knees, presenting his book to his "most redoubted Lord," the Duke of Burgundy. He wears the Saracen dress which he had been obliged to assume and has near him the horse that carried him during all of his astonishing ride. We have not entirely dismissed him from mind; we shall have occasion, from time to time, to resummon him as an authority, an eye-witness of the things he observed in the Levant, with such clarity and judgment, five hundred years ago.

Even before letting him out of sight this time, it is perhaps best to recall him for a few moments to have him relate an event which happened after the departure of his friends and shortly before the commencement of his own home journey—an incident highly typical of the exigencies which foreign merchants of those times might have to face in the pursuit of their calling. Sir Bertrand tells us:

"I met, near Damascus, a very black Moor, who had rode a camel from Cairo in eight days, though it is usually sixteen days' journey. . . .

"This courier was the bearer of an order from the Sultan. A galley and, two galliots, of the Prince of Tarentum, had captured before Tripoli, in Syria, a vessel from the Moors; and the Sultan, by way of reprisal, had sent to arrest all the Catalonians and Genoese who might be found in Damascus and throughout Syria. (35). This news which my Moucre told me did not alarm me; I entered boldly the town like the other Saracens, because, dressed like them, I thought I had nothing to fear. . . . By virtue of this order, my host, who was a Genoese, was arrested, his effects seized, and a Moor placed in his house to take care of them. I endeavoured to save all I could for him and, that the Moor might not notice it, I made him drunk."

The return voyage from Palestine of the good ship *Notre Dame et Saint Paul*—for such was the real name of the "galley of Narbonne"—was not so fortunate. Its passenger, Sir André Toulongeon, who had shown such solicitude for the safety of his venturesome friend, was himself never to reach his Burgundian home. Being created that same year, 1432, a Knight of the Golden Fleece, Philip the Good's celebrated order, he was not, in life, to wear its elaborate decorations; for, as its records show, "he was then a pilgrim and died on the road." (36).

The other Burgundian passengers were probably

safely landed, most likely at the port of Genoa, to continue their journey overland through Savoy, Burgundy, Champagne, and Picardy, to the court of their
Duke, then held at Ghent in the County of Flanders;
as his subjects they would not have been safe in France,
with which they were nominally still at war; apparently they were not on board during the evil fortunes
which were to mark the end of the ship's voyage.

The vessel itself, with Jacques Cœur and the other
French merchants—its charterers—its owner, captain
and crew, and its precious cargo of "spiceries" and
Egyptian and Syrian ware, while nearing Montpellier,
its final port of destination, met with bad weather off
the northern coast of Corsica. A leak was sprung and
shipwreck followed. The owner of the ship, Jean Vidal,
the captain, Augustin Sicard, and the six merchants
threw themselves into a boat and landed on the island
near the town of Calvi. They set about the rescue of
their comrades remaining on the ship—apparently the
crew—as well as the cargo, but in order to accomplish
this found it necessary to call in the aid of the islanders.
This was fatal to them. Conducted by the captain of
the place, whom the ancient record calls Raynuxto,
and elsewhere Rotmulo, de Larcha, the Corsicans
threw themselves on the shipwrecked mariners, relieved them of their purses and personal possessions,
and despoiled them of their clothes, "denuding them
even to their shirts," as the recital goes. Vidal and
Sicard were retained prisoners, the one for fourteen
months, the other for nearly three, awaiting the payment of their ransoms, fixed at 800 and 100 gold ducats
respectively. (37). The other merchants were released,

but the goods of all had been lost; that portion of them which had been saved from the wreck, about one-sixth of the total merchandise, became the pirates' booty. Raynuxto de Larcha possessed himself, among other objects, of some spices belonging to two of the merchants, which he caused to be dried and renovated in an oven at his Château de la Raquette, where, we are told, he kept a spicer for that purpose. As for the merchandise losses of Jacques Cœur, the documents do not give the details. But, besides his share in the general bill of damages, there was adjudged to him a personal indemnity of ten gold ducats, this being the appraised value of his clothes and the pocket-money of which he had been robbed. In this respect, his loss was placed below that of some of his companions in misfortune, above that of others, showing that at this stage of his career his habit "was not expressed in fancy," however richly we may find him apparelled at a later period.

For that part of the narrative which relates the incidents of this mishap we are indebted to an ancient manuscript record of the proceedings of the joint commission afterward appointed by the Kings of France and Aragon—to which latter kingdom the island of Corsica then belonged—to hear and determine the claims for damages in favor of the French merchants growing out of the actions of the Corsican pirates which we have just recited. This document, which has within comparatively recent years come into the possession of the Municipal Library and Musée Fabre of Montpellier, is a *mélange* of Latin, Catalan, and old French. For the incidents of the shipwreck we have borrowed heavily, almost textually, from the digest thereof, made by Mademoiselle L. Guiraud, in her scholarly work on *Jacques Cœur* to which we shall have frequent occasion hereafter to refer. (38).

The ancient document does not inform us how Jacques Cœur fared in dispensing with the hospitalities of the pirates; it leaves him on the rocky coast of Corsica, clad only in his shirt, some hundreds of miles from his native town of Bourges. We know, however, the brave motto he had chosen by which to steer his life: "To VALIANT HEARTS NOTHING IS IMPOSSIBLE." With the comfort and guidance of this indomitable creed, we leave him to extricate himself from his predicament as best he may.

CHAPTER VI

JEANNE D'ARC'S DEATH. MERCHANTS DURING THE MIDDLE AGES. FAIRS. PERILS BY LAND AND SEA

When Jacques Cœur sailed from Montpellier on his ill-starred voyage to the Orient in May, 1432, just one year had passed since Jeanne d'Arc had suffered martyrdom in the market-place of Rouen. In the circles of the court, the etiquette seems to have been to observe silence with regard to this tragic event; the people at large were too occupied with their own distress to be very demonstrative in their grief. None the less, the worthy townsfolk of Bourges, who had shown the young heroine such practical devotion, must have been cast into the deepest dejection by the news.

The reverberations of it reached even the Orient. Our friend la Brocquière, at Constantinople, was asked embarrassing questions by the Emperor, John Paleologus II, about his "most redoubted Duke's" part in the affair.

"I was lodged," says the traveller, "with a Catalonian merchant who having told one of the officers of the palace that I was attached to my Lord of Burgundy, the Emperor caused me to be asked if it were true that the Duke had taken the Maid of Orleans, which the Greeks would scarcely believe. I told them how the matter had passed, at which they were greatly astonished."

Jeanne, we know, was not taken by the Duke, but

by the soldiers of his *beau cousin* and general, John of
Luxembourg, who sold her to the English. The Duke
rejoiced over her capture as being "by the grace of
our Blessed Creator," and spread the news of it to all
his loyal vassals, that they, too, might have cause for
thanksgiving. Apparently, the Greeks of Constantinople found it difficult to believe that a Christian
prince could have been concerned in a transaction
so base. We cannot envy la Brocquière his work of
explanation and can only congratulate him that the
defense of his master's conduct did not have to be
made before infidel Arabs and Turks, who could not
be expected to comprehend such matters.

What led Jacques Cœur to leave his native city to
associate himself with a group of other merchants from
the south of France in a commercial venture to the
Orient?

In all probability the step was partly the natural
reaction of a bold and ambitious spirit to the initial
reverse which he had suffered as a Director of the Mint
at Bourges; it was mainly, however, due to a purpose
much more definite. The career of a local city dealer
had become too small for him. Having observed, at
close range, from a merchant's standpoint, the demands of the court, and those that radiated from it,
in an era when the nation's purchasing power was
therein so largely centred, he set himself the task of
supplying this market, through a complete commercial organization—one that would include production,
transport, and distribution to an extent new to the
kingdom of France.

Far from being discouraged by his initial failures,

THE SIEGE OF ORLÉANS.

Miniature from the manuscript of the *Vigiles de Charles VII*, by Martial de Paris, 1484. A cannon in the foreground.

JEANNE D'ARC.

Imaginative drawing by the clerk of Parliament in one of his registers.

JEANNE AT THE STAKE.

Miniature executed in 1484. Probably not a portrait.

E. Lavisse, "Histoire de France." Librairie Hachette, Éditeur.

of his stumbling-blocks he made stepping-stones and marched ever forward toward his goal. Master spirit that he was, he first studied his problem at each of its stages, and later set about it with a fixity of purpose and a surety of insight that never failed or faltered.

There were then no large factories as in modern days; capital, as we know, was not sufficient to support them. There were never more than four or five hands in the same shop, including its head, for the word workman applied to master as well as man.

In each community all of the artisans of the same craft were banded together into a guild which regulated all of the conditions of the work and extended aid to its members in times of distress. The guild had its hall, its officers, even its patron saint, and its banner under which its members assembled for public ceremonies and marched in time of war.

In order to become a master craftsman, it was first necessary to serve an apprenticeship, the length of which was fixed by the rules of the order. The apprentices lived at the house of their master, and often the artisans as well. Shop and factory were one, and the work was done before the eyes of the customer, as in Oriental bazaars at this day. Hours of labor then were longer but holidays came more frequently.

The practice of the Middle Ages was to manufacture in small quantity according to the needs of the community—to produce on the spot all that was to be consumed there. Communications were too rudimentary and too interrupted to permit a different policy; the modern economic ideal of manufacturing where most advantageous was out of the question.

Although restricted in its extent, the interchange of commodities between cities, towns, and countries necessarily existed. The tendency of commerce was to concern itself with articles which represented the maximum of value with the minimum of bulk; this was due to the difficulties of transport, which also led, naturally, to the establishments of fairs; these latter were an especial feature of the commercial and social life of the Middle Ages.

Inasmuch as the largest crowds gathered on days of religious festivals, fairs were usually held so as to include some one of these occasions, and were often designated by the name of the saint in whose honor the fête was held. (39).

In the north of France, the most noted fairs had been those in Champagne, in the cities of Provins and Troyes, where the proximity of the headwaters of the Rhine, the Rhône, and the Seine formed a natural meeting-point for the commerce of these great waterways. These marts had been ruined by the One Hundred Years War, and the Italians now sought the rich cloth of Flanders directly by the water route to Bruges, or through the intermediary of the fair at Geneva, which sprang into a new importance, as a result. Charles VII tried to rival the latter by establishing fairs at Lyons, where one still continues to be regularly held.

The great meeting-place for commerce in southern France was at Beaucaire. Fairs were also held on the plain of St. Denis near Paris, at Bourges, and at many lesser places throughout the kingdom.

Although the University of Paris was then the largest and most reputed in the world—larger by far than any modern institution of learning—we wonder whether the old chronicler can be entirely trusted, who tells us: "When the scholars of Paris, with all their masters, went, ranged in two lines, in great ceremony, to purchase at the fair of Landit, which was held near St. Denis, the parchment necessary for the work for each year, the head of the procession was already arrived in the plain of St. Denis, when the rear had not yet quitted the rue St. Jacques," the old street of the Écoles at Paris. (40).

The King had the sole right to institute fairs; sometimes the privilege was asserted by one of his powerful vassals encroaching on the royal prerogative. The emoluments were usually leased or farmed out; we shall find Jacques Cœur interesting himself as one of the partners in the farm-lease of the fairs of Pézenas and Montagnac. The royal revenues were, as we know, largely collected on this system. The King wrested from the provincial assemblies what he could in grants of taxes. The task of collecting them he willingly parcelled out to whomsoever, for an assured profit, would help him perform this function of his government and guarantee to the royal treasury the highest returns.

The great fairs lasted several weeks; purchasers and dealers from all countries came to them by thousands. They were opened and closed by the blowing of trumpets and no business outside of the hours thus fixed was permitted. Sales were regulated by the representatives of the sovereign authority under whose auspices they were held, as transactions on a stock exchange are to-day regulated by its governors.

They were not only a convenience to trade; they

stabilized prices as well, and tended to prevent the
wide fluctuations to which the narrow margins between
local supply and demand would otherwise have given
rise.

Like the expositions of modern times, they were not
entirely given over to commerce; they also afforded
diversion, and the booths of the acrobat and juggler
were to be found side by side with the stalls of the
merchants.

With their moving crowds of people from all parts
of the world—Venetians, Florentines, Genoese, Barcelonians, Provençals, Jews, and even Mussulmans—
mingling the apparel of all countries, of all classes, in
an era noted for its striking display of colors and its
extravagance in costume, the minstrel's music vying
with the traders' cries, the fairs of the Middle Ages
have perhaps never been equalled as spirited scenes of
human animation.

The rivers were then what the railroads are now,
the main arteries of commerce. With the Seine joining
the capital to Rouen and the Channel, and the waters
of the Mediterranean and the Atlantic Ocean so nearly
connected by the Rhône and the Loire, France is particularly fortunate in inland waterways. The boatmen
formed themselves into traffic associations; the league
at Paris was particularly strong, and it is from its
trade device—a ship—that the seal of the city has been
taken.

One of the legacies which fell to France as a result
of its history as a Roman province, had been an excellent system of roads, which even to-day forms the
framework of the country's highways. Lyons was the

centre of the main routes, which, five in number, radiated from that point to Mayence, on the Rhine; to Boulogne, on the Channel, passing through Paris; to Brest, via Bourges; to Bordeaux and to Marseilles. These ways, solidly built by the great master road-builders of all time, had been placed in order during the reign of Philippe Auguste some two hundred years before the times of which we speak. In Jacques Cœur's day these roads had fallen into sad disrepair; their splendid grades and directions, however, still remained.

On the highways all travel was on horseback—infirm people and *"grandes dames"* went by litter—and all transport was by pack-saddle. Goods which would not bear packing into bales or bundles were stored in trunks or boxes slung on either side of the horse. For mutual safety the merchants went in caravans, themselves armed and frequently escorted by armed men, as one travels in savage countries at the present time. More than thirty days was required to make the journey between Paris and Marseilles, to which now about twelve hours are given. The trip from Montpellier to the capital took about twenty-four days; several more, if the route lay through the valley of the Rhône and Burgundy. (41). The mountain route—now associated with memories of Robert Louis Stevenson—was probably the safer, though rougher. It enabled the caravan to stop at Le Puy, that the merchants might worship at its far-famed cathedral shrine, to which Jeanne d'Arc's mother, Isabelle Romée, had resorted, to offer prayers for her daughter's safety. The ancient Velay capital still retains much of its quaint, mediæval aspect.

The progress of the caravan was plagued by the in-

numerable halts, caused by the necessity of paying
tolls and duties on the goods and exhibiting the safe-
conducts which the merchants were compelled to buy
from the lords of the country through which they
passed—documents which were not always honored by
the issuer.

Levies were made by every baron chieftain whose
castle guarded the roadside, not always cloaked by
claim of right, not even one as preposterous as that of
Sir Richard Venable, an English knight, turned bandit,
who, in Lower Normandy, in 1434, sold and signed
his passports as "King of France and England." (42).

Tolls were to pay to enter, and tolls to leave, each
city, each bridge, sometimes even at the fords. France
has not yet completely rid herself of these communal
charges at her *octrois*.

The merchant's calling was hazardous beyond all
others. The story of Jacques Cœur's initial voyage
has given us some idea of its dangers on sea in small
boats, exposed to the elements and lurking pirates;
the perils by land were even greater.

"There is no sport or joy in this world but that of
men-at-arms and warriors," says Aimerigot Marches,
a brigand who has retired from his vocation with regret. "How we rejoiced when we rode seeking adventure and were able to find on the way a rich abbé, a
merchant, a caravan of mules laden with cloth, furs,
spices, or silks! All was ours or let to ransom as we
saw fit. Each day we would have new riches. The
yokels of Auvergne and of Limousin provided us with
abundance and yielded us politely wheat, corn, well-
baked bread, oats, straw, good wine, beef cattle, flocks,

fat sheep, poultry, and fowls. We were clothed like kings, and when we raided, all the countryside trembled before us. *Par ma foi, cette vie était bonne et belle.*"

Although the above extract from Froissart relates to conditions at an earlier period of the One Hundred Years War, it is equally apt to illustrate the times which we discuss. Witness Olivier de la Marche on the subject of the latter:

"The whole kingdom was full of towers and fortresses, the guardians of which lived by rapine and plunder; and in the centre of France and the neighboring countries (*i. e.* Burgundy, Provençe, etc.) assembled all manner of people, collected into companies, calling themselves *écorcheurs*. These raided and travelled from country to country, and from province to province, seeking adventure and supplies; so that they found the means of living, they respected not the lands of the King of France, the Duke of Burgundy, or any other prince; they made prey of whatever fell into their hands, and all were in accord as far as plunder went. Their chief captains were the Bastard of Bourbon, Brusac, Geoffroi de Saint Belin, Lestrac, the Bastard of d'Armagnac, Rodrigues de Villandrando, Pierre Regnault, and Antoine de Chabannes, Count of Dammartin; and although Poton de Xaintrailles and La Hire were two of the principal and most renowned captains of the French party, yet were they engaged in this pillage and this *écorcherie;* but," he adds, "they fought against the enemies of the country. . . . The said *écorcheurs* did much mischief and injury to the poor people of France, and merchants and others."

In all records and documents of the era, one is struck

by the number of bastards; their presence well illus-
trates the moral laxity produced by generations of
warfare and violence; Philip, Duke of Burgundy, is
said to have left fifteen of them. These illegitimate
scions of noble houses, perhaps not unnaturally, gravi-
tated to scenes where they could "live like nature's
bastards, not her sons," and we find many of them
among the leaders of the *écorcheurs*.

These latter gentlemen were at their worst for the
ten years prior to the establishment in 1445 of a regular army in France; after that they vanished. All the
chronicles of the times are full of harrowing recitals of
their brutal conduct and sadistic cruelties; we shall
present but a few examples.

Listen to the complaint addressed to the King by
the Bishop of Beauvais with reference to these armed
ruffians:

"O God! the tyrannies which they commit! Some
they roast, others have their teeth pulled, others are
beaten with heavy clubs, and never do they let up on
them until the victims pay of money more than they
are worth. And they do not take only men, but women
and girls. . . ." (43).

A document of Montpellier states that some of these
people, appearing in Languedoc "had done infinite
evils, both to merchants and to other people coming
to the fair of Saint-Ylaire, at Montpellier, as a result
of which there was no one who dared come to or go
from the said fair." (44).

"In the year 1435," says the King's historian, Jean
Chartier, "there came in the Champagne country three
or four thousand men of war, who ravaged the region

severely, and there was neither man, woman, or child whom they did not strip even to the shirt. And when they had pillaged all, they held the villages to ransom; and their captains were one named Chabannes and two bastards of Bourbon, and the people colloquially called them *écorcheurs* or strippers.''

"And the reason why they had this name," says the chronicler, Monstrelet, "was that all the people who had encountered them, whether of their faction or not, were stripped of their garments, even to their shirts; and therefore, when they returned home, thus stripped and undressed, it was said of them that they had been in the hands of the 'strippers,' in mockery of their misadventure."

So much for the dangers to be met with in the homeland. In foreign countries there were other perils to fear. Alien merchants were regarded as hostages, and their goods as pledges for the right conduct of their own country and that of their compatriots; la Brocquière has given us an excellent example of the practical application of this theory.

In Mussulman lands there was an additional and more terrible prospect to face—that of being taken, held, and sold in slavery; for the amelioration of this evil, the activities of two benevolent societies were constantly employed, the Order of Our Mother of Mercy and the Order of the Trinity for the Redemption of Captives. (45).

From the notarial registers of Montpellier a local historian has extracted a vivid picture of the miseries of the merchant subjects of the King of France, trading in the domains of the Sultan of Egypt, prior to the negotiation by Jacques Cœur of the commercial treaty, of which we shall hereafter learn. Incidentally, for much of the material on which it draws, history is greatly indebted in Latin countries to the fulness, completeness, and clarity of the legal instruments of the civil law and its system of enregistration. The document in question recites:

"The city of Montpellier has suffered a great loss of merchandise and property in Alexandria, where there have been seized some merchants of the said city [Montpellier] with others of the said country [Egypt], of which some have died there and those who are alive have been imprisoned in the said place of Alexandria in horrible and inhuman dungeons. And afterward they have been led to Quayre [Cairo] where they now are in great distress in the hands of the Sarrazins, who, besides, have deprived them of all merchandise in their possession, both their own goods and those which they had on order from other merchants, which amounts to the sum of 60,000 francs; and also as the result of this affair, a number of women and children have become and remain in great poverty and misery, and others there are who had their money placed on the venture, who have thereby fallen into the state where they do not have, nor will they have in time to come, the wherewithal to carry on their merchantry, but will be obliged to wander through the land as mendicants; for some of them are aged and do not know any other trade by which to gain their livelihood—which is the most poignant grief in the world, to be rich and in good condition in one's youth and to become poor in old age." (46).

CHAPTER VII

SHIPPING, COMMERCE, AND BANKING DURING THE MIDDLE AGES

WE need not be surprised to find that the losses occasioned by the misfortunes of the Montpellier merchants in Egypt were so wide-spread in their effects. The business framework of a maritime trade adventure was then a most complicated structure—more so, perhaps, than in modern days when plenitude of capital and corporate organization permit of larger business units. In the ill-fated voyage of the "galley of Narbonne" no less than thirty-six individual claimants for damages appeared in the subsequent proceedings of reprisal.

Outside of Venice, with its great mercantile fleet and extensive navy-yard, and the other rich commercial Italian republics, ships were then comparatively scarce. Henry V of England had been obliged to hire them from the Netherlands in order to complete the transport of his army of 15,000 men to the shores of France. (47).

In comparison with the contemporary craft of northern waters, the ships then employed in the Levant trade were large; they sometimes had two decks, one in Genoa is mentioned as having three; that of Paolo Centurione of the latter city was of 1,000 tons. (48). Sails were not entirely relied upon; as in Roman days, oarsmen were also frequently employed to propel the

boat in time of calm; in galleys of war they were, as
we know, an important factor even down to times
comparatively modern; in one of the two illustrations
of Jacques Cœur's vessels printed in our text a bank
of five oarsmen can be counted on the side.

Fiske, the American historian, in commenting on the
similar Spanish and Portuguese caravels of the end of
the fifteenth century, says:

"With their length seldom more than thrice their
width of beam, with narrow tower-like poops, with
broad-shouldered bows and bowsprit weighed down
with spritsail yards, and with no canvas higher than a
topsail, these clumsy caravels could make but little
progress against head winds, and the amount of tack-
ing and beating to and fro was sometimes enough to
quadruple the length of the voyage. For want of me-
tallic sheathing below the water-line, the ship was
liable to be sunk by the terrible worm which, in Hak-
luyt's phrase, 'many times pearceth and eateth through
the strongest oak.'" (49).

In order to recruit the crew, impressment was sometimes resorted to. The "immemorial usage," by which
Lord Mansfield justified the legality of this practice,
dates back at least as far as the fifteenth century,
and the taverns and pleasure-haunts of Montpellier
and Marseilles, like those of English ports in the days
of Nelson, were visited by the press-gang, in search of
"able-bodied rogues and vagabonds and persons following no lawful calling." The merchant marine was
then the only navy, and was sometimes given, by
royal ordinance, powers which, in later days, although
only properly applicable to ships of war, were very

generally assumed by commercial craft, without other warrant than complaisant public opinion.

As we shall see, the operations of the press-gang were to make trouble for Jacques Cœur. The drag-net thus employed could not have been expected to work invariable justice; it was charged that it had failed to do so in the incident we are about to relate.

One day, as later was testified, several bailiffs of the city of Montpellier and divers of Jacques Cœur's agents "laid hands on certain knaves, ruffians, taverners, and other disorderly people and embarked them on the Galley *Saint Jacques* which was about to sail." Among the persons thus seized chanced to be a certain German, claimed to have been a pilgrim, and afterward, by the sheriff of the city, who in his official rôle had played a part in the proceeding, stated to have been an *"homme honnête et de bonne conversation."*

The alleged palmer, apparently objecting to this summary method of seeing the Holy Land, strenuously demanded to be set ashore, but Jacques Cœur, we are told, refused his consent. One of the citizens of Montpellier, who had himself been a victim of the press law, with its rough presumptions as to disorderly persons, testified that "the said German jumped into the sea and was drowned, although every effort was made to save him. And before his leap he wept and said that they had made a mistake as to him."

It is difficult to see how this sad mishap, in its worst aspect as regards Jacques Cœur, can represent anything more serious than error in judgment on the part of one whom the policy of the state invested with the duty of decision. The difference between a pilgrim, whose person was inviolate, and a vagabond, subject to impressment, was then more sharply defined in theory than was justifiable in practice; true, many pious men proved their devotion by making the long and arduous journey to the Holy Sepulchre and lesser sacred shrines; on the other hand, we know that the church sent penitents on these journeys to atone for the most atrocious crimes; the religious zeal which inspired the Crusaders, had, in the fifteenth century, lost much of its fire, and many cloaked themselves with the pilgrim's garb as a cover for irresponsible wanderings which imposed upon the religious hospitalities of the way. Jacques Cœur had been himself to the Holy Land; his fleet carried many pilgrim passengers; he was probably a far keener judge of a genuine palmer than the less travelled, and moreover, as we shall see, prejudiced, citizens of Montpellier who testified against him.

Much as in Sweden and Norway to-day, ships then were usually the property of several, sometimes of many owners; rich nobles and bourgeois availed themselves of them as outlets for the placement of their funds. Merchants combined to charter vessels for particular voyages, dividing and subdividing the tonnage among themselves; thus, we find Philbert de Heves and Pierre Teinturier of Montpellier, uniting, in 1443, to hire one-third of the cargo space of a ship then at anchor in the harbor of Nice; often the captain and owners reserved a share in the venture beyond their freight-money. (50).

If any of the merchants were unable to finance their part in the undertaking, they borrowed from shore-folk, occasionally women and children—widows and orphans, perhaps, of former traders—lenders, accustomed to such speculations, who advanced their funds in return for shares in the borrowers' expected profits.

The merchandise, carefully described and valued in the agreements, was bartered in the Levant for goods of analogous worth; sometimes this exchange was balanced by specie. Although the practice of exporting the latter from the kingdom, we shall see, was frowned upon by public ordinance, the inhibition was probably not strictly observed, for we find that in the voyage of the "galley of Narbonne" Philbert de Heves' only interest in the venture was represented by 1,000 gold ducats, for which he had given exchange on Alexandria to the vessel's owner, Jean Vidal, with which to purchase pepper and ginger in that city. (51).

In the instance of this vessel, as we learn from the proceedings for reprisal, the total freight-money, receivable by owner and captain, was two per cent of the value of the goods on the outgoing voyage and a like proportion of the appraised worth of those purchased in exchange; the charterers had also to pay the wages of the sailors who, in addition to food and clothing, received a small fixed stipend; to this the owner added a modest share of his commissions.

Thus were constituted veritable limited joint-stock companies, created by instruments which, for precise definition of individual rights and careful guard against contingencies, are not excelled by good examples of the present-day practice of business men and lawyers. Indeed, one cannot but be impressed by the completeness and the competency of the legal documents of the age under discussion. Whether it be a question of

wills, general powers of attorney, bills of lading, ship
charter-parties, receivership proceedings, court pleadings or joint-stock companies, legal forms and proce-
dures have changed but little through the intervening
centuries, and many of the ancient models, with slight
verbal change, might be made to serve analogous conditions of modern business.

Bills of lading for carriage by land were equally
carefully drawn and, quite naturally, saved the carrier
harmless from all responsibility where the real dangers
lay, "*exceptis aqua, igne et periculo malarum gentium.*"
Apparently these were hazards which the merchant
must himself absorb; no one was to be found at this
period so rash as to indemnify against loss by violence
and *force majeure* on inland shipments in the realm of
France. (52).

Maritime insurance, however, was not unknown; in
1433, Barcelona, where Jacques Cœur had an important branch house, framed highly developed regula-
tions which served as the models for other countries;
at about the same time marine risks were underwritten
in Genoa. (53). Hallam, in his *Middle Ages*, says that
the practice was of earlier date; but that it is not mentioned in the maritime codes of the fourteenth century. (54).

Short sales, selling what is not possessed, with the ex-
pectation of acquiring it in time to make the agreed delivery, were also engaged in by Genoese traders. (55).

In Jacques Cœur's day, banking was mostly in the
hands of individuals. Charles VII in 1423 borrowed
from François Surrat, a merchant of Geneva. (56).
A considerable part of the funds required to commence

his war against the French was loaned to Henry V by merchants of London, among them the renowned Sir Richard ("Dick") Whittington. (57).

The principal dealers in money and exchange in these days were, however, the Lombards; the Jews had been earlier banished from both the French and English kingdoms. (58). The Italian bankers then enjoyed an enormous advantage. On them, naturally, devolved the function of remitting to Rome the funds attributable to the Holy See from trans-alpine benefices. The flow of money, thus controlled, was balanced against the purchases of raw materials by the Italian merchants; indeed, it would be an interesting historical study to investigate the extent to which the then existing mercantile and maritime supremacy of the republics of Italy was due to the part taken by their financiers in the movement of church funds toward Saint Peter's.

The two colossal Florentine banking-houses, the Bardi and Peruggi, called by Villani "the pillars which supported the great part of the commerce of Christendom," which, in 1345, had crashed as a result of heavy loans to Edward III of England, had been succeeded by the still more illustrious Médicis of which the great Cosimo was now the head. (59). Commines tells us that the latter frequently furnished Edward IV of England with many hundred thousands of florins, and Hallam states that the customs of the latter country then were often "farmed to Italian bankers for loans not always punctually paid."

The city of Cahors, in southern France, famous at an earlier period for its dealers in money and exchange, had then lost much of its business, as a result of the English domination of Guienne and the general decline of French commerce during the wars. (60).

The first great public bank, established on modern lines for the accommodation of individual merchants, was probably that of Barcelona, formed in 1401. (61). The banks of Venice, founded as early as 1170, and that of Genoa, incorporated in 1407, seem to have specialized in loans to their individual states; however, we find the former, in 1246, transmitting 2,500 marks to a private citizen of Frankfort, a sum deposited with it for the purpose by Pope Innocent IV, and the latter, during the days of Jacques Cœur's power and influence in Languedoc, and very probably at his solicitation, making advances to that province in anticipation of its collection of taxes. (62). The Genoese institution, called the Office of Saint George, originally incorporated as an association of local creditors who had made unfortunate loans to the republic on the security of its revenues, rose to enormous financial and political power in that state.

The rate of interest current in the different countries depended then, as now, upon too many varying factors to give much weight to particular examples. In 1435, however, it is stated to have been as low as ten per cent in Barcelona. (63). In France and England, considerably higher rates prevailed, largely due to exhaustion from continual warfare; the latest French historian places the yield on capital at twenty per cent in the former kingdom at this epoch. (64).

All lending of money for profit was then called usury, whether the rate was reasonable or not. It was denounced as a sin by the theologians of the Middle Ages, though generally employed in practice. The Romans had been much more liberal in this regard and freely recognized the right of capital to earn, though limiting its exorbitant demands. Thus Cicero, writing from Cilicia, of which he was then the Governor, to his friend Atticus, states that he has established twelve per cent as the rate for that province, with "the assent of the most grasping money-lenders." (65).

In the fifteenth century, however, the ethical attitude had changed; the slowly moving wheels of economic laws had yet to compel the admission by ecclesiastics of the absurdity of principles that never should have been imposed. The Church itself found it desirable to receive regular returns on its placements of capital to maintain some of its religious houses; accordingly, it purchased from landed proprietors the right to receive their rents, giving the owners the privilege of redemption after a stated period. Opinion being taken of two of its most renowned legists as to whether this constituted the offense of usury: "No," said the learned doctors, "not if the right of repurchase was out of mind when the deal was made"—by which bit of metaphysical casuistry a safe way was pointed out whereby the wicked demons could be easily exorcised from future investment transactions in line with ecclesiastic purpose. (66).

One of the most awkward points of conflict between the doctrines of the Church and the practices of men of affairs was over the matter of commerce with infidels. No distinction was attempted between the subjects of the Egyptian Sultan and the Turks, the latter the enemy of the former and of Christendom as well; traffic with both was equally condemned. Inasmuch as the luxurious products of the Levant were then the principal material objects of Occidental desire and the entire eastern and southern shores of the Mediterranean were possessed by the Mohammedans, this inhibition of the churchmen, if faithfully obeyed, would have left but little scope for the enterprise of the Christian merchants of southern Europe.

The history of this contest between theory and practice is set forth by the French historian Clément as follows:

"During several centuries the Popes had believed that to forbid commerce with the Levant was an excellent means of combating and ruining the infidels; they aimed further at preventing the odious traffic of the Venetians who carried off or bought children along the shore-fronts whom they sold to the Saracens. Such was the origin and principal motive of the interdictions. Some Venetian merchants, having transgressed them, were visited with excommunication; then, on their death-beds, wishing to re-enter into grace with Heaven, the majority of them bequeathed their property to the churches. A great many wills of this character having been attacked by the families of the testators, Venetian theologians and casuists decided that the merchants had done nothing sinful, but the Pope condemned these decisions as heretical. A compromise was arrived at after long negotiations, and Pope Benedict XII forbade solely commerce with the infidels, without an express authorization from the Holy See. From this time on, the sale of authorizations became a source of papal revenue. At first individual and special, these authorizations circulated later like bills of exchange, and ship-owners passed them from one to another by indorsement." (67).

CHAPTER VIII

LEVANTINE TRADE. MEDITERRANEAN PORTS

In seeking commercial influence and advantage in the Orient, the present-day policies of European statecraft are but repetitions of the aims of enterprising merchants and bodies politic of the Middle Ages. Perhaps only when we recall that the New World was discovered and the Cape of Good Hope rounded in an effort to regain the Levant trade by other routes, after the old ways to the East were blocked by Turkish invasion, can we have some conception of its relative importance in the first half of the fifteenth and prior centuries when man's whole world consisted of the Mediterranean and the peoples clustered around it. It was the glitter of this great prize, more, perhaps, than missionary zeal which lured the first discoverers out on the mighty main beyond the Pillars of Hercules and led them, in its quest, to dare what was to them the appalling risk of sailing off the edge of the world.

To Western eyes the Crusades had disclosed such a vision of the riches and luxury of the "gorgeous East" as has made them, ever since, the favorite poetical metaphor for wealth and magnificence. Constantinople, the noble capital of the Eastern Roman Empire, at the time of its taking by the Crusaders in the year 1204, had been much the largest and most resplendent city in the world. Its gilded marble palaces, its works of art, its treasures of gold, silver, and jewels, had formed a striking contrast to the comparative crudity and poverty of the Western nations of that age. Ville-hardouin, the chronicler of the Fourth Crusade, has left us a naïve record of the impressions which its glories had made upon him and his fellow followers of the Cross.

"They looked longingly at Constantinople," says he—"those who had never before seen it—for they could not believe that the world could contain a city so rich, when they saw the high walls and strong towers which enclosed it and the noble palaces and lofty churches, in number which would have been beyond belief if they had not seen them with their own eyes, and the length and breadth of the city, which was truly the sovereign city of the world." And, again, in telling the story of its sack and pillage:

"The booty was so great that one could not find words to tell you the amount of gold, silver, plate, and precious stones, of satins, silks, furs, and of all the rich goods which therein were found. Never since the world was created has the like been gained from one city." (68).

When Jacques Cœur brought to its inglorious end his first commercial voyage to the Orient, he must have been impressed, as was la Brocquière, by the evi-dences of the fact that the great commercial advan-tages, originally given to the French by the establish-ment, during crusading days, of the Latin Empire of Constantinople and the Christian Kingdom of Jeru-salem, had all been lost. To the people of the Orient all foreigners then were "Franks"; practically all trade with eastern Mediterranean ports, however, belonged

to the Italians and Catalans or was tributary to them.
(69).

La Brocquière goes through all Palestine, Asia Minor,
and Constantinople and, although keenly alive to his
country's prestige, despite his Burgundian prejudices,
finds no compatriots but Jacques Cœur and his small
party of French merchants. Perhaps it was from home-
sickness on this account that, after meeting traders
from Venice, Genoa, Florence, and Barcelona, we find
him theorizing as to whether a certain Berkat, once a
prominent figure in Damascus affairs, then long since
dead, might not have been a Frenchman, because of
the *fleur-de-lis* carved upon his former habitation; in
Constantinople, visitors from France were of such rare
occurrence that the Emperor, on hearing of his arrival,
sends for him to inquire news of Jeanne d'Arc, whose
martyrdom was then two years old.

Their geographical position, as well as the constant
stream of papal money flowing toward them, had early
enabled the cities of northern Italy "to profit alike by
the barbarism of the West and the civilization of the
East." The Crusades, "from which the inhabitants of
other communities gained nothing but relics and
wounds"—and again we borrow from Macaulay's
rich and vivid phrase—"brought to the rising com-
monwealths of the Adriatic and Tyrrhene Seas a large
increase of wealth, dominion, and knowledge." Ville-
hardouin tells us that the Venetians had charged 85,000
silver marks for the transport, by their fleets, of the
soldiers of the Cross, on the occasion of the Fourth
Crusade. (70). In addition, they had bargained for a
share of the booty, a part of which may be seen to-

day in the four famous gilt horses which adorn St. Mark's Square.

Their control of shipping undoubtedly enabled the Italian dealers to profit from the war spoils of other peoples as well. Thus many a valiant trans-alpine leader, whose bold part in sieges and battles, under the banner of the Cross, had gained for him, in the general allotment, some of the precious works of classic or antique art, too bulky or too heavy to be carried with him on the campaigns toward Jerusalem, must have been at the mercy of the Italian ship-owners, who alone had the bottoms to carry away these treasures.

Sheltered between the rival zones of Papal and Imperial power, setting off, the one against the other, the influences of Popes and Cæsars, the Italian cities had consolidated the political and commercial advantages thus easily secured, and by the fifteenth century had become true urban republics, sharing only with Barcelona the maritime domination of the Mediterranean.

Perfumes from Arabia, Persian rugs and velvets, rubies from India, pearls from Ceylon, Chinese silks, spices from Sumatra and Java, which had found their way toward Europe during the days of the Roman Empire, continued, during the Middle Ages, to reach the eastern shores of the Mediterranean by lines of travel almost as old as commerce itself.

The two main routes traversed by these commodities, during the fifteenth century, were largely controlled by the Venetians and Genoese, whose large fleets and effective commercial organizations in the Levant ports assured to them an advantage, against which the merchants of other nations found difficulty in contending.

The water route was by way of the Indian Ocean and the Red Sea to Egypt, where, at Alexandria, the depots and commercial outposts of Venice collected the traffic for the vessels of that republic; the route by land was by caravans across Turkestan to the Caspian, thence again by camel to the Black Sea, where it was met by the ships of the traders of Genoa, whose colonies at Pera, a suburb of Constantinople, and Caffa, in the Crimea, enabled her to dominate the waters of the Euxine. (70a).

In addition to these principal Asian travel ways, there were several minor ones. An intermediate path led from the Persian Gulf along the Euphrates River, through Damascus, to Beirut and other Syrian harbors; it was this which we find Jacques Cœur intercepting on his first commercial voyage. The caravan in which our friend la Brocquière had ridden had journeyed northward along the Red Sea, through Syria and Anatolia, to the then highly important commercial port of Brossa on the Sea of Marmora. The trail from Timbuctoo to Tunis, by which gold from the Rio del Oro was carried on camel-back to the Mediterranean, was soon to meet with active competition by sea, following the great voyage of discovery, down the Guinea coast, made in 1433 by the Portuguese mariner, Gil Eannes.

Checked in her early attempts to monopolize the Eastern trade by her bitter and continuous wars with Genoa, her commercial and maritime rival, Venice, in Jacques Cœur's day, seems still to have maintained

CONSTANTINOPLE.
From an old engraving.

her superiority in the Levant. Although no longer, as
during the reign of the Latin Empire, the most favored
traders in Constantinople, the Venetians still continued to be the most influential there. "There are
merchants from all nations in this town," says la Brocquière, "but none so powerful as the Venetians, who
have a bailiff that regulates all their affairs, independent of the Emperor and his officers. This privilege
they have enjoyed for a long time!" and he adds: "The
Turks have also an officer to superintend their commerce, who, like the Venetian bailiff, is independent
of the Emperor; they have even the privilege that if
one of their slaves shall run away and take refuge
within the city, on their demanding him the Emperor
is bound to give him up." Pera, the Genoese suburb
of Constantinople, he describes as "a large town, inhabited by Greeks, Jews, and Genoese; the last are
masters of it, under the Duke of Milan, who styles
himself Lord of Pera. It has a podesta and other officers, who govern it after their manner"; and he records
a similar practice there followed with regard to fugitive
Turkish slaves. The Duke of Milan was then ruler as
well of Genoa, which, as so often during this epoch,
had sought outside help to settle its internecine strifes.

The intense hostility and jealousy existing between
the rival Venetian and Genoese republics is illustrated
by an incident also related to us by la Brocquière. "I
met at Pera," he states, "an ambassador from the Duke
of Milan, named Sir Benedicto de Fourlino. The Duke,
wanting the support of the [German] Emperor Sigismond against the Venetians, and seeing Sigismond em-
barrassed with the defense of his Kingdom of Hungary

against the Turks, had sent an embassy to Amurath
[the Turkish Sultan] to negotiate a peace between the
two princes.

"Sir Benedicto," he records, "in honor of my Lord
of Burgundy, gave me a gracious reception. He even
told me that, to do mischief to the Venetians, he had
contributed to make them lose Salonica, taken from
them by the Turks; and certainly in this he acted so
much the worse, for I have since seen the inhabitants
of that town deny Jesus Christ, and embrace the Mohammedan religion." Sir Benedicto, we are rejoiced
to find, did not succeed in his noble mission to the
heathen.

La Brocquière contents himself with the statement
that "Venice is a great and handsome town," and with
a discourse on the wisdom of its government; its grandeur was then too well known to require but passing
comment from so wide a traveller. A somewhat later
and more renowned chronicler has given us a less reserved description of it as it was before Da Gama's
epoch-making voyage of discovery, in 1499, sheared it
of its glories.

"I was," says Philippe de Commines, then an ambassador to the Venetian republic, from his sovereign,
Charles VIII of France, "conducted through the principal street, which they call the Grand Canal, and it
is so wide that galleys frequently cross one another;
indeed, I have seen vessels of 400 tons or more ride
at anchor just by the houses. It is the fairest and best
built street, I think, in the world, and goes quite through
the city; the houses are very large and lofty and built
of stone; the old ones are all painted; those of about

one hundred years' standing are faced with white marble from Istria—which is about a hundred miles from Venice—and inlaid with porphyry and serpentine. . . . In short, it is the most triumphant city that I have ever seen, the most respectful to all ambassadors and strangers, governed with the greatest wisdom, and serving God with the most solemnity. . . .

"In this chapel [Saint Mark's] their treasure—of which so much is said—is kept, and intended only for the decoration of their churches; there are twelve or fourteen rubies, the largest I ever saw; one of them weighs seven, the other eight, hundred carats, but both of them are unpolished; there are twelve other stones in cases of gold, with the edges and fore part set richly with very fine jewels. There are also twelve crowns of gold. . . . But this is not a treasure of equal value with ready money," says the practical King's Minister, "and indeed they have not much of that kind of treasure; for the Doge told me in the Senate House that it is a capital crime among them to suggest collecting a treasure of that nature. . . . After they had shown me their treasure, I was carried to see their arsenal, where their galleys are equipped, and all things necessary provided for their navies; which perhaps are even now the finest in the world, and were formerly under better order and regulation."

In the Doge's reply to his inquiry as to hoarding specie, Commines had elicited an expression of one of the striking enactments of Venetian policy, so opposite to the statecraft of other nations much slower, in that age, to perceive that money is but the standard by which real wealth is measured and an instrument for

its exchange. "He who would bring home the wealth
of the Indies must carry the wealth of the Indies with
him," goes the Spanish proverb; the gold and silver
pieces of Venice were then being employed by its merchants in uses far more serviceable to the state than
would have been gained in amassing it in idle public
treasure. They were hoarded, 'tis true, but not in the
city of Saint Mark's or by its inhabitants. Their secret
hiding-place was disclosed, centuries later, when Lord
Clive in India received from his native ally that splendid honorarium which was to bring down upon a great
name the censure of his countrymen. "The treasury
of Bengal was thrown open to him [Clive]. There
were piled up, after the usage of Indian princes, immense masses of coin, among which might not seldom
be detected the florins and byzants with which, before
any European ships had turned the Cape of Good
Hope, the Venetians purchased the stuffs and spices
of the East. Clive walked between heaps of gold and
silver, crowned with rubies and diamonds, and was at
liberty to help himself." (71).

An Italian historian has preserved a speech of the
Doge Mocenigo, extolling the virtues of peace, in opposition to the war against Milan then being debated,
which gives us a vivid and detailed picture of the
proud position of the Venetian republic and some
statistics of its trade in the early years of the fifteenth
century.

"Every week," said he, "we receive from Milan
17,000 to 18,000 ducats; from Monza, 1,000; from
Como, 3,000; from Tortona and Novara, 2,000; from
Pavia, Cremona, and Parma, each a like amount; from

Bergamo, 1,500. The bankers all agree that the Milanese must each year pay 1,600,000 ducats to settle with us. Tortona and Novara each buy annually 6,000 pieces of cloth; Pavia, 3,000; Milan, 4,000; Cremona, 40,000[?]; Coni, 12,000; Monza, 6,000; Brescia, 5,000; Bergamo, 10,000; Parma, 4,000; in all amounting to 94,000 [sic] pieces. These cities, besides, send us gold of the value of 1,558,000 sequins. We do with Lombardy a commerce of 28,000,000 of ducats. The Lombards buy from us, each year, 5,000,000 pounds of cotton, 2,000,000 pounds of thread, 4,000,000 pounds of Catalonian wool and a like amount of the French variety, cloth of gold and silks of the value of 250,000 ducats; 3,000 cartons of pepper, 400 packages of cinnamon, 200,000 pounds of ginger, sugar to the value of 95,000 ducats; needlework and embroidery, 30,000 ducats; 4,000,000 pounds of dye-woods; vegetable dyes, 50,000 ducats; soap, 250,000 ducats; *slaves*, 30,000. I do not count the production of salt.

"Consider how many vessels the carriage of this merchandise maintains in activity, whether to deliver them to Lombardy, or to bring them from Syria, Roumania, Catalonia, Flanders, Cyprus, Sicily, from all points of the world. Venice gains two and one-half to three per cent on the freight. See how many persons make their living from this movement of the traffic: brokers, workmen, sailors, some thousands of families, besides the merchants whose profits reach not less than 600,000 ducats.

"Know that each year Verona takes 200 pieces of cloth of gold, silver, and silk; Padua, 200; Treviso, 120; Friuli, 50; Feltre and Belluno, 12; that you supply to these different communities 400 cartons of pepper, 120 packages of cinnamon, 100,000 pounds of sugar, and 200 cakes of wax per year.

"Florence sends you merchandise of the value of 16,000 sequins, and 350,000 in spices and takes in return Spanish and French wools, seeds, silks, gold and silver thread, wax, sugar, and jewels.

"In short, the commerce of Venice places in circulation each year 10,000,000 sequins. . . . Our housing is valued at 7,000,000 ducats; its annual rental at 500,000. Three thousand merchant ships carry on our trade; 43 galleys and 300 smaller vessels; these, manned by 19,000 sailors, secure our naval and maritime power. Our mint has coined 1,000,000 ducats within the year. . . .

"To you alone," said the Doge in conclusion, "are both land and sea equally open. You are the canal of all riches; you supply the entire world; the whole universe is interested in your prosperity; all the gold of the world flows to you." (72).

Genoa, bold, energetic, but turbulent republic, supporting almost ceaseless hostilities with both Venice and Catalonia on the high seas, was engaged within in never-ending strife. Repeatedly, after the fourteenth century, at the price of the republic's independence, the partisans of its powerful contending families invoked a foreign prince's aid. Thus, as we have found, Filippo Maria Visconti, Duke of Milan, was now its master and "Lord of Pera" as well. Famagosta, long the capital of the island kingdom of Cyprus, was now, as la Brocquière informs us, a Genoese possession. This city, like the colonies in the Crimea, from which Genoa maintained a line of commerce with interior Asia, had been purchased for the republic by its famous state bank, the Office of Saint George, which, amidst the general civil confusion, remained the only stable element in Genoese affairs, and was permitted to govern its outlying territorial acquisitions in a manner analogous to the early operations of the British East India Company.

Famagosta, then one of the most flourishing cities of the world, so the chroniclers tell us, is now famous only as the scene of Desdemona's tragic honeymoon. Rudolphe of Saxe, a German bishop, whose eyes, fortunately for us, were not entirely closed to lay affairs, has left a most engaging picture of Famagosta and Cyprus, as they were in the century preceding Jacques Cœur's time.

"There exist in the isle of Cyprus," writes he in 1341, "the most extravagant and the richest lords of Christendom. There a fortune which brings in 3,000 florins a year is no more thought of than a revenue of three marks in Germany. But the Cypriots spend all their wealth in the chase, tournaments, and amusements. The Count of Jaffa, whom I knew, kept more than 500 hunting-dogs.

"The merchants of Cyprus have also acquired immense riches; and it is not surprising, for their island is the most eastern outpost of Christendom; as a result, all ships and all commodities, from whatever shore they may have come, are obliged to stop at Cyprus. Furthermore, pilgrims from all lands, who desire to journey abroad, must first land upon this isle. Thus one is informed, at each hour of the day, from sunrise

to sunset, by letters or by the word of mouth of constantly arriving foreigners, of the news and gossip of
the remotest countries; consequently, the Cypriots
have special schools to teach all the known languages.

"As for the city of Famagosta, it is one of the wealthi-
est cities in existence. Its inhabitants live in the greatest opulence. One of them, at his daughter's wedding,
gave her for her head-dress alone, jewels which were of
more value than all the ornaments of the Queen of
France, so say the French knights who have visited us
in Cyprus. A merchant of Cyprus, one day, sold to
the Egyptian Sultan for his royal sceptre, a golden
apple enriched with four precious stones, a carbuncle,
an emerald, a sapphire, and a pearl. These jewels cost
60,000 florins; some time after the sale the merchant
wished to repurchase it and offered 100,000 florins; but
the Sultan refused. . . .

"There is, in any shop of Famagosta, more wood of
aloes than five carts can haul. I say nothing of spices;
they are as common in this city as bread, and sold in
equal quantity.

"As for precious stones, cloth of gold, and other
articles of luxury, I know not how to tell of them; I
would not be believed in our land of Saxe.

"There are also in Famagosta," the observing
churchman adds, "a multitude of courtesans; they
make considerable fortunes there, and many of them
possess more than 100,000 florins; but I hesitate to
say more of the riches of these unfortunates." (73).

Cosimo de Médici, greatest of merchant princes, of
the famous banking and commercial house described
by Commines as "so renowned and triumphant over

Christendom," then swayed Florence by his wise and
benign citizenship. His life, devoted to the arts of
peace, brought lustre on his native land and seem-
ingly influenced not a little that of the subject of
our memoir.

The Florentines were great manufacturers of fine
cloth; this industry, we are told, occupied one-third
its people. They took the primary products of the
looms of Flanders, France, and England, and rework-
ing them by processes of shearing, fulling, and dyeing,
akin to magic in their results, transformed them into
fabrics of great richness, beauty, and costliness, making
the world, on buying back its products, pay heavily
for the stamp of Florentine craft and taste thus added
to them. It was at Florence, and in association with
two of its citizens, that Jacques Cœur, toward the
close of his business career, established a silk-factory,
the only foreign industry in which he is known to have
engaged. (74).

The Florentines, above all others, were the bankers
of Europe. "The tables of Italian money-changers
were set in every city," and those of the Florentines
were the most numerous and active of them all. They
peopled in Paris an entire street, like that frequented
by them in London, inaccurately called "Lombard"
after the money-dealers of Florence.

One of the republic's authors, somewhat boastfully
discoursing on the superiority of its fabrics to those of
Venice, asserts:

"Their better quality is recognized at the court of
Rome, at that of Naples, in Sicily, at Constantinople,
Pera, Chios, Bursa, Gallipoli, Salonica, Adrianople,

and everywhere the Florentines send their cloths, have their banks, factories, and consulates. As for silks and gold and silver brocades, we produce, and we will always continue to do so, more than your Venice, Genoa, and Lucca combined. Ask of the merchants who frequent Marseilles, Avignon, Lyons, Geneva, Bruges, Antwerp, and London; they find everywhere strong banks, magnificent exchanges, esteemed merchants, warehouses, churches, and consulates belonging to the Florentines. Inform yourselves of the banks of the Médicis, the Pazzis, the Capponis, the Brandelmontis, the Corsinis, the Falconeris, the Portineris, and other houses so numerous that their names alone fill pages. In these establishments it is not haberdashery, hardware, sewing-thread, fringes, strings of beads and glassware that one deals in," says the Florentine writer in slighting allusion to the commodities of the rival republic; "here the commerce is in ducats, brocades, and cloths *de luxe*." (75).

Meanwhile, Brunelleschi was putting the finishing touches on the cupola of the famous Duomo, and the city of Giotto was being still further enriched by the peerless art of Donatello, Ghiberti, della Robbia, and Fra Angelico.

The high-spirited Catalans, always jealous of their local liberties, the price of their allegiance to the Aragonese Crown, vied with the Italian cities on the seas, and, in their Barcelonian capital, set up commercial usages and institutions the most progressive of their day. Their sovereign, Alfonso the Magnificent, shortly after Jacques Cœur's return from Damascus, fell heir to the Kingdom of Naples in addition to his own, which legacy he was enabled to maintain only after bitter warfare with René of the House of Anjou.

The unsuccessful candidate, thenceforth contenting himself with ambitious royal titles to Naples and other kingdoms, none of which he possessed, governed amiably his county of Provence, whose chief city, the ancient seaport of Marseilles, had shared in the ruin of his cause. Though for his other domains owing homage to his brother-in-law, Charles VII of France, the sceptreless King René ruled the beautiful Provençal land in nominal fealty to the German Emperor.

PART II

THE MERCHANT PRINCE

"Seest thou a man diligent in his business? he shall stand before kings; he shall not stand before mean men." (Proverbs 22 : 29.)

CHAPTER IX

JACQUES CŒUR ORGANIZES FRENCH COMMERCE

"The King's household"—writes Thomas Bazin, the Bishop of Lisieux, who had enjoyed great favor under Charles VII and, therefore, could portray with authority the men and events of that reign—"was at this period administered by a man of the utmost industry and genius, Jacques Cœur, of Bourges, of a plebeian family, but endowed with great mental ability, unflagging perseverance, and rare prudence. Lord Steward of the household of the King, in addition to the tasks of this office he continued to devote himself, as before, to vast commercial operations which brought him great riches, and with them high place and wide renown. The first in his day, he caused to be constructed and equipped ships which transported to Africa, throughout the Levant, and even to Alexandria in Egypt, cloths, woollens, and other articles fabricated within the realm. On the return voyage these ships brought back different varieties of silks and all sorts of spices, and perfumes which were marketed in the provinces reached by the waters of the Rhone, or in Catalonia and other neighboring lands, *a practice which was then entirely new in France*, for theretofore this commerce had long been carried on through the medium of other nations, notably, the Venetians, the Genoese, and the Barcelonians.

"Such was the source of the immense riches amassed by Jacques Cœur. Among other ways, he gave proof

of his opulence in causing to be erected with such unusual despatch at Bourges, his native city, that house,
so richly ornamented, so spacious, and yet, withal, so
magnificent, that neither princes of the blood, nor the
King himself, had any residence comparable to it.

"But, at the same time that he possessed this immense fortune, Jacques Cœur was wholly devoted to
the King and zealous in the interests of France. It
was due to no fault of his that the country found itself in a critical situation. While the great lords, enriched by the largess of the King, pretended poverty,
and found a thousand false and frivolous pretexts for
refraining to come to his aid, Jacques Cœur offered to
lend him a considerable sum, and placed at his disposi-
tion, for the accomplishment of that work, at once so
sacred and so urgent (the expulsion of the English from
Normandy), 100,000 écus. Thanks to this assistance,
the French brought siege to Falaise, Domfront . . ."

It is not surprising to find much that is undisclosed
in the history of a life lived five hundred years ago.
Only in rare instances, such as that of Jeanne d'Arc,
every act of whose daily being became the subject of
the minutest theological study, or that of the early
Médicis, whose posterity perpetuated their renown,
are the gaps in the careers of the uncrowned heroes
and heroines of this epoch sufficiently filled in to satisfy
the inquiries of succeeding generations; the glorious
ogival churches of thirteenth-century France are the
sole monuments to preserve the memories of peerless
architects whose names, even, have failed to descend
to us.

Contemporary chronicles have clearly recorded the

rôle played by Jacques Cœur in freeing French commerce from the control of strangers; the results of his efforts stand out boldly, but the earlier steps of the progress by which he attained them are still obscured.

To the scattered French commerce of his day, Jacques Cœur supplied an element, then unknown in his country, but indispensable to enable it to withstand the strenuous rivalry of other maritime nations—organization. Indeed, this factor, even now, is none too much appreciated in France, where imagination is preferably employed in skilful craftsmanship and brilliant invention rather than in the creation of comprehensive business structures, unconnected with the state.

With the true eye of a master spirit Jacques Cœur saw that, in those days of special privileges, only by solidifying the home markets could French traders hope to compete with the Venetians and Genoese, each with their highly developed commercial machines and jealously guarded spheres of Levantine influence.

Thus, two years before setting out on his eastern voyage, we find him forming a partnership with the brothers Godart, two of his former companions in the Mint at Bourges, to deal in "every class of merchandise, including that required by the King, Monseigneur the Dauphin, and other nobles, as well as other lines in which they (the partners) can make their profit." Of this association which lasted for nine years, when, in 1439, it was terminated by the deaths of the two Godarts, we know nothing further than the recital of its purposes and the bare facts of its existence. The simultaneous demise of his partners remains a mystery; lives were uncertain in those troubled days. The

pre-eminence over all his fellow merchants so quickly
attained by Jacques Cœur during the term of this co-
partnership, seems to show that the joint arrangement
did not command his entire efforts, but was rather a
price, necessarily paid, at this stage of his business
career, for court influence and local representation.
There are, too, some indications that, even after his
earlier difficulties there, he continued relations with
the local Mint at Bourges, and biographers have as-
signed to him the direction of its affairs throughout
his life. It is unlikely, however, that his later connection with this institution differed any from those existing after the conclusion of his management of the
Paris Mint to which he was later called; his period of
active service over, he retained a share in the emoluments of the office in consideration for his voluntary
withdrawal from it—an arrangement then not un-
common with regard to public posts, and one which
has been frequently practised down to times more
modern. (76).

When Jacques Cœur fixed upon Montpellier as the
centre of his operations, the French Mediterranean
coast was then only a fraction of its present extent.
Roussillon, with its harbor of Perpignan, belonged to
the Crown of Aragon; Provence and its port of Marseilles, as we have seen, to the House of Anjou.

Commerce with the Levant might then be carried
on from three principal French ports; Narbonne, Montpellier, and Aigues-Mortes. Encroaching sands have
since made inland cities of the former two; the fortified point of embarkation for Saint Louis's ill-fated
Crusades, then, as now, far from firm land and reached

by causeways over intervening flats, still raises its
stanch thirteenth-century walls amidst the shallows
of the Gulf of Lyons, a monument to the religious zeal,
though not to the commercial sense, of that devout
but impractical monarch. These factors, silting sands,
and, in the case of Aigues-Mortes, its isolation, adding
to the effects of endless warfare, had brought all three
harbors to the verge of ruin and decay. By letters,
confirming those of the preceding reign, Charles VII
had granted to Aigues-Mortes a monopoly of the Mediterranean coasting-trade. Although prevented by its
remoteness from itself enjoying these royal benefits, the
favored port was enabled to confer them upon the neighboring city of Montpellier, then joined to it by canal.

Besides thus sharing in these coastwise privileges,
Montpellier, in its foreign trade, had a monopoly of
its own; Pope Urban V, its special patron, had relaxed
on its behalf the Church's ban against traffic with the
infidels; six ships from that port were permitted to
make, each, one yearly voyage to Alexandria and return; it was doubtless the possession of this latter right
which decided Jacques Cœur to select it as the headquarters for his maritime trade.

When he began his operations there we have no
certain knowledge; patient local researches have produced no dates for them prior to 1440. The vast commercial results already achieved by him by that time,
indicate that he must have commenced to create them
soon after his return from the Orient in 1432, or even
shortly before. (77). He completed his organization
rapidly; his progress was made with giant strides.
Within twenty years from the time of his initial reverse

at the Bourges Mint, he reached the zenith of his career, when the contemporary chronicler, Mathieu de Coucy (or d'Escoussy) could say of him that he sold "not only to the court but in many other places in the said realm of France, and without it, every sort of merchandise that the brain of man could think of or imagine, at which many persons, nobles as well as merchants and others, marvelled greatly. He had fully 300 factors under him, distributed in many and divers places, both on the sea and land."

In the heyday of his prosperity, he had for his branch houses and town residences—it is in some cases difficult to distinguish between them—more than thirty buildings; two at Paris, one on the rue Rambuteau, where to-day there is a bust of him with an inscription, another on the site where now stands the Palais Royal; two at Tours, where he maintained his great central depot of supplies for the court; four business houses and two residences at Lyons; buildings at Saint Pourçain, Sancerre, Beaucaire, Béziers, Narbonne, Perpignan, and Marseilles; several at Montpellier; eight at Bourges, including his magnificent palace there which still commemorates his taste and former grandeur. (78).

As for his ships, the records of the administration of his confiscated estate show that he owned and operated from French home ports, four large galleys and three lesser vessels; earlier historians have assumed that these represented his entire maritime force. Transacting, as he did, nearly all of his country's commerce, at home and abroad, one would have been surprised could he have handled it with so small a merchant

fleet. That he owned other vessels, recently produced
public documents of the city of Barcelona have now
established. (79). On the French expedition of 1448
for the relief of Finale, in the Republic of Genoa, he
commanded a squadron stated, by chronicles of that
day, to have been equipped at his expense and to have
been composed of eleven ships of various tonnages;
though the narratives are silent regarding their ownership, one would be at a loss to account for these craft
in the naval service of France, otherwise than by attributing them to Jacques Cœur, then all-powerful in
his country's maritime trade. The muster, on comparatively short notice, of such a squadron, presupposes his possession of other vessels not readily recall-
able from long voyages to Eastern ports. France, it
must be remembered, had then only one safe harbor,
Rochelle, on the Atlantic and Channel coast; all of its
seaports there were held by England; Dieppe, although
recovered in 1435, was constantly menaced by English arms.

His factors and the masters of his ships he bound to
him "by hoops of steel." History has few more inspiring records of loyalty and devotion than the example of these qualities given by them in their master's time of trouble. The memory of it was still fresh
in men's minds, although the details had become somewhat confused, a century later, when Étienne Pasquier
writes of it in a letter to his friend, the Sire de Mari-
lhac, King's Counsellor and Master in Ordinary of the
Paris Chamber of Accounts:

"It is indeed as you say; I imagine that France
never produced a man, who by his industry, without

any special favor of the prince, arrived at so much eminence and riches as Jacques Cœur.

"He was, in his way, both King and Emperor; and, as we discover the grandeur of old Rome by its ruins, I may say the same of him. . . .

"As for his sentence, but that is on record, I should say it was altogether a calumny; but I cannot speak falsely in stating that it was the jealousy of the great men of Charles VII's court which concocted this tragedy. . . .

"Judge, I pray you, if I am not right in saying that he was a monarch in his way, since one of the chief points of his accusation was a correspondence which he had with the Sultan of Egypt; and remark also, that the Pope became the principal intercessor with the King, that his life might be spared.

"And, again, perhaps the most marvellous part of the story is, that after his condemnation there should be found sixty or eighty men, his former subordinates, who through him had become possessed of great wealth, who were ready to lend him each a thousand crowns to aid him in his difficulties, so that he was able, after a time, to re-establish his fortunes. (80). This service, mind you, not being founded on any other ground than the obligations they owed their master, for his goodness to them in the days of his prosperity.

"Nothing is more surprising than that a simple citizen should have been able to create such a fund of gratitude, except that beings so grateful should be found to remember him in his adversity.

"It may well be said of him that he was another Alexander, who produced many kings."

CHAPTER X

HIS FACTORS

Jacques Cœur's factors were the heads of his branch houses, having full power to engage their master or to bind his credit in any way; some of them were themselves great personages in their day.

First of them all, called in a document of the times his "head clerk," was William de Varye. His relations to his principal were rather those of a junior partner. Although all Jacques Cœur's factors participated in the profits of his operations, de Varye's interest was especially intertwined with that of his chief; their names are joined as defendants in the confiscation proceedings of which we shall later hear; in the royal edict of restitution de Varye comes in for a third share with Jacques Cœur's children in the partial restoration of their patrimony.

Charged with the control of the great central depot at Tours, from which were furnished all the needs and desires of the court and nobility of France, from cloth of gold and precious stones to supple coats of mail and plate armor, de Varye was a good man for a courtier to know during Charles VII's reign. Did the great soldier, Dunois, Lieutenant-General of the Kingdom, wish a costly ruby for the scabbard of his dress sword, or Charles of Orleans, the Poet-Duke, lately returned from captivity in England, fancy a silver shoulder-piece and Turkish buckler to heighten his soldierly array; did other princes of the blood crave ornaments for their royal splendor—all these objects could be had from the dazzling supply guarded by the faithful William. Did the Admiral or Marshal of France require *brigantines* for war, or ells of black or crimson velvet for their state appearance, or, perchance, the Queen's mother, Yoland of Aragon, need a gown, the Dauphiness, Margaret of Scotland, "some silks and sables to make a robe for our person" to be worn at the fêtes of Nancy, or Margaret of Anjou a queenly wedding-trousseau for her marriage to Henry VI of England; was the Queen of France obliged to borrow 400 écus on her "great pearl," or did the King's mistress, Agnes Sorel, "Dame of Beauty," covet diamonds to enhance her charms; did some great churchman require gold vessels for his cathedral's service or jewels to garnish its reliquaries; was a Scottish archer of the King's body-guard to be rewarded for his valor by a gift of coat of mail with azure velvet covering; was the French herald-at-arms, the royal chaplain, the court painter, even the King's laundress in need of money or supplies —all alike were furnished from this famous treasure-hoard at Tours. (81).

It is hard to leave this enchanting depository; these were but a few of its possessions. We shall have a longer peep into it by and by when the King's officers come to throw it open and take in charge its contents. As for its guardian, Jacques Cœur had him apppointed Controller-General of Finance in Languedoc, in 1448, and when Rouen was recaptured the following year one of its houses was granted to de Varye "from those confiscated of the English." (82).

Antoine Noir directed the import and export business at Montpellier; his brothers, Huguet and Rostain, seem to have been in charge of the branch at Lyons, and possibly one at Avignon as well. When the King's process falls heavily upon their master, these three, by their bold and prompt action, succeed in saving a portion of his estate from the general ruin. Fleeing to the papal jurisdiction at Avignon, in the language of the King's letter denouncing their presence there, they "had taken, seized and carried off from the houses of the said Argentier [Jacques Cœur] situated in our cities of Lyons and Montpellier, certain sums of gold and silver coin and bullion, rings, jewels, and other things of great price and estimation, books of account, papers and other property." One of the most piquant episodes of the entire legal process taken against Jacques Cœur is provided by the strenuous efforts of Charles VII and his ministers to lay hands on these fugitives, their assets and records, and the clever diplomacy of the Papal Legate, the Cardinal de Foix, by which the royal purpose was defeated. We cannot now be attainted for *lèse-majesté* if we express relief on learning that Antoine, probably accompanied by his brothers, protected by a safe-conduct from the Pope and guarded by the Cardinal's officers, quitted Avignon and, traversing Provençe, gained Italy in safety. Shortly afterward he appears in Florence, where the money and property, which had been left meanwhile in the Cardinal's care, is duly transmitted to him, later to form part of that general accounting of Jacques Cœur's factors which Étienne Pasquier has so eloquently though somewhat inaccurately described.

Those who had loyally protected him did not do so

without cost. For the complicity of their government in this affair royal letters of reprisal were issued against the citizens of Avignon whereby their persons and their goods were made subject to seizure wherever found on the King's highway, to be detained by Charles VII's officers until the Crown should be reimbursed in full for the abstractions of the brothers Noir. All markets in the French Kingdom were thus closed to Avignese merchants, some of whom were arrested, despoiled, and imprisoned under the royal decree. Eighteen months of fruitless negotiations passed before the sovereign wrath was sufficiently appeased to lift the heavy penalties thus visited upon the papal fief. (83).

CHAPTER XI

HIS SHIP-CAPTAINS

JACQUES CŒUR's ship-captains were, with one exception, rare persons indeed. The tie existing between him and these gallant merchant mariners is one of the beautiful foregrounds in this picture of mediæval intrigue and oppression, showing all the brighter against the dark and stormy sea of troubles which, together, he and they so bravely faced. Jacques Cœur not only could appraise precious stones, fine fabrics, and tempered steel; he was equally keen in judging men. None of the nobler human relationships owes so small a debt to nature or, perhaps, partakes so much of attributes divine, as when a man of assured success, unprompted by the call of blood, chooses some promising junior as his *protégé*, forms and fashions him for the tasks of life, and, in due season, cheerfully makes room for him on the stage of their mutual endeavor. Rulers often hate and distrust their successors; and while his sovereign, Charles VII, fearful lest the heir apparent should intrench upon the paternal power, ate his selfish heart away with jealousy of his own unscrupulous son—later to starve his body for fear of him—Jacques Cœur, like Alexander, as Étienne Pasquier has so aptly said, busied himself with the creation of many kings. (84).

Foremost of them all was the dashing Jean de Village, a true hero of romance if there ever was one. His early years were crowded with adventures and his later ones with honors well deserved. Close though the asso-

ciation was between them, Jacques Cœur sought to
make it closer still and so consented to the union of this
gallant young sailor prince with his own niece Perrette,
and in the marriage settlement dowered the bride with
a handsome *dot*. (85).

It was through a mission of Jean de Village, who was
his factor at Marseilles as well as commander of the
galley *La Madeleine*, that Jacques Cœur established
those relations with the Sultan of Egypt which greatly
enhanced the French commercial influence in the
Levant; it was this faithful agent who, on the news of
his master's arrest, sailed away from Montpellier in
command of Jacques Cœur's fleet, to anchor it in the
safer refuge of Marseilles, under the friendly jurisdiction of King René; it was again devoted Jean who,
with the will to do and the soul to dare, planned and
executed that thrilling rescue of his master, which will
be later told.

These last actions brought him into contempt of the
King's process, made him an exile from his native land,
and even led to a short imprisonment of his wife and
children; several years passed before Charles VII's
grace was granted him, based on the grounds "that the
said Village is well trained and experienced in the matter of navigation and may be able to serve us thereby," as the royal pardon reads. It is largely from the
recitals of this instrument that we know the story of
Jean's early life, and we will let them tell it in the
quaint law language of the fifteenth century, much of
whose flavor is unfortunately lost in translation.

"Charles, by the grace of God, King of France, let
all present and to come know: We have received the

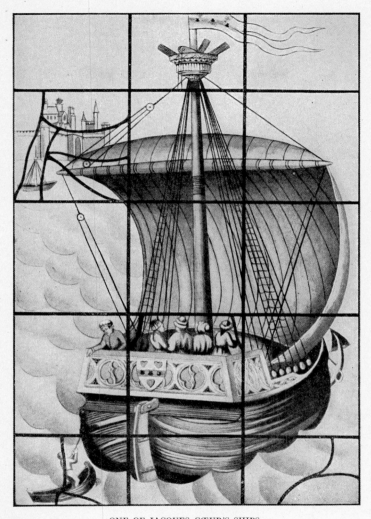

ONE OF JACQUES CŒUR'S SHIPS.

Stained-glass window formerly in Jacques Cœur's house; now in the Bourges Museum.
Arms of Jacques Cœur in the stern of the ship.

E. Lavisse, "Histoire de France." Librairie Hachette, Éditeur.

humble supplication of Jean de Village, native of our
said city of Bourges, stating that he might have been
about fifteen years old, a youth living in the said city
of Bourges when, because he had a great desire to advance himself in the business of merchandising, and
that the late Jacques Cœur, who then was of good and
great authority under us, carried on a very great merchantry both on land and sea, the said suppliant found
means of entering the service of Jacques Cœur; who,
after he was with him a certain while, because of the
confidence which he had in the said suppliant, gave
him his niece to wife and advanced him strongly, and
gave him some important charges in his affairs, and
especially at sea, in the conduct and guidance of his
galleys; on which the said de Village, the suppliant,
has trafficked in the business of merchandising for the
space of from ten to twelve years, and commanded the
said galleys, and in so doing has traded with the Moors,
Turks, and other foreign nations, both in the countries
of the Levant, Barbary, Myour [Majorca ?], the Ponant
and elsewhere, without permission or license from us;
in making which voyages, this suppliant, on several
occasions, has carried on his galleys and withdrawn
from our said kingdom and transported into the said
foreign lands a great quantity of alloyed silver, both
minted and in the form of plate, and among other
things, in a voyage which he made to the Levant, when
he was at Rhodes, he delivered to Bernard de Vaux
and Lazarin d'Andrea, of Montpellier, a certain quantity or sum of solid silver, which he had in his said
galley—he did not remember clearly the amount—to
be minted, and which silver was minted in the said

place of Rhodes by the said de Vaux and Lazarin, with nine or ten pence of alloy, or thereabouts, and was by them marked with a silversmith's mark in the establishment where the said silver was coined; which mark, on his advice, was that of a clover-leaf. And this [coin] he transported to Alexandria, there to sell it and spend it, as was done; *and has on his said galleys passed along other merchandise, and also a number of Moorish, Turkish, and other foreign personages, when they travelled from one country to the other.*

"And also the said suppliant, Village, made a voyage to the Levant during which he went to Cairo and had an audience with the Sultan and delivered to him letters from us, which the said Jacques Cœur, his master, had handed him, and by the order of his said master, presented to the said Sultan as gifts from us, a small *jazeran* of mail, a steel cross-bow, four small jacks of steel for bending the cross-bow, equipped with their quivers, six battle-axes, six fancy arms, and a small cup of enamelled gold and silver; to receive in return from the said Sultan certain foreign objects and garments of his country to be carried back to us, which was done and we were presented with them in our said city of Bourges.

"And, besides, the said suppliant was in company with the late William Gimart when he, Gimart, returned to Alexandria from the port of Aigues-Mortes, a Moorish slave, who from the said place of Alexandria, had, as they said, been carried off by Michael Teinturier, of Montpellier, in a voyage which the said Michael had theretofore made to the said place of Alexandria, being at the time captain of one of the said galleys; which Moorish slave the father of the said Michael Teinturier took by boat from Montpellier to the said port of Aigues-Mortes so that he might be sent back to the said place of Alexandria, because on account of him the Sultan was making great threats of detaining the Christian merchants who thereafter might go to the said place of Alexandria, as the Grand Master of Rhodes and others informed the said Jacques Cœur, his master, and the merchants of the said place of Montpellier.

"After these events and while the said suppliant was thus in the service of his said master, this Jacques Cœur, for certain faults committed against us by him, was, by our commandment and ordinance, placed in arrest, and it was ordained by us that all his goods should be seized and placed in our hands, as was done, and certain of our officers were commissioned to go likewise to take and seize the said galleys, together with the goods therein belonging to the said Jacques Cœur; and there were given to the said suppliant many commands and injunctions, under heavy penalties from us, that he should surrender the said galleys and the goods of the said Jacques Cœur, which he did not obey, as he should have done, although he had always offered to place the said galleys of which he had charge, in our possession or that of our officers, at any time that he would be given a release from us and from his said master. And finally, they were delivered and surrendered by him and his companions to our said officers and commissioners; and in surrendering them, there was made a certain stipulation between him and his said companions and our said officers and commissioners, by which the said sup-

pliant and his companions were [acknowledged as be-
ing] bound to render account to the said Jacques
Cœur, their master, or to any one in his stead having
sufficient power, of all the employments and under-
takings, both in the matter of their joint association and of any other things whatsoever that they
should have or might have had of their said master."
(86).

The story of Jean de Village's embassy to the Sultan of Egypt referred to in the above recital, resembles
a tale from *The Thousand and One Nights*, then being
woven and pieced together in the domains of that
potentate. "There is not on the face of the earth a
more agreeable country than Egypt with its Nile,"
says one of the characters in that greatest of all story-
books; "he who hath not seen Cairo hath not seen the
world."

One of a party of Florentine pilgrims who journeyed
there in 1384 has given us a more reliable description
of this land as it was under the rule of the Circassian
Mamelukes, and before the blight of Turkish conquest descended on it. On entering the harbor of Alexandria, the travellers' boat was deprived of sails and
rudder to prevent its leaving without acquitting the
Sultan's tribute. Boulak, the port of Cairo, appeared
to have as many ships anchored at its wharves as
Genoa or Venice. Cairo itself seemed to them as populous as their own Florence and all the rest of Tuscany
besides. The merchants of entire Europe came to its
marts for their sugar and spices; numerous jewellers
offered for sale precious stones and pearls in bazaars
set up opposite the Sultan's palace. Even the Italian

travellers accustomed to luxury were astonished at the extravagance displayed in the dress of the Egyptian women. (87).

As a result of the avidity of the agents of the Sultan and the prejudices of his government in favor of other nations, the commercial relations between his subjects and the French were strained and, at times, completely disrupted. It was in order to remedy this situation and to keep open this great market to the merchants of France that Jacques Cœur had persuaded Charles VII to send Jean de Village as an envoy to the Egyptian ruler.

The mission succeeded perfectly. The French were granted the right to be treated, in the Sultan's domains, on the same basis as Venice and others of the nations more favored there, and thus, thanks to Jacques Cœur and his competent young aide, was founded in the Levant that commercial influence of their country which, at a later epoch, was to reach such a flourishing state under the brilliant direction of Colbert, Louis XIV's talented minister.

Behold the letter of Abou-Said-Djacmac-el-Daher, granting Charles VII's requests, which, as an interesting record of the times, we give in full, minus its florid Eastern salutation:

"The Grand Sultan sends thee this letter to assure thee that good friendship and accord reign between us. Thy letter we have seen and read, and believe that thou dost wish us well, as we do thee.

"Thy ambassador, a man of honor, a gentleman, whom thou callest Jean de Village, has come to our Sublime Porte, and has presented thy letter together with the presents thou hast sent me, and I have received them; and what thou hast written that thou desirest of me, that have I done. Accordingly I have made a peace with all thy merchants for all my countries and seaports, as thy ambassador has requested of me.

"The said ambassador came in great state and has taken his presents in great love and pleasure for the love of thee.

"That which thou hast desired, is decreed and done; I have commanded all the lords of my dominions, and especially the Lord of Alexandria, that good-fellowship be shown to all the merchants of thy land, and to all others having liberty therein, and that honor and pleasure be done unto them; and when the consul of thy country is come, he shall have high favor amongst the other consuls.

"And I have ordained that good-fellowship shall be extended to the pilgrims of thy country, who go to Jerusalem and Saint Catherine; for the said ambassador has also begged this of me, and nothing shall be taken of them but what is customary to pay to other sultans; they shall be despoiled by none, nor injury of any sort done to them. And all that the said ambassador has asked for the pilgrims, and all other things, have I done for thy love, and thy ambassador departs from our Sublime Porte with his answers. And I have clothed him in a robe of state according to custom, in honor of thee, which I have given him, having told the said ambassador that I consent that a consul shall be sent from thee to reside in my dominions in order that peace may be between us.

"I send thee a present by the said ambassador, to wit, a balm made from our holy vine; a beautiful leopard; three porcelain bowls from Sinan [China]; two large platters of open-work porcelain, two bouquets of porcelain, a wash-basin and *lavoir-es-mains* of finely wrought porcelain; a jar of fine green ginger; one of almond kernels; a jar of green pepper, some almonds, and fifty pounds of our fine *bamouget* [balm?]; and a quintal of fine sugar.

"God lead thee to salvation, Charles, King of France." (88).

It was an established custom in the Orient never to appear before a superior without bringing gifts, a practice with which the Bible has familiarized us. Jacques Cœur was too well versed in Eastern ways to allow his envoy to present himself empty-handed to the Mussulman ruler. Although the benefits of the embassy were gladly welcomed by the King of France, and the Sultan's return gifts eagerly accepted by him, the presents made by Jean de Village which aided in eliciting them were to bring great trouble upon Jacques Cœur and his youthful emissary, and for this reason they are mentioned in the pardon which the latter, in the end, obtained.

The captain of the galley *Saint Michael* was William Gimart. Like Jean de Village, he too had been born at Bourges; had espoused his employer's relative; was beloved and trusted by Jacques Cœur. He exhibited every proof of devotion that de Village did and more; for Gimart was "faithful unto death." What degree of relationship connected his fiancée, Jeanne Heymar, with Jacques Cœur we do not know, but we must approve the latter's generosity when he writes the expectant bridegroom the following letter:

WILLIAM GIMART,

Place to my charge two thousand écus, current money; that is to say, one thousand écus which I have promised you on your marriage to Jeanne and one thousand écus with which I have settled your account with Jehan Sirac, for the value of one thousand ducats; and, further, place to my said charge all that you may have to spend to clothe and dress your said wife, for all of which I promise to be responsible at the end of the joint arrangement which we have with one another, on your producing this voucher, which I have signed with my sign manual, hereunto affixed.

At Béziers the XXII day of May.

in the year one thousand CCCCLI.

JA. CUER. (89).

Let us hope that it was not for the bonnets of her trousseau, but for newer ones, that Jeanne's husband, several years after, reclaims from Jacques Cœur's confiscated estate at Montpellier "a wooden press for shaping women's hoods and head-gear, which he said belonged to his wife," and which the King's Procurer-General, after an inquest, gallantly surrenders. (90).

After his patron's arrest, with Jean de Village, Gaillardet, and Jean Forest, other ship-captains, William Gimart sailed his galley to Marseilles's friendly port, there to be withheld from the King's process until a favorable composition could be made. With them, also, he took part in the thrilling rescue of their chief;

he joined with them and Jacques Cœur's factors in the final settlement with their master at Rome which evoked Étienne Pasquier's praise. Here, however, the parallel ceases. While Jean de Village returns to Marseilles to become King René's admiral and to found a titled house, William Gimart, leaving wife and small daughter, Analette, sails with the naval expedition conducted by Jacques Cœur against the Turks. As a document of the time states, "the said late Gimart went off with . . . Jacques Cœur, his master, who had charge of a certain ship of war, sent by our Holy Father (the Pope), to go to meet the enemies of the faith, in which employ he was for some time, and, sad to say, in a certain encounter had by him and other Christians with the said enemies, he, the said late Gimart, was killed and slain by these enemies of the faith in Turkey." (91).

Michael Teinturier was a different sort of man. The son of a local merchant whose losses had led him to seek remission of his taxes, his family was none the less an influential one at Montpellier. Jacques Cœur had chosen Michael to captain the galley *Saint Denis*, but relieved him of this command as a result of the following incident already alluded to in connection with Jean de Village, but of which we now give the version set forth in the formal charge against Jacques Cœur, brought by Teinturier, who became the principal witness for the prosecution on this count of the indictment.

"The said Jacques Cœur is also charged by information with the following: In 1446 the galley *Saint Denis*, owned by him, being at Alexandria, and having for its captain Michelet Teinturier, a youth of *four-teen or fifteen* years of age, a Christian from the land of Prester John, held as a slave by a Saracen, boarded the galley *Saint Denis*, and threw himself on his knees before the said captain crying 'Pater Noster! Ave Maria!' and proclaiming that he *wished to be* a good Christian and that for this reason he had fled from the house of his master the Saracen; and that the said Michelet caused him to be brought in the galley as far as our city of Montpellier, where the said youth remained for more than two months with certain of the townsfolk and merchants, and also with Master Pierre du Moulin, then Archbishop of Toulouse, serving him as his groom, during which time the said youth acted as a Christian, going to church, hearing mass like others of the faith, and was allowed his freedom and liberty without any restraint whatever, such as slaves are accustomed to. Nevertheless the said Jacques Cœur, coming to Montpellier, summoned the said Michelet Teinturier before him, and received him very harshly, saying many bitter things to him, and reprimanding him severely for having brought the said slave from Alexandria, and for having robbed his master of him, in consequence of which his galleys would in future suffer; and that the said Michelet Teinturier excused himself, and related to the said Jacques Cœur how the case stood, and that in his opinion there would not be much danger to the vessels, inasmuch as the Saracen master of the youth would probably rather have fifty ducats than his slave. Nevertheless, the said Jacques Cœur paid no attention to these explanations and opinions, but insisted that the youth should be restored to his master, and that should any harm come to any of his galleys through this matter, he would ruin the said Teinturier and his father as well. And he sent also for Isaac Teinturier, father of the said Michelet and repeated the same words that he had used with the son, swearing to God to destroy him, body and goods, if he did not immediately repair what had been done. Whereupon the said youth was seized by men under Jacques Cœur's orders and command, acting solely on their private authority, and imprisoned and held in the prisons of the bailey of our said city of Montpellier; there he was detained by force and against his will and desire for a space of two months and more, and until the galleys of Jacques Cœur were ready to transport him back to Alexandria, there to deliver him to his Saracen master, where he has since renounced the Christian religion; (the said Jacques Cœur) having thereby committed several great and enormous crimes, such as those of *lèse-majesté*, public force, private imprisonment, unprivileged deportation from our jurisdiction, assault, and so forth."

When Michael Teinturier enters the witness-box at Jacques Cœur's trial, this youthful slave suddenly becomes "a man of twenty-four or five years." The "land of Prester John," claimed by the captive as his birthplace, was a geographical myth of the Middle Ages, the fabulous home of a lost Christian people whom credulous followers of the Pope were forever seeking as allies against the growing Mohammedan power. Thus, la Brocquière meets at Pera a romancing Neapolitan who relates some absurd fables and revolting marvels regarding this nebulous region, to which the Burgundian traveller attaches the sage comment, "but I know not whether what he said be the truth and I shall not therefore warrant any part of it." Teinturier's fugitive may have been an Abyssinian or a native of some other semi-Christian country, but his artful use of the Frankish legend almost certainly presupposes imposture on his part, a conclusion which his subsequent conduct strengthens; we learn from one of the prosecution's witnesses that on his return to Alexandria the captive reverted to the religion of the prophet. "You are a wicked people in France," he is quoted as having said. "I was a Christian in your country; in this one, I am a Moor and live like a dog. The Catalans would not have returned me." (92).

This was not the first glimpse of slavery that Teinturier had had; his action in this case was not the yielding of a sensitive soul to its own promptings on being suddenly confronted with the baneful effects of that inhuman institution. He had witnessed its operations in his own home city. Although the African slave-trade, only started several years before, had not then fully developed in Europe, the notarial registers of Montpellier, for this period, as indeed those of all southern France and Spain, are marred with records of the buying and selling of Mohammedan captives, a traffic conducted in defiance of the ban of the Church. (93).

For defense, Jacques Cœur stated that he had not believed that the slave's conversion was real; that by a treaty between the two nations the French had agreed to refrain from interference with an institution generally recognized in the lands of the Sultan; that several of his fellow merchants had strongly protested

Teinturier's action, urging that it compromised their safety; and that he had received word from the Grand Master of Rhodes of the intention of the Saracens to commence reprisals on the first favorable opportunity. Consequently he and his agents at Montpellier, after mature deliberation and consultation, had decided to return the slave to his master, considering that they were but performing an act of good faith in obeying the articles of a treaty.

CHAPTER XII

THE ARAB EMPIRE. PAPAL AND ROYAL LICENSES. PILGRIM PASSENGERS

As a matter of fact, Teinturier's action, though small in itself, was as pregnant with mischief as many another trifling incident which, happening at a moment especially inopportune, has precipitated war between nations and brought misery to thousands. It jeopardized a policy which Jacques Cœur was painstakingly building. He believed that Europe, in its attitude toward the infidels, should restrict its enmity to the Turks. The Arab Empire had been the intermediary between western Europe and the Asiatic world, the channel by which the great inventions of the compass, paper, and powder had reached the Occident from China. In the East, its caliphate at Bagdad was then in partial decline, owing to struggles with the Turks and the devastation of the Mongolian raider Tamerlane; although its western arm at Cordova was losing its long-continued hold on Spain, the central Arabian power at Cairo still flourished, in Jacques Cœur's day, with but little diminution of its ancient vigor. Arab mathematicians and astronomers were the continuators of the knowledge of the ancient Greeks, their alchemists the forerunners of our modern chemists, and their medical treatises then the classic text-books in Montpellier's celebrated college of physicians. From Egypt, where the science of irrigation was greatly advanced, were being introduced into Europe many trees

and plants for which modern civilization is heavily indebted; rice, sugar-cane, apricots, asparagus, beans,
hemp, and the mulberry-tree, so useful in the manufacture of silk, and probably other fruits and vege-
tables, all came from the banks and deltas of the Nile.
The emphasis placed upon the rarity of the almonds,
delivered by the Sultan to Jean de Village for presen-
tation to Charles VII, would seem to show that France
was thereby being endowed with a specimen new to
the nurserymen of that kingdom. The Arabs excelled
in metal work; Damascus steels and Toledo blades
were renowned for swords and armor; their brasses
were unsurpassed and their carved ivories and mother-
of-pearl work were the models of elegance and taste.
Their famous mosques at Cordova and Toledo and the
Alhambra at Granada still bear silent witness to their
perfection in architecture and the arts. (94).

The Moors in Spain were an important agency in
imparting Eastern culture to the more backward Eu-
ropeans of the Middle Ages and the rapid rise of the
commerce of Catalonia undoubtedly owed much to its
proximity to the Saracen realm of Granada, an advantage partially shared in by Montpellier as the
natural French port for Spanish trade.

The Sultan at Cairo was, like European rulers, himself menaced by the rising tide of aggression of the
Turks, with whom his subjects were united only by
the tie of a common religion and by whom they were
to be submerged less than a century later.

We find Jacques Cœur's efforts constantly aimed at
establishing peaceful commercial relations with the
Arab power and distinguishing between its chivalrous

and industrious peoples and the cruel and nomadic
Ottomans. By the intervention of his factors the Venetians were restored to their trading privileges in the
Sultan's domains from which they had been excluded
in 1442. The year before the Teinturier incident,
through Jacques Cœur's intervention, the Knights of
Rhodes, who had recently sustained a forty-day siege
by the forces of the Sultan, were enabled, with papal
consent, to conclude a treaty of peace with their late
enemy, which provided for the release of the Rhodian
captives then held in Egyptian slavery; the liberated
prisoners were repatriated on the vessels of Jacques
Cœur. (95).

The date of the compact between France and the
Sultan, negotiated through Jean de Village, is somewhat uncertain. The chronicler de Coucy fixes it in
1447, the year *after* the incident of the slave, although
the order of its recital in de Village's pardon would
point to its having preceded that event; Jacques Cœur,
in his defense, as we have seen, excused his conduct as
being obedience to an existing treaty, a plea which
does not seem to have been controverted. De Village's successful mission was but the fruition of friendly
relations with the Arab power, established by his principal during years which had preceded it. It is of little
import whether Teinturier's ill-judged action imperilled the formal treaty or merely the prospects of making it; in any event, it threatened the tranquillity of
Rhodes, the famous island bulwark against the Mussulman power.

Jacques Cœur's trade with the Levant was carried
on with express permission of the Holy See. As we

have found, his privilege at first was local, depending upon papal favor enjoyed by the city of Montpellier; later it became a special personal license without reference to the home port from which his vessels sailed. The first of these indulgences was procured for him by Étienne de Cambrai, then Canon of Narbonne and later Bishop of Agde, whose relations with Jacques Cœur were intimate, if, indeed, they did not involve mutual participation in affairs. (96). Preceded by less formal permissions, a bull of Pope Eugenius IV, dated September 6, 1446, conferred upon Jacques Cœur, his factors, mariners, and agents, full authority to traffic with infidels in any sort of wares. Nicholas V, so loyal a friend to the great merchant after his fall, confirmed his predecessor's action in October, 1449. (97). The Church then maintained suzerainty over all heathen lands and peoples; Eugenius IV's concession to Jacques Cœur was but a different exercise of the same power which that Pope had drawn upon in 1442 in his memorable grant to Portugal, under the protection of which, before the century's end, Da Gama was to find the long-sought route to India

The commercial prestige and protection secured by Jacques Cœur as a result of his favor with the Sultan and the confidence shown him by the Pope was but cumulative to that which he already enjoyed through his relations with the King. With the recapture of Paris from the English in 1436, the derided "King of Bourges" had become the King of France. The improvement of the finances of the kingdom and the regularization of its tax receipts had enabled Charles VII to apply to the maintenance of his household a

definite part of the revenues which theretofore had
been consumed by the expenses of the war. Accordingly, in 1438 the office of Argentier was created and
Jacques Cœur called upon to perform its duties. The
post was one of intimate and personal relations with
the King and royal family. Its functions were somewhat analogous to those of the Lord Steward of the
Household in England at the present time, allowance
being made for the diminution in the scope of the office
resulting from the general curtailment of royal power
which has taken place since the fifteenth century.
Charles VII's Argentier was a functionary to whom
all the departmental treasurers were bound each year
to turn over the revenues belonging to the King and
to be employed in his establishment, and who, in turn,
was required to report his transactions to the Chamber of Accounts.

Thus, commercially, Jacques Cœur was thrice armed
against the harassment and dangers which beset the
less enterprising traders of his day. Was a Saracen
governor at Alexandria disposed to collect an undue
tribute or port charge from the good ship *La Madeleine,*
the Sultan's safe-conduct, produced by Captain Jean
de Village was magic to soften the Mussulman's exactions; did William Gimart's boat need a snug berth
in the harbor of Rhodes, the Grand Master of the
Order of Saint John of Jerusalem only too gladly accorded a favor asked for in the name of an owner so
trusted by the Church; at Barcelona and at Genoa, the
ships of the Argentier of Charles VII had a prestige
almost as great as though they belonged to that sovereign himself. It would have been a hardy pirate who

would have dared to attack vessels protected by such an aggregation of Mediterranean power. The comparative safety and immunity thus secured for Jacques Cœur's ships caused them to be prime favorites in the passenger trade, and the transport of pilgrims to the Holy Land and back must have been a considerable item in their profitable operations.

The fashion of going on a pilgrimage, as we all know, was very general throughout the Middle Ages. Although it had abated much since the flaming days of the Crusades, in the fifteenth century it was again on the increase, owing to the fact that Turkish encroachments in the East kept the fate of the Holy Sepulchre constantly before men's minds. (99). La Brocquière, himself a pilgrim, has familiarized us with the completeness of the arrangements made for the accommodation and protection of these wayfarers, confirming the fact that, in Jacques Cœur's day, there was a steady stream of devout travellers wishing to see with their own eyes

> "those holy fields,
> Over whose acres walk'd those blessed feet,
> Which fourteen hundred years ago were nail'd,
> For our advantage, on the bitter cross." (100).

CHAPTER XIII

SLAVE TRAFFIC. IMPORTS. SOCIAL STATUS OF MERCHANTS

A COMPARATIVELY recent author whose painstaking and scholarly local researches have added much to our knowledge of Jacques Cœur has been the first of his biographers, during five hundred years, to attribute to him participation in the scandalous slave-traffic then not unknown on Mediterranean shores and waters; unfortunately this theory has been followed in the latest compilation of the history of France. (101). The accusation we believe to be as unfounded as that made during the great merchant's life-time, of poisoning the mistress of the King. The modern charge is based solely upon the language of the recitals contained in the letters of remission granted to the masters of his vessels. As we have already seen, the inherent nature of these documents is such as to require them to be strictly construed; the person to be pardoned was encouraged to boast of his crimes, almost to invent them. As nowadays in the charters of corporations, in jurisdictions where full liberty of defining corporate purposes is allowed the applicants, we find enumerated every conceivable object of which the grantee, on the remotest contingency, might have need, so, in these fifteenth-century indulgences, the suppliant for forgiveness wracked his brain for items of past conduct which, on any theory, under any ingenious information which might be laid against him in times to come,

116

could be interpreted as amounting to transgressions of the law. Thus we have found in Jean de Village's pardon a confession that he had "on his said galleys passed along other merchandise and also a number of Moorish, Turkish, and other foreign personages when they travelled from one country to the other." The statements of the remaining captains, although less explanatory than that of de Village, are entirely consistent with the view of the facts, which, it seems to us, all mean to state: that in their coastwise passages between different Mussulman ports, Jacques Cœur's vessels acted as true common carriers and transported, alike, Christian lord and Saracen grandee, with their suites, even though the former's body-servants were held in feudal fealty, the latter's in Mohammedan bondage.

As for regularly engaging in the slave-traffic, as such, the idea is almost preposterous. Jacques Cœur was, for one thing, far too keen a merchant to imperil his large passenger service in the carriage of pilgrims by mingling with these religious devotees the victims of an institution anathematized by the fathers of the Church. How long, think you, would his license from the Pope, which brought him the envy and jealousy of his less trusted fellow merchants, have been permitted to continue, if the religious meditations of the palmers on their way to or from the Holy Sepulchre were to be broken in upon by the clank of manacles and irons? Would the faithless Michael Teinturier, the discharged ship's captain, have confined his accusation against his master to the one incident of the returned slave if he had had whole boat-loads of bondsmen to inform about? It is true that Jacques Cœur's vessels carried slaves, and Christian slaves at that, but they carried them out of the bondage of Egypt and delivered them, as free men, to the mild and just rule of the Grand Master of the Knight Hospitallers at Rhodes.

The post of Argentier was one which brought to the great merchant just the market which he required for his Eastern importations. On the other hand, it involved the reciprocal duty of making advances for the maintenance of the royal establishment. The furnishing of Charles VII's household could only have been undertaken by one who, like Jacques Cœur, had the necessary commercial organization and capital to buy the supplies in Levantine and other foreign markets, transport them to central depots, and have them on hand when demanded by the royal needs. The profits were doubtless large, but the credit risk was none too good. It was probably as much in tacit recognition of this latter fact as for Jacques Cœur's eminent fitness for the place, that the King's supplier and banker was invested with an office which enabled him to act as trustee for the security of his own credits. We should not allow our twentieth-century notions to be shocked at the dual rôle of seller and buyer which this arrangement involved; the machinery thus invoked was in full accord with the principles and practices of the fifteenth century. (102). Nor should we feel any compunctions at Jacques Cœur's other efforts to secure unequal favors for his commerce. His was the day of special privilege; his century knew no different way.

Neither the King's household, nor even the court, absorbed all of the commodities dealt in by Jacques Cœur; his market was the entire kingdom, with for-

PORTRAIT OF CHARLES VII.

Painting by Jean Foucquet in the Louvre.

E. Lavisse, "Histoire de France." Librairie Hachette, Éditeur.

eign customers as well. We have peeped at a few of
the articles which William de Varye had in his great
emporium at Tours; a glance at some of the merchandise in Antoine Noir's branch at Montpellier may,
perhaps, be worth our while.

First there were "all the perfumes of Arabia"—musk,
incense for the churches, spikenard, eau-de-rose, and
essence of violets; spices announced their presence,
breathing "Sabean odors from the spicy shore," cloves,
ginger, cinnamon, and pepper; dyes and colors were
to be seen, durable and fine, such as we still admire in
Fouquet's miniatures and King René's illuminations
—cochinelle and cinnabar for the reds, indigo and lit-
mus for the blues, saffron and henna for the yellows;
drugs were here of every kind and nature, including
some which have, fortunately, disappeared from our
pharmacopœia, as the curative "Bezoar stone," taken
from the stomachs of Persian and Indian monkeys and
baboons, which, set in gold and precious stones, rich
people then wore around their bodies and believed to
be a panacea for human ills; here the gourmet might
find confections for his palate, such as candied fruits
from Damascus, sweets of lemon and other flavors,
liquorice, nutmegs, and sugar from Egypt and Candia.
Here, too, were metals and ostrich feathers, precious
stones for the vain, coral rosaries for the devout,
velours, taffetas, and cloths of gold—in fact, as the old
chronicler so aptly puts it, "every sort of merchandise
which the brain of man can think of or imagine." (103).

Jacques Cœur's business was not entirely that of
trade; he interested himself in production as well. Besides his silk-factory at Florence, he had a paper-mill

at Bourges; in the country round about Lyons, mines of silver, lead, and copper were leased and operated by him. (104). His widely extended facilities made him the favorite intermediary for the transfer of funds, both within the kingdom, and to and from places abroad.

Differing from conditions in the Italian republics, and in a degree from those in all the other European countries, the status of a merchant of the fifteenth century, however great, was relatively low in the French social scale, as compared with that of the haughty nobles and powerful churchmen of the realm. It was appreciation of this fact, over a century later, that prompted the artful Mary Queen of Scots, then Queen of France as well, to taunt her formidable mother-in-law with the scornful appellation of "*la fille de marchand*," thus reminding Catherine de Médici, at the proud court of France, of the commercial origin of her celebrated Florentine family. It was in protest against these conventions that, in still another century, a great French author writes:

"However, I need not say which is more useful to a nation: a lord, powdered in the tip of the mode, who knows exactly at what o'clock the King rises and goes to bed, and who gives himself airs of grandeur and state, at the same time that he is acting the slave in the ante-chamber of a prime minister; or a merchant, who enriches his country, despatches orders from his counting-house to Surat and Grand Cairo, and contributes to the felicity of the world." (105).

PART III

KING'S MINISTER

"In that fierce light which beats upon a throne."
(Tennyson, "Idylls of the King," Dedication.)

CHAPTER XIV

TREMOUILLE'S FALL. TREATY OF ARRAS. RE-CAPTURE OF PARIS. REORGANIZATION OF FRENCH FINANCES. ARGENTIER. ENNOBLEMENT

SHORTLY after Jacques Cœur's Eastern voyage the course of events in France took a turn favorable both to himself and his country. In 1433 the King's favorite Tremouille was set upon, wounded, and forcibly driven from the court. The fickle Charles VII, although not a party to this action, easily allowed himself to be persuaded of its benefits. The passing of this baneful figure ended the long period of fruitless intrigues and an era of accomplishment under the party of the Constable Richemont began. The good influence at the court of the Queen's mother, Yolande of Aragon and her sons Charles and René of Anjou, commenced now to assert itself.

In September, 1435, the long feud between Charles VII and the Duke of Burgundy ended amidst the general rejoicings of the people. Philip the Good, who, as a prince of the blood royal of France, had begun to sicken of the rôle of his country's enemy, found his budding patriotism accelerated by indiscreet provocation by his English allies. (106). His instinctive dislike of seeing the crown of his ancestors on a stranger's head revived as his passion for vengeance on his father's murderers wore out. After the signing of the Treaty of Arras, Philip "warred no more on the holy

Kingdom of France," as Jeanne d'Arc had so earnestly
implored him. The treaty did not humble Burgundian
pride; on the contrary, it fed it, and during Philip's
life-time his duchy retained most of the attributes of
an independent power. The sermon, preached to commemorate this peace pact, took as its text: "How good
and how pleasant it is for brethren to dwell together
in unity!" Mediæval churchmen were not given to
humor, and it is therefore reasonable to suppose that
the application of this preachment was intended for
future governance, and that the royal princes were not
being lauded for having so well dissembled their love
in the past. (107).

The death of the Regent Bedford, thus deserted by
his Burgundian ally, followed shortly after the Treaty
of Arras, in which he had impolitically refused to join;
although the rich provinces of Normandy and Guienne
had been offered to the English Crown, the condition
attached to their tender—that they be held in vassal-
age to Charles VII and his successors—was deemed by
Henry VI's representative unbecoming to the pride of
an English King who had been proclaimed King of
France as well.

The loss of this skilful general and able adminis-
trator did much to weaken the English cause. Paris,
which had given its allegiance rather to the Duke of
Burgundy than to his English allies, was quickly re-
taken by the Constable Richemont at the head of the
troops of united France.

Charles VII thus finishes his rôle of pretender to his
ancient crown; in possession of its ancient capital he
is recognized as King of France in substantially all the

realm, except the two provinces whose peaceful concession to England the Regent Bedford had so scornfully rejected but which the English still firmly held.

For the reconstruction of his partially recovered realm the King of France had need of a very different class of ministers than the self-seeking courtiers who had satisfied the whims and truckled to the tastes of the nomad "King of Bourges." The reconstruction of the shattered credit of the nation could not safely be intrusted to those whose sole remedy for empty coffers had been to force the debasement of the coinage. The time had passed for dependence on temporary expedients and false worths. The King could still stamp a face value on men as on pieces of money, but the necessity of recreating public confidence required that there be real metal back of both. During the burst of energy and even statesmanship which Charles VII now displayed—so foreign to his past conduct as to lead historians to seek beyond him for its cause—he began to surround himself with those ministers whose ability, loyalty, and patriotism caused him to be known in history as the "Well-Served," and enabled his country not only to throw off the English yoke but to take the front rank in position and power among the nations of Europe.

The campaign for the capture of Paris had completely exhausted Charles VII's funds, in spite of heavy contributions demanded of the city by the Constable. The King did not immediately enter his newly regained capital, but continued to remain at Bourges and governed Paris from there. One of his first administrative acts with regard to it was the appointment of Jacques

Cœur as Director of the Paris Mint. The latter had now become the greatest merchant in the kingdom; as such, he had the largest personal interest in the stabilization of its currency; as such, his financial opinions commanded respect. He must have known too well the sinister effects on commerce of alterations in the coinage to accept the office without a thorough understanding that its policy was to be one of reform, totally different from the regime which had prevailed during his connection with the Mint at Bourges. Therefore, in all likelihood having first satisfied himself that his sovereign's aims were in line with his own, he accepted the charge. Backed by his own strong credit and aided by his own organization, he bought, on terms of future payment, great quantities of gold and silver which he converted into coin, used to meet the soldier's wage. The pieces which he minted were of a weight and fineness which restored honor to the money of his country. His system of reform was carried into the financial enactments of the period, and he mustered all his forces to rectify the finances of the realm. (108).

The number of mints in the kingdom was decreased and their policy made to accord with the central one at Paris. Among the directors of these institutions who were retained in office, after this sweeping reduction in their staffs, we find the name of Ravant Ladenois, Jacques Cœur's old superior in the Mint at Bourges. The selection of these two former associates to play important rôles in the national currency reform—a choice made after deliberation by the financial counsellors of the King—is fairly convincing evi-

dence of the moral worthlessness of the charges brought
against them in their earlier service to the state.

It is probably to this period of his public zeal that
we should assign the very curious letter, of incomplete date, written by Jacques Cœur to the bailey of
Saint-Benoit, near Chinon, on the subject of counter-
feit money. As authentic examples of the correspondence of the great merchant are few, it is perhaps worth
repeating in full:

MONSIEUR DE BARBANÇOYS

I recommend myself to your good graces in the
highest degree possible, and may it please you to know
that yesterday, after vespers, there came to me a man
with whom I was unacquainted, who said that he
wished to speak with me on condition that I would
promise to keep his communication secret, without
discovering or revealing to any living soul that he had
approached me; who, having been granted this audience, told me that the receiver of taxes at Saint-Benoyst
had acquaintance with some alchemists, through whom
he caused to be made alchemical écus, which he used
in paying the men-at-arms, and had already, to the
knowledge of my informant, exchanged five ingots
which were not gold as they seemed but were counter-
feited gold made by the said means of alchemy, and
that the said receiver and the said alchemists are in
the habit of meeting by night at a tavern of the said
Saint-Benoyst, where hangs the sign of the "Wild
Man" [l'ôme sauvage]; and there they plan to exchange
still other ingots; which leads me to request you, by
these presents, to cause to be spied upon and watched,

the said receiver and all who come into the said tavern, and all who meet there, and take them prisoners, remanding the said receiver to Bourges, and, further, to inquire fully into the said business.

And this cannot but be a matter of great usefulness in the service of the King, our sire. And, personally, Monsieur de Barbançoys, I recommend myself to you and pray God that he may grant you long and happy life.

At Bourges the VIII day of April. (108*a*).

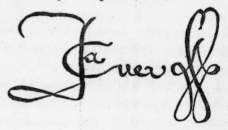

Two years after his appointment to the Paris Mint Jacques Cœur became acting Argentier, to which office, as we have found, he was shortly to succeed in title as well as in fact. The keeper of the King's purse, who himself had an individual claim upon it as furnisher to the royal household, was a rôle which only a strong man, confident of his ability, rectitude, and influence would dare to undertake. The creditor had too strong a debtor; the controller of the royal expenditures was called upon to restrain too many demands. The King's process obviously could not run against the King, who could always pay his debts by condemnation of his creditor; checking the royal expenditure was irksome to the monarch, and more unpopular still with the troop of greedy courtiers ever clamorous for largess. The rôle was not unlike that of one who enters the cage of a lion to regulate its diet, having a personal interest in the food which he might hope to conserve. Nevertheless, it is difficult to criticise Jacques Cœur for his assumption of this situation; it was the inevitable reward of eminence in his calling. A man's part in life was hazardous in France during the fifteenth century; that of a merchant more than others, that of a great merchant most of all. The furnisher of a King, perhaps, ran equal risks, both to person and to property, whether or not he followed his supplies over the threshold of the palace.

The high position which he held in the royal household, plebeian though he was, made it fitting that he receive a rank in keeping with his duties; accordingly in April, 1440, the King, "in consideration of his merits and the services which he has rendered, both in his office of Argentier and otherwise," granted him letters of ennoblement for himself, his wife, and their posterity. He filed with the royal herald armorial bearings in which the hearts (*cœurs*) were the reproduction of his own name, and the escallop shells an allusion to his patron saint James (Jacques), joining thereto that famous motto which his whole life justified so well:

"To Valiant Hearts [Cœurs] Nothing Is Impossible." (109).

CHAPTER XV

JACQUES CŒUR'S PERSONAL APPEARANCE. TRUCE OF TOURS. FRENCH PROSPERITY

PERHAPS, at this stage, we should pause in studying the story of his life to observe the appearance of this hardy personage whose energy and industry had ranked him among the *noblesse* of France. Records of his estate show that Charles VII's court-painter, Jacob de Litemont, and even the celebrated Jean Fouquet himself were in the redoubtable merchant's debt; the great Italian artist, Piero della Francesca, is said to have painted him. Unfortunately no unquestioned oil-portrait of him, painted from life, has yet come to light. Alone, the engraving by Grignon, which appeared in Godefroy's work on Charles VII, nearly two hundred years after Jacques Cœur's death, is conceded to have reproduced some authentic original.

Happily, however, we have some fresh and vivid descriptions of his personal appearance given by those who testified during his trial when the question at issue was as to Jacques Cœur's being tonsured and apparelled as a *clerc*. Upon this evidence hinged his motion for a change of venue to the jurisdiction of the ecclesiastical courts. We will cite but two of the seven depositions which were taken on this point.

The first witness was André Vidal, watchman at the Toulouse Mint, formerly in Jacques Cœur's personal service. After being duly sworn André says:

"I was a servitor of Jacques Cœur for eighteen

months or thereabouts, and was such at the moment
of his arrest. With regard to the tonsure, I have been
present several times, each time to hold the candle,
when Jacques Cœur was being shaved. On my oath
I swear that I have no recollection whether the barber
or barbers whom I have seen shave him, tonsured him
or not.

"I have seen Jacques Cœur shaved by two barbers,
the one named Hannequin, who was his barber at the
time of his arrest and who had been engaged as such,
shortly before Jacques Cœur went on the embassy to
Rome; the other was a tall young man of the city of
Bourges, whose name I do not know, but who at present
resides with Monseigneur the Archbishop of Bourges
[Jacques Cœur's son].

"With regard to his habit, I have seen him in the
past wear one without a collar, the sleeves of the doublet
being striped with red against a black background.
During his visit to Normandy, I have seen him wear
a hat covered with velvet with large silk folds on top;
long-pointed laced shoes. I have also seen him wear
generally a short robe, reaching half-way to the knees,
gathered at the shoulders and open at the sleeves, red
or green-and-gray shoes, and robes of all colors, several of them being without a collar, in the style that
gentlemen of the court are wont to attire themselves."

Aubert Panois testifies: "I have several times seen
the barber shave Jacques Cœur, the King's Argentier,
both in the city of Montpellier and elsewhere; I did not
notice whether or not the barber tonsured him on these
occasions. I recall that in the month of July or August,
1449, at Jacques Cœur's house at Chinon, I saw one

named Hannequin, Jacques Cœur's barber, shave his
master. Afterward he rubbed his head for a long time
with a towel, and it seemed to me that he did not tonsure him. I have no recollection of ever having seen a
tonsure on Jacques Cœur, and yet I have been often
with him.

"I have seen Jacques Cœur wear a large hat of scarlet brocade and a robe without a collar, reaching half-
way to his knees, gathered at the sleeves, heavily bor-
dered with sable and slashed at the sides. This was
in 1447, 1448, and the years following. I have never
seen Jacques Cœur wear a long robe except during the
past year, two months before his arrest, in the month
of May, 1451. Then I saw him wear, at Montpellier,
a long robe, I do not recall of what color, trimmed
with vair; I have seen him wear hose of scarlet and
other colors and long-pointed laced shoes. Whether
at the time two months before his arrest or always
when I have seen him, he was dressed like a layman.
More I do not know." (110).

The question of Jacques Cœur's right to claim the
jurisdiction of the ecclesiastical courts will be more
fully considered when we reach his trial. We have
anticipated events in calling these witnesses, merely to
obtain their description of his personal appearance.

The reorganization of the finances of Charles VII,
enabling him to maintain and equip a regularly paid
soldiery, began to be reflected in successes in the war.
After the Treaty of Arras, the advantage was greatly
with the French and the tide of battle which had flowed
against them during one hundred years of sporadic
warfare, now began to ebb in their favor. French

superiority in artillery contributed most to this result. Owing to better marshalled finances, access to the foundries of Flanders, which Burgundy's adhesion gave, and due to their possession of a master artilleryman in the person of Jean Bureau, the French were much quicker than the English to take full advantage of this important arm, then just coming into general use in besieging fortified places. Henry V had captured Rouen and Meaux with the ancient catapults, ballistæ, and trebuchets inherited from the Romans; at the siege of Orleans these bulky war-engines were ranged side by side with the early form of cannon. (111). Meaux, which had taken the English nine months to capture, was now regained in a fortnight by the bombardments of Jean Bureau.

Although national pride rebelled against a humiliating conclusion to a war of conquest so brilliantly begun, the counsellors of the English King, seeing their realm so nearly exhausted by the never-ending warfare, decided to negotiate a truce. The English ambassadors with their retinue, headed by the Earl of Suffolk, and escorted with great pomp on the last stages of their journey by Charles of Orleans, long Suffolk's captive in England, appeared at Charles VII's court, then held at Tours, and entered into *pourparlers* with the delegates of France. The peace congress was held during the spring of the year, and its sessions were intermingled with gay and lively revels by the followers of the two courts. The English Earl and Pierre de Brézé, the latter a great friend of Jacques Cœur and now Charles VII's chief minister, arranged an archery contest in which the prize was carried off by an archer of the French King's Scottish body-guard; the popular young Dauphiness of France, Margaret of Scotland, led the rival courtiers in a May-party gallop in the royal park and along the banks of the Loire; most fateful incident of all in shaping the destinies of the French court, Agnes Sorel appeared among the ladies in waiting, and openly received the admiration of the King of France. (112).

By way of cementing the resulting truce Margaret of Anjou, René's daughter, Charles VII's niece, was espoused to young Henry VI of England. Great ceremony attended this latter function. An ancient chronicle, this time an English one, informs us that after the service in the church, "all the people, filled with joy, shouted 'Noel!' clapping their hands together. The Queen of France then approached the bride and placed her on the right hand of the Queen of Sicily, the former's mother (to whom she gave her own right arm). Thus departed the Kings and Queens for the Abbey of Saint-Julien in the said city, where a great supper had been prepared for them.

"The Queen of England was there accorded her due precedence, at the right hand of the Queen of France, with the (Papal) Legate on the left. The Dauphiness and the Duchess of Calabria were seated with the Earl of Suffolk. The two Queens were served simultaneously with each course in turn. There were various subtleties and divertisements between the courses. Thus two giants entered carrying great trees in their hands. After them came two camels carrying turrets on their backs and a pantomime of men at arms combating, who fenced against each other with their lances. Immediately after supper, the Queens, the lords, and ladies danced until a late hour. Then all mounted on their horses and went home to their great houses." (113).

Jacques Cœur had been a member of the Royal Council, *étroit et privé*, two years before the peace conference at Tours; in all probability he was appointed one of his sovereign's advisers when he was ennobled in 1441. (114). His exceptional training and experience were doubtless of great service in the consideration of the commercial clauses of the treaty.

The truce with England opened suddenly for France an era of great prosperity. Commerce was established between the two nations and Jacques Cœur shipped goods to be sold in England. Rouen in the north and Bordeaux in the south, both still held by the English, became great fairs for the interchange of commodities between the two peoples. The trade balance across the channel heavily favored the French, but was settled by English credits established with the Flemings. Although England itself was then almost entirely an agricultural country, the fifteenth-century world was largely clothed with English wools, wrought in Flanders. The great wool-market, or staple, as it was called, was at Calais, then an English city, where, Commines tells us, "it is almost incredible what prodigious returns they [the great merchants of London] make from thence twice every year; there their wool lies till the merchants themselves come over, and their chief vent is into Flanders and Holland." Nevertheless, the wise policy of Edward III in encouraging the Flemish weavers to bring their art across the Channel was beginning to be justified and in the inventory of Jacques

Cœur's estate, we find the black and gray cloths of England's infant industry selling in competition with those of Dinan, Lille, and Rouen. (115).

After the Treaty of Arras, Flanders, which belonged to the Duke of Burgundy, opened the rich markets of Bruges, Liège, and Ghent to the merchants of Charles VII. Bruges, besides marketing the product of its own looms, was the principal centre of exchange for the commodities of northern and southern Europe. Here the celebrated Easterlings, of the free cities of the Hanseatic League, came to barter the hides, tallow, pitch, and lumber of the Baltic for the more highly finished products of the Mediterranean. From the competent authority last mentioned, we learn that Bruges in 1471 "is a place of trade and of great resort for foreigners of all nations in which more commodities and merchandise are disposed of than in any town in Europe." Commines also says that it was a town as large as Rouen and there is ample reason for believing that at the period of the Truce of Tours, Normandy's capital was the richest and most populous city then belonging to the English crown. (116).

Grand seigneur, Argentier, and Counsellor of the King, Jacques Cœur, rich and powerful, did not relax in the extension of his commerce.

"In the affairs of his calling," enthusiastically writes Georges Chastellain, chronicler of the Duke of Burgundy, who, as we shall see, had a personal acquaintance with Jacques Cœur, "there was no equal to him in the world. He had increased in fortune from 100 to 100,000, and then to a number of millions, by sheer ability. The glory of his master he made redound in every land, and the flowers of his crown he made flourish in far distant seas. All the Levant he visited with his ships, and there was not in the waters of the Orient a mast which was not decorated with the *fleur-de-lis*."

CHAPTER XVI

TURKISH CONQUESTS. KNIGHTS OF RHODES

No sooner did the rainbow of peace glow in the western horizon than lowering war clouds mounted once more, high in the eastern sky. The crushing defeat and slaughter which, at the beginning of the century, had been administered to the Turks by the Tartar conqueror Tamerlane, had plunged the Ottoman Empire into anarchy, and, for nearly a generation, retarded the progress of its arms. The Sultan Amurath II had mended his nation's shattered power and was now engaged in a memorable series of battles with the Hungarian hero Hunyady, who had kept the Turks at bay for another score of years. The latest news from this war-front was most disconcerting to the Christian powers. The Sultan's overwhelming victory at Warna permitted the Ottomans to resume their campaigns against Constantinople, now tottering to its fall.

The Turks owed much of their military success to the lack of unity which was opposed to them; the principal cause of their victories, however, was the superiority of their regular army over the undisciplined European chivalry, encumbered with its armor's heavy weight. Neither the Turkish cavalry—the *spahis*, as they were called—nor their celebrated infantry, the janizaries—the latter recruited from Christian proselytes, trained from infancy to be fanatical soldier-zealots—wore any defensive armor worthy of the name. (117). Like Samson of old, the Turkish soldier

> "Ran on embattled armies clad in iron,
> And, weaponless himself,
> Made arms ridiculous."

The strongest outpost of Christendom, short of Constantinople, was the island of Rhodes. Here, since 1309, the warlike order of Saint John of Jerusalem had guarded the commerce of Europe against the attacks of the Mussulman pirates, and maintained a strategic stronghold in the midst of the infidel power.

The Arabs, to whom Jerusalem is a holy city, had respected the shrines of Christian piety. Unlike the Turks they had ever shown themselves tolerant, and had never placed obstacles in the way of the pilgrimages to the Holy Sepulchre.

Nevertheless, the Knights of Rhodes, originally driven out of Jerusalem and Palestine by the Saracens, regarded the Sultan of Egypt as their hereditary enemy with whom their feuds had been of longer standing than their encounters with the Turks. Thus the year 1444—that of the Peace of Tours and of the Hungarian defeat at Warna—found Rhodes strongly invested by the forces of the Mameluke ruler; 18,000 infantry and a large body of cavalry landed on its coast and laid siege to its fortified capital. After one of the heroic defenses which has made the name of their order glorious, the chivalric Knights of Saint John, under their aged Grand Master Jean de Lastic, succeeded in beating off their assailants and forcing their withdrawal.

Despite this victorious resistance, the situation of

the Christian order was one of the greatest peril. Weakened by the attack of the Egyptian Sultan and having reason to fear repeated incursions from so strong and resolute a foe, the Knights saw their other infidel enemy growing ever stronger at the expense of their coreligionists in the East.   It was to them only too apparent that the strategical position of their island between the Bosphorus and the Levant, would call for its reduction by the Turks, once the latter were disengaged from their main objective in front of Constantinople. The urgency of their plight was represented to the Pope; fruitless appeals were likewise made to the princes throughout Christendom, too occupied with their own quarrels to be helpful to their brethren.

The Pontiff Eugenius IV had been greatly chastened by the Christian defeat at Warna. The battle had been the direct result of a breach of a formal truce between the Hungarians and the Turkish Sultan. The Papal Legate, the Cardinal Cæsarini, had counselled King Ladislas that good faith needed not to be observed in compacts made with pagans. (118).   Whether in reaction from the casuistical doctrine which had proven so maladroit at Warna, or whether prevailed upon by counsellors more practical than the ill-fated Cardinal, the Pope authorized the Grand Master of Rhodes to terminate the ruinous warfare with the Egyptian ruler, who was himself, as we have seen, in danger from the Ottomans. To effectuate the amicable arrangement there was need of skilful and delicate intermediation. The hostilities between the two adversaries had been of long duration; three hundred and fifty years of crusades and combats had marked the clashes of

their arms. Their mutual deeds in battle were renowned in song and story, associated with the names
of paladins, such as Saladin and Godfrey Bouillon; the
wide breach of contending religious faiths parted their
sympathies.

It is a clarifying commentary on the subject of our
memoir that for this difficult negotiation, "one alone
appeared eligible to the Knights, one whose great repu-
tation inspired confidence, whose successes proved his
great capacity, whose credit was equally conspicuous
in the East as in the West, and whose intimate relations with the Egyptian Sultan opened a free course to
negotiations; they fixed unanimously on Jacques Cœur,
the great merchant, and resolved to intrust him with
their interest and their safety." (119). It was not
customary, during the Middle Ages, any more than it
would be now, for private individuals to arrange treaties
except as commissioned agents of their sovereign.
Power then sprang from office even more generally than
it does to-day. Popes, Emperors, Kings, and Doges, in
person or through their ambassadors, played the leading rôles in the settlement of international affairs.
Charles VII's Argentier had, as such, no relation to
the task for which the Knights of Rhodes sought a
delegate; it was the man Jacques Cœur who was
wanted for the special duty in hand. That a mere individual, solely on his own prestige and credit, should
be selected by an outside power to concern himself in
its questions of peace and war, is an incident without
precedent in the history of his times, if indeed it has a
parallel in the annals of any age.

The success which crowned his mission we already

know. It only remains to add that, largely through this fortunate result, the warlike order of Saint John of Jerusalem occupied its island stronghold for nearly a century longer,

> "Streaming the ensign of the Christian cross
> Against black pagans, Turks, and Saracens."

CHAPTER XVII

CHURCH SCHISM. FINALE NAVAL EXPEDITION. EMBASSY TO ROME

THE last years of the life of Pope Eugenius IV were embittered by an ecclesiastical schism. (120). While engaged in an effort to effect union with the Greek Church, dissension spread in his own. The Council of Basle upheld the rights of the civil power against what the latter regarded as encroachments by Saint Peter's. The secular authority asserted itself with the greatest daring. Reform of the relations between Church and State was strongly demanded by most of the Christian Powers. When, however, the assembly, exasperated by the Pope's resistance to its programme, undertook to depose him and elect a successor, it lost the adherence of France and Germany, theretofore the strongest supporters of its policy.

The Council's choice of a pontiff was rather a singular one; it raised to the Papal See an abdicated ruler, who had sought seclusion from state affairs in a hermitage of his own creation. Amadeo VIII, Duke of Savoy, had called together the nobles and prelates of his duchy and, after recounting the events of his reign in a speech from the throne, had announced his intention of retiring from the world to seek, at the end of his days, the repose and tranquillity which had been denied him as the wearer of the ducal crown. After formally abdicating in favor of his son, with the six courtiers whom he had chosen as companions in his

retreat, he immured himself in the monastery which
he had caused to be built at Ripailles on the banks of
Lake Geneva, there to be Grand Master of the order
of chivalry which he had instituted. This unusual
ceremony had taken place while the Council of Basle
was still in session; whether or not by design, it had
attracted the attention of the members of that assembly. The historian of the Duke of Savoy assures us
that Amadeo, in his solitude, led a life austere and
penitent, making it all the more difficult to account
for the origin of the French proverb, *faire ripailles*,
which denotes taking pleasure in a jovial retreat. (121).

The Church was thus again confronted with the
very crisis which it had so recently undergone and
which its Councils had been assembled to remedy,
"when two Popes, each with a doubtful title, made all
Europe ring with their mutual invectives and anathe-
mas." The Papacy, during the fifteenth century, was
the symbol of an authority which was supported by
universal belief, the only effective brake upon the un-
trammelled wills of many of the princes who represented the civil power. "The plain Christian people,
brought up in the belief that it was a sacred duty to
be in communion with the head of the church, were
unable to discover amidst conflicting testimonies and
conflicting arguments, to which of the two . . . priests
. . . the headship of the church rightfully belonged."
(122). The confusion of ecclesiastical leadership was
especially unfortunate in view of the Turkish onset
in the East which made it all the more important that
there be opposed to it unity in the army of the Christian faith.

Charles VII had taken an advanced position in the general movement for the limitation of papal power; in his own kingdom he had especially curtailed it. His celebrated edict of 1438, known as the Pragmatic Sanction, had proclaimed rules of ecclesiastical policy abolishing in France many of the privileges and practices theretofore enjoyed and exercised by the Holy See in all of the countries owing it the allegiance of their faith. The effect of this had been to reduce the revenues derived by Rome from benefices in France and to limit the papal power in church elections within the Gallic realm.

The fathers of the Council of Basle had, therefore, good reason to expect Charles VII's support of their action in proclaiming the deposition of the reigning Pope and the election of the ex-Duke of Savoy in his stead. They were soon undeceived. The French King promptly announced his continued obedience to Eugenius IV, and prayed the members of the Council and "Monsieur of Savoy" to devote themselves to ending the dissensions of the church, a work to which he pledged his own assistance. Owing largely to the troubled condition of his realm, the papal division lasted for seven years before his promise was redeemed.

In 1447, during the truce with England, Charles appointed an embassy to reason with the Savoyard claimant to the tiara, in the hope of arriving at an accommodation which would heal a schism which the King had characterized as "pestilential and horrible." This delicate mission was intrusted to Jacques Juvenal des Ursins, Archbishop of Rheims, Jean d'Étampes, Bishop of Carcassonne, Robert Thibault, Master of Theology and—among these formidable churchmen—a practical man of affairs in the person of Jacques Cœur. The ambassadors found Amadeo not unwilling to yield his pretensions, on terms which would reserve for him special dignities and honors, when the situation became further complicated by the death of Pope Eugenius IV and the election of Nicholas V as his successor at Rome. This right of substitution, should it be exercised in the case of its nominee by the Council of Basle, would tend to perpetuate the dual headship of the Church. Charles VII, with the concurrence of England and certain German princes, hastened to acknowledge the new Pope selected by the conclave of Cardinals, and sent to him an embassy of which Jacques Cœur was again a member.

This legation had a dual rôle to perform—it carried the sword as well as the olive branch. The stormy republic of Genoa was then in the throes of one of the domestic crises so common in its history. Under the preceding reign France had exercised for a time certain suzerain rights over the turbulent state which Charles VII, now relieved from battling with the English, was ambitious to restore. The fortified château of Finale, a minor Genoese fief on the Ligurian coast, held in the interests of France by the Marquis Galeotto of Caretto, was strongly invested by land and sea by the forces of the republic.

Accordingly Jacques Cœur, accompanied by that sturdy old warrior Tanguy Duchâtel, of bridge of Montereau fame, now the seneschal of Beaucaire, in April, 1448, sailed from Marseilles in command of a fleet of eleven vessels provided by the enterprising merchant and outfitted at his expense. It is not entirely clear whether their colleagues on the papal mission were embarked with them or had taken an overland route, later to rejoin them in time for the collective appearance of the envoys at Rome. The question is of little importance, as, for the matter first in hand, men of action were required and the choice of them was proven to have been well taken. Eight of the transports contained provisions and munitions of war for the relief of Finale; these supplies being safely landed in the besieged port, the admiral of the expedition, with its three largest vessels, pursued by the naval forces of Genoa, which he successfully eluded, sailed away for the Roman port of Cività Vecchia, on his ambassadorial and ecclesiastical errand.

The envoys made their ceremonial entrance into Rome in a most impressive manner. More than 300 horses richly caparisoned and harnessed figured in the cortege. "No living man," says Jean Chartier, the royal chronicler of France, "ever saw so honorable an embassy enter Rome; so great was the magnificence, that such a company was never before heard tell of, which turned greatly to the honor of the King and Kingdom." Pope Nicholas V wrote to Charles VII that the residents of the Eternal City did not remember for sixty years to have seen a legation so numerous, or one composed of men so illustrious. Jacques Cœur was accorded especial consideration by the sovereign Pontiff. Shortly after his arrival, having been taken with a fever, the Pope caused him to be borne to the Vatican "in order that the papal physicians might minister to his health with the same great care that they would show to the person of His Holiness himself, should he be ill." (123).

The embassy happily accomplished its purpose. In the end Amadeo was induced to content himself with lesser honors than Saint Peter's chair. The ex-Duke became a cardinal, a bishop, legate and vicar of the Holy See in the duchy of Savoy; he obtained ecclesiastical rank only junior to that of the Pope; it was provided that when he should appear before His Holiness, the latter would rise from his chair to receive him and kiss him on the mouth, "without exacting from him any other marks of respect or submission"; finally he was permitted to retain the habit and ornaments of the pontificate, save only the famous Fisherman's Ring, the dais, and the insignia of the cross upon his shoes. (124). With these concessions to his religious pride, Amadeo confessed to the assembly that had chosen him that Nicholas V, and not he, was, after all, the true shepherd, and retired to his monastic retreat there to satisfy himself with the worship which was naturally due so distinguished a Grand Master of the Order of Saint Maurice from its knightly members.

The ending of the schism caused rejoicing throughout Christendom. Nothing in Charles VII's reign brought him more glory than this successful stroke in the cause of church unity; naturally the emissaries whom he employed to accomplish it shared in their sovereign's honor. "To conduct which peace and to bring it to an issue, the Very Christian King of France and his ministers labored valiantly," the royal chronicler comments. "And to this end, in order to accomplish it, he employed *grandes finances*; hence he is entitled to very great praise and recompense." As for Jacques Cœur, his labors on this occasion obtained for him the loyal gratitude of that great humanist Pope, Nicholas V, which was to stand him in good stead in his days of adversity to come.

CHAPTER XVIII

NEGOTIATIONS WITH GENOA. LANGUEDOC.
"SWEETMEATS"

THE relief of Finale, so dashingly accomplished on the way to the fulfilment of the diplomatic errand at Rome, was but a minor episode in a complicated chain of events, intrigues, and negotiations in the relations between Genoa and France which had their inception half a century before. The republic, exhausted by several hundred years of strife both at home and abroad, had reached at the end of the fourteenth century a stage in her history when she had need of a protector. The liberties of neither of her great Guelf and Ghibelline factions were safe with the other seated in the Doge's chair; the rights of both were in danger from the aggression of the Duke of Milan by land and the King of Aragon by sea. Faced with this dilemma, the republic had given herself to France and for half a generation the viceroy of Charles VI had governed Genoa with the same authority as though he were its Doge. Ever open to foreign intrigue through the ambitions and animosities of its powerful families, Genoa had thrown off the French yoke only to invite another, and, successively, the Marquis of Montferrat and the Duke of Milan had become its suzerains. In 1435 the republic had recovered its independence, but not its liberty; vainly the better citizens strove to give stability to the elections of their Doge and council. The

Fregoso family, rulers during the early years of freedom, had been violently driven out of power by the Adornos, who now governed with the aid of a strong body-guard of Catalans, supported by Alfonso V of Aragon, while the Fregoso faction maintained an active cabal at Nice in the duchy of Savoy and intrigued for the support of France. The Fregosos during their interval of power had strongly sustained Charles VII's brother-in-law, René of Provence and Anjou, in his struggle against Alfonso for the throne of Naples; the Genoese fleet had carried him back to Marseilles at the end of his ill-fated expedition to validate his claim to this one of his several empty royal titles.

. Jacques Cœur, who seems always to have been a member of the Angevin party at the French court, had already begun to concentrate an increasing number of his commercial ventures at Marseilles. In February, 1446, he took out formal citizenship papers there and established in the Provençal port the centre of his Mediterranean operations, a step which was dictated by the increasing silting of Montpellier's harbor, and the decline of its commerce in consequence of this and other causes. (125). Charles VII's ambition to reassert his father's dominion over Genoa was naturally a project which appealed especially to the enterprising merchant. The commercial advantages, enjoyed in the East by the Italian state, with its settlement at Pera, a suburb of Constantinople, its colony at Caffa in the Crimea, its ownership of Chios and the rich city of Fumagasta in the island of Cyprus, were only too apparent to France's great Mediterranean trader. Accordingly he took a keen and eager interest in all the

royal plans for attaching Genoa to France and iden-
tifying the commercial interests of the two Powers.

The Fregoso cabal put into Marseilles with their
ships of war and sent word to the French King of their
desire to make him suzerain of Genoa, should it be his
sovereign pleasure to accept. Charles VII promptly
sent an embassy to treat with them and to devise ways
and means to carry out a purpose with which he was
so heartily in accord. Jacques Cœur, although not the
official head of this mission, seems to have played in it
the principal rôle. From Marseilles the French envoys
went to Nice, there to complete their arrangements
with Janus de Campo Fregoso, Benedict Doria, and
other Genoese noblemen attached to the Fregoso cause.
(126). As a result of the joint plans, Janus took the
field in the name of the King of France and, at the head
of troops at least partly furnished by Charles VII, succeeded in capturing several places on the Genoese
shore-front; meanwhile, Jacques Cœur, Tanguy Duchâtel, and the other French legates, with a fleet which
they had provided and equipped, held themselves in
readiness at Nice to co-operate with the campaign by
land. At this point Janus seems to have determined
to forestall his Gallic allies. Entering Genoa with one
galley and a small band of chosen companions, fighting under the banner of France, he put to flight the
Adornos, and caused himself to be proclaimed Doge of
Genoa January 30, 1447. This done, furling the banner of the *fleur-de-lis*, he politely dismissed the Seigneur de Saint-Vallier and the other Frenchmen who
had aided him to carry out his successful stroke.
Charles VII's ambassadors at Nice were naturally

GENOA.

From an old engraving.

perplexed and astounded at Janus's action, the more so in view of the latter's repeated protestations that the affair would have "a good ending."

Jacques Cœur reported the matter to the King's ministers in a letter dated February 17: "I cannot believe that Janus would so betray us. Nevertheless, one cannot guard oneself against a traitor. If the King is willing to approach as far as Lyons and the men-at-arms should be marched past that city, I make no doubt but that we will have that which we demand for the King's honor, and more surely than we will have it in any other way."

Counsel was taken with the Dauphin, then in Dauphiny, and a plan of action agreed upon, with the approval of a member of the house of Doria, which involved an immediate demonstration against Genoa by the King's representatives, a show of force in Italy by the French Prince at the head of an army, and the co-operation of the republic's fleet under Benedict Doria, who still continued to protest his loyalty to France.

Early in March Jacques Cœur and the other ambassadors, sailing from Villefranche east of Nice, entered the harbor of Genoa and summoned the recalcitrant Janus to carry out his pledges. The demand was crushingly rebuffed. The newly installed Doge announced that he had won his honors with the sword and would defend them with that weapon if need be.

The diplomatic naval expedition was not in sufficient force to capture Genoa by direct assault, unaided from within. "For to approach the walls of Genoa without a considerable body of forces was ridiculous and impracticable by reason of the numbers and the courage of its inhabitants"; so says that excellent military authority Commines in speaking of another French enterprise, half a century later to assert the same ambitions. Defeated in their hopes, Jacques Cœur and his fellow envoys sailed home to Marseilles, and the "affair of Genoa" took its place among history's lost causes, to be revived, however, by succeeding French monarchs, ever ready to respond to the lure of Italy. (127).

Jacques Cœur's intrepid philosophy, so tersely expressed in his famous motto which he was just beginning to have carved in stone on his stately mansion at Bourges, then in course of erection, did not permit him to abandon a project so easily. Thus we find him in continued and earnest correspondence with Campo Fregoso by letter and by secret emissary for eighteen months after the rebuff of the French ambassadors in the port of Genoa, an intercourse which was only closed by the death of Janus. The letters on the side of the Argentier are missing, the wily Doge probably having regarded them as too compromising to be preserved; copies of his own missives, which he took care to make sufficiently non-committal, were faithfully kept. There are six of these documents in the archives of Genoa. (128). The duplicate of the first of them, written August 28, 1447, was sent to the Argentier at Piacenza, a city in the duchy of Milan, about sixty miles from Genoa. The sudden death of Philippe Maria Visconti, a fortnight before, without lawful issue, had left the ducal throne vacant and caused a lively scramble over the succession. Jacques Cœur had probably gone to

Italy in the interests of the French claimant, Charles
of Orleans, cousin of the King. In assertion of that
Prince's title, Charles VII's troops, already occupying
Asti as a result of a concession by the late Duke, were
about to take the field against the forces of the newly
declared Milanese republic. The presence of French
soldiers so near to Genoa, and the vigorous preparations then on foot in France to establish the Orleans
claim, created a favorable occasion to urge upon the
elusive Janus the fulfilment of his broken pledges.
That Charles VII's able minister was not slow to take
advantage of this convenient opportunity, is shown
by the Doge's letter which, in view of its brevity, is
given here in full, translated from its Latin text.

To that August and Illustrious Man, Lord
    Jacques Cœur, Argentier of the King and
    our Very Dearest Friend.

We have listened, august and illustrious man, our
very dear friend, to your young Parisian, Alvere, and
we have fully noted all that he has reported to us.
And so, to-morrow morning, we are sending to you
[an emissary] of ours, one Terdo, judging that he will
be able to find Your Excellency in that city [Piacenza];
whom, if perchance Terdo does not encounter on the
way, he will go as far as Piacenza, in order that, either
there or on the road he may meet Your Excellency;
to whose aggrandizement we and ours eagerly defer.
Dated XXVIII August [1447].   JANUS, DUX.

Times were troublous now in Lombardy; fierce ambitions were unloosed over the Milanese succession;

French troops were on the march from Asti to besiege Alessandria; that scheming *condottiere*, Francis Sforza, who had espoused the late Duke's natural daughter and was soon to annex his throne, had crossed the Adda with his mercenaries, seeking to enlarge his power in the Milanese domain. The adjoining republic of Genoa, whose war-time force was chiefly on the sea, began anew to feel the need of protection. We find its Doge, on September 5, despatching two letters to the Argentier, one following the other in rapid haste. The intermediary between the two is now Francis Calvari, and Janus, who now appears to be taking the initiative in the negotiation, sends him to Jacques Cœur "with full instructions on all matters." At this stage the negotiations seem to have met with reverses, and the Argentier to have attempted to coerce the Doge with reminders of the French King's power. Thus on September 25 Janus writes him: "As for your exhortation to us, in your wisdom, that we should take care at this time to be of service to the amplification of the majesty of the King, in so far as is consistent with our dignity and best advantage, we accept your warnings in very good part, as counsels which we do not hesitate to act upon in true love and sincerity of mind. In consequence, we say that it has always been among our especial desires that occasion should be given us of gratifying that most illustrious King, and of working for his dignity and grandeur."

Such was the state of affairs when, on October 17, the comparatively small French army in Lombardy was almost completely destroyed by the forces of the Milanese republic. (129). The adventurous Argentier, deep in the enemy's country, unsupported by soldiers of his own nationality, must have found himself in a position from which it could not have been easy to extricate himself. His correspondence with Campo Fregoso was broken off, not to be resumed until nearly a year later. The loss of French prestige beyond the Alps, resulting from the disaster of Alessandria, was not without its effect on the policies of the artful Doge. Charles VII did not carry his operations in Italy any farther. Like the aspirations of his brother-in-law René to the throne of Naples, his cousin of Orleans's ambitions as to Milan and his own pretensions to Genoa were allowed to end in disappointment.

Not that the royal hopes were completely abandoned. Finale was relieved, as we have seen, in order to keep open a convenient side-entrance for a possible future movement against the obdurate city. As for Jacques Cœur, we find him, a year later, during the course of his embassy at Rome, profiting by the prestige gained by his sovereign on that occasion, to renew negotiations regarding Genoa, efforts which ceased only with the death of Campo Fregoso, shortly after sending the last of his letters to his "Very Dear Friend." (130).

From 1441 to 1451, with the exception of the year 1449, Jacques Cœur was one of the commissioners representing the King at the sessions of the "States" of Languedoc. This province formed one of the four principal subdivisions for the collection of the revenue of the kingdom, and it was the duty of the commissioners to adjust with its legislative assembly, Languedoc's share of taxes payable to the royal treasury.

The *aide*, an impost on sales and products, and the *taille*, a property rate, were, in theory, gratuities to the sovereign. The amount of these contributions was a matter of bargain between the assembly and the King's representatives, arrived at only after continued grumbling on the one side and pressure and threats of royal displeasure on the other. Once the imposition was voted, Jacques Cœur seems to have been charged with the duty of apportioning it among the dioceses which, in turn, distributed it among the different localities. The system was a primitive and random one, in accord, however, with the administrative methods of the times. Edmund Burke said of it, at a later period of its application: "Rational people could have hoped little from this their tax in the form of a benevolence; a tax weak, ineffective, and unequal." "Better the public enemy than the tax-gatherer" runs the Persian proverb, which finds its apt illustration in the case of Bordeaux, which city, soon to be freed from English rule, rather than pay the unequal French taxes, reverted to its old masters across the channel and was brought back to its native allegiance only after a bitter struggle.

The duties of the King's commissioners in administering a revenue scheme so imperfect naturally brought them unpopularity; it brought them, however, emoluments as well. The assemblies seldom adjourned without voting substantial honorariums, called "sweetmeats," to each of the several royal representatives. These were all granted in open parliament by a body loath to appropriate except to carry out a practice which was the universal custom of the age. The "States" of Languedoc, whose harbor of Montpellier was then contending with Marseilles as the home port of the great merchant's fleet, awarded him on one occasion a substantial sum, "for the expenses by him laid out to support the volume of trade by means of galleys, ships, and other vessels"; at another time it accorded him a grant "to compensate him for the expenses which he had laid out for the army in connection with the conquest of Normandy." Both appropriations were freely voted in public sessions with words of accompanying praise. Nevertheless, the very openness of these transactions caught the eye of envy, and the unsuccessful merchants of Montpellier, instead of blaming the Lord for the drifting sands which were destroying their harbor, blamed Jacques Cœur, on whom they had been accustomed to rely for everything, and treasured up against him the all too inadequate rewards which their province had bestowed upon his public spirit in its days of greater prosperity. (131).

PART IV

PROSPERITY

"A man in prosperity resembleth a tree, around which people flock as long as it hath fruit; but as soon as it hath dropped all that it bore, they disperse from beneath it and seek another."
(Nur-ed-din and Enis-el-Jelis, *One Thousand and One Nights*.)

CHAPTER XIX

JACQUES CŒUR'S HOUSE AT BOURGES. HIS MANORIAL ESTATES

"FEBRUARY 9, 1815.—After breakfast Madame de Staël told father that she believed greatly in heredity; undoubtedly he had inherited his talent for finance from their common ancestor, Jacques Cœur."

"April —, 1817.—Father again went to see Madame de Staël. He came back very depressed, as he fears she will not last long. She was very excited, talking about Jacques Cœur, from whom she is descended through the Gallatins. Cœur was certainly an extraordinary man. I never heard that any of our family benefited by his fortune. I intend some day going to Bourges to see his palace, which they say is the finest Renaissance palace in existence. If Jeanne d'Arc had not had those absurd visions we might be rich [?]. Madame de Staël says that both she and father get their brains from Cœur; they certainly got nothing else."

"October 19, 1822.—To my great pleasure, he [father] proposed that we, he and I, should go to Bourg[es] and see the fine palace of Jacques Cœur. This has been a pleasure long postponed."

"October 25, 1822. [Bourges.] It has, indeed, repaid us to come here. I never realized what Renaissance architecture was and what a wonderful man was Cœur—almost a magician. His origin is hardly known —but, at one time, the richest man in France until

Charles VII stripped him of his fortune to carry on his wars against the English, then, by way of gratitude, threw him into a prison on a trumped-up charge of poisoning Agnes Sorel, the former's mistress. He was absolved of this charge; went to the East and made another fortune [?]. One of his daughters married a Lenthène, their daughter Agnes a Tudert, and Sarah Tudert a Gallatin, our direct ancestor." (132).

Thus wrote young James Gallatin over a century ago, in the diary which he kept while serving as secretary to his brilliant father, Albert Gallatin, early American finance minister, then representing his country at the court of France. The youthful diarist is excusably inaccurate; his reasoning in associating the Maid of Orleans with his own fortunes is hard to follow; even his genealogical tree, as he describes it, lacks several of its connecting limbs. His boyish and enthusiastic reaction to the charm and beauty of Jacques Cœur's town house at Bourges is, none the less, a naïve and faithful record of the impression made upon every one who views this fascinating example of fifteenth-century art. Jacques Cœur, the architect of his own fortunes, one can readily see was largely the architect of his own dwelling. Spacious, magnificent, and elaborate in all its parts, he stamped it with his native force and adorned it with his graces.

From the moment one enters the *porte-cochère*, underneath the two false windows, from each of which a house-servant, carved in stone, leans outward, peering expectantly down the street, on the lookout for the master's possible return, the house is pervaded with the spell of its owner's personality. On the balustrade above the entrance, in graceful stonework pattern, amidst alternate cockle-shells and hearts—the emblems of his name—is wrought his intrepid theme:

The tower of the interior courtyard is studded with stone sculptures, telling of Eastern lands; inside the mansion, over the doorways, leading to the different rooms, graphic scenes are carved, proclaiming each apartment's use. Religious subjects lead the way to the portal of the chapel, a veritable gem of devotional art.

Like many modern merchant princes, and others whose busy lives oblige them to conform their conduct to routine rules of practice, Jacques Cœur made use of maxims. In stone and stained glass he extolled the golden virtue of silence. "The very roofs of this curious house," says an English visitor, "are covered with sculpture, and open lacework parapets bear the favorite mottoes; every pipe and gargoyle is wrought and ornamented, every chimney wreathed and decorated, every window surrounded with devices." (133).

Thus in that amiable period of the Renaissance, when the architects and sculptors no longer clove to the rigid conventions of antique art, Jacques Cœur builded him a house, the most perfect standard of sumptuous dwelling of his age. He endowed it with his own individuality and gave it personal expression without detracting from its type. Like the Sphinx of Egypt, one feels that it has a message to convey, whose meaning constantly eludes. Michelet has, perhaps, come the nearest to interpreting it, although one feels that in the rendition he has not been entirely fair.

"One should visit at Bourges," he writes on the subject of Jacques Cœur, "the curious house of this equivocal personage—a house full of mysteries as was his life. One sees, on examining it closely, what it reveals and what it conceals; throughout, one seems to sense two opposing characteristics, the boldness and the defiance of the parvenu, the pride of Oriental commerce, and at the same time the reserve of the King's Argentier. Nevertheless boldness triumphs; the parade of mystery is like a challenge to the passer-by.

"This house, projected somewhat into the street, as though to see and study those who come, keeps itself entirely apart; at its false windows, two servitors, carved in stone, have the air of scrutinizing the public. In the court, small *bas-reliefs* present the humble images of labor, the spinner, the sweeper, the wine-grower, the peddler; but up above this false humility the equestrian statue of the banker juts forth imperially. In this triumph behind closed doors, the great financier does not disdain to inform all of the secret of his fortune; he explains it to us in two devices: one, is the heroic rebus: '*A vaillans (cœurs) rien impossible.*' This device is peculiar to the man, to his audacity, to his naïve pride. The other is the petty wisdom of the merchant of the Middle Ages: '*Bouche close. Neutre.*

Entendre dire. Faire. Taire.' Wise and discreet maxim which he should have followed by not proclaiming it! In the beautiful hall above, *le vaillant* Cœur is still more indiscreet; he caused to be sculptured for his own daily amusement, a burlesque joust, a donkey-back tournament—a durable mockery of chivalry which would naturally greatly offend certain classes." (134).

Valet de Viriville is perhaps, on the whole, equally interpretative and more just. "Jacques Cœur," says he, "had known his century by seeing it at close range. The greatest affairs, the greatest personages were familiar to him. More than once he was constrained to find them petty. The rank which his birth denied him he had purchased by his own merit and with his own gold, and Jacques believed the score to be evened. One of the grotesque figures or cornices sculptured on the tower, belonging to what is called the Treasury, represents a blackamoor slave, a *fellah* of the Orient, who holds, in the guise of an heraldic support, the helmet or casque of an ennobled merchant, draped with his mantling and emblazoned with two hearts. Another subject on the same tower shows us two cavaliers, armed cap-a-pie, fencing, each striving to transfix the other with his blade. At the right, a masked peasant, crouched, lies in wait for the wayfarer, armed with a cudgel which he holds in his hands. On the other side, *une fille d'armée*, a vulgar Briseis, awaits likewise the result of the clash of arms. It is the satirical picture of war in the fifteenth century. Another scene, the archness of which is no less Gallic, decorates the chimneypiece of one of the reception-rooms and relates to tournaments. Here the con-

testants are shepherds and swineherds, mounted bare-
back on donkeys, with old ropes for stirrups. They
point broomsticks gravely at each other, as though
they were lances, carrying basket-lids in place of shields
or bucklers.

"Jacques Cœur also had the gift of good sense. These
judicious railleries, then perfectly apposite, anticipated
by more than one hundred years Cervantes and *Don
Quixote*. Proverbs, they say, are the wisdom of nations.
Jacques Cœur took delight in many of these popular
adages. He also shared in the taste for rebuses, so
wide-spread in the fifteenth century." (135).

Jacques began the erection of his Bourges mansion
in 1443; an inscription on the clock of the chapel's
spire pronounced it as having been completed in July,
1450; his wife and family had been installed in it three
years before. Yet, when the King's officers came to
seize it in July, 1451, "it was not in perfect order and
awaited the said Cœur to put the finishing touches on
it; for the workmen who roamed throughout the house
had ruined and destroyed a great deal," indicating that
artisans have been much the same in every age. Still,
many of the rooms were already furnished and the
testimony in the confiscation proceedings by Jacques
Cœur's steward, Guillot Trépant, gives us an idea of
some of his master's personal treasures with which he
embellished his home. We learn thus that tapestries,
some embroidered with the arms of the King, some with
those of the Argentier, adorned the principal apartments; the walls of one chamber were decorated with
red embroidered taffetas, those of another with dam-
asks portraying "*personnages de Nabugot-de-Nozor*";

others with different fabrics of various colors and patterns. As for the plate, it was of a magnificence which gave rise to the common report that Jacques Cœur was served from gold and silver, the King from pewter. Much of this ware was carried with him on his journeys from one of his town houses to another; some of his tapestries, even, were transported to sustain his state whilst an ambassador at Rome. The kitchen, his steward complains, "was so poorly equipped that when the said Cœur came and held banquets and fêtes, pewter utensils were rented and other articles borrowed." (136).

It is a singular instance of the perversity of human affairs that this building which commemorates a name associated with judicial iniquity should, now for a century past, have served as a temple of justice. (137).

While engaged in building his own house Jacques Cœur erected a beautiful sacristy for Bourges's majestic cathedral, and on the site of the old sacristy, a chapel. Nor did he restrict his munificence to his native city. Paris and other cities felt its benefits. "During his life-time," writes an author of the sixteenth century, "Jacques Cœur of Bourges, merchant and afterward Argentier of France, founded the College of Good Children and the Chapel Sainct-Cler, in the Rue Sainct-Honoré." (138).

In addition to his town residences in Bourges and elsewhere, Jacques Cœur possessed an incredible number of manor-houses and estates. Scattered throughout the kingdom, but principally in the provinces near Bourges, and including within their bounds many villages and parishes, more than twenty of these great country places were acquired by him during the latter part of his life—properties which, for the most part, had theretofore belonged to the greatest families of the realm. One of the largest of them had been bought of Charles, Duke of Bourbon, cousin of the King; of the Marquis of Montferrat he purchased baronial estates in Puisaye, the best-known of which was the château and domain of Saint-Fargeau, whose ownership was contested by the family of Charles VII's former favorite, la Tremouille.

These acquisitions have been attributed to an overweening ambition to found a powerful house, whose titles of nobility and influence would be based on ownership of land. Although the King's Argentier could not have been entirely blind to considerations such as these, Jacques Cœur's chief reason for his policy was probably a simpler one. Real-estate investment was then practically the sole outlet for the safe placement of accumulated funds. The rent-rolls and yield from cultivation of these properties represented a sure return on capital which the careful husbandry of the capable merchant would almost certainly increase. One hundred years of intermittent war and almost continuous disorder had greatly reduced the condition of the great French nobles. In the fifteenth century most of them were in financial straits. The war, in bringing ruin to their tenantry, had adversely affected the landlords. Many, whose domains had escaped its devastations, had paid heavy ransoms to the English for the redemption of themselves or their relatives. Charles VII's reform of taxes had deprived them of the benefit of road and river tolls and other feudal

JACQUES CŒUR'S HOUSE AT BOURGES.

tributes. There was, however, a more fundamental reason for their exigencies, totally unrelated to their misfortunes: prodigality was their special virtue, glorified in song and story and prescribed for them by the laws of chivalry. (139).

Many of them had recourse to the rising middle class of townsfolk—merchants and public officials—a rank which, during this century, was beginning to establish itself in France, and which, possessed of ready money in a period of currency shortage, was naturally called upon to take the buyer's and lender's end of bargains with the hard-pressed nobles. The financier of the King's household, whose daily duties brought him into close touch with the courtiers and whose wealth had become proverbial, could scarcely avoid playing his part in a movement then so general. (140).

These transactions were not without their dangers to those who represented capital. The age had outgrown the days described by Fiske, when "the fashionable method of compounding with your creditors was . . . to inveigle them into your castle and broil them over a slow fire." Yet the position and authority of the great nobles, now still further exalted by martial leadership in war time, towered so high that those who followed peaceful arts found themselves greatly overshadowed.

That subtle and acute statesman Machiavelli advises princes that, if constrained to put any to death, they should do so only when there is manifest cause or reasonable justification. But, above all, they must abstain from the property of another. "For," he adds, "men will sooner forget the death of their father than the loss of their patrimony." And so Charles VII's needy nobles, compelled by stern necessity to part with their ancestral estates to a class whose birth they had been taught to despise, bitterly resented these transactions, although of their own seeking.

CHAPTER XX

ARMY REORGANIZATION. RENEWAL OF THE
WAR. RECAPTURE OF ROUEN. JACQUES
CŒUR'S LOANS. HIS PROSPERITY, EMI-
NENCE, AND HONORS. HIS FAMILY

CHARLES VII profited by the truce to reorganize his
soldiery. With the double aim of suppressing the marauding free companies and driving the English from
his kingdom, he established the first regular army in
France. At this epoch, outside of England, the attention of military Europe was confined almost entirely
to cavalry. Accordingly, the King of France gave his
first care to this arm of the service and organized fifteen
compagnies d'ordonnance, so called because of the royal
proclamation ordaining them. Each company was
composed of ten lances. Each of these units, in turn,
contained six mounted men: the *chevalier,* or man-at-
arms proper, wearing full armor weighing from 150 to
175 pounds, his steed being likewise encased in steel;
three archers, an equerry, and a page.

The captains of these companies held their commissions directly from the King and were removable at
the royal pleasure. These officers were, for the most
part, drawn from among the most celebrated chiefs
of the *écorcheurs.* With adequate provision made for
their pay, the troops were distributed in garrisons
throughout the kingdom, and almost immediately restored order as though by magic. The highways and
countrysides became safe, and commerce and agricul-
ture revived.

Having in 1445 reorganized the cavalry, three years later Charles VII gave his attention to the infantry. Borrowing from the fighting methods of the English, he established a militia of archers and crossbowmen, sworn to join the royal standard at the first call to arms. (141).

The brothers Bureau, Gaspard and Jean, gave their attention to the artillery and assembled, says the royal chronicler, "the largest number of huge bombards, great cannon, *veuglaires*, serpentines, mortars, *crapeaulx d'eaulx*, culverins, and *ribaudigues* that ever the memory of man had seen in possession of a Christian King." (142).

Charles, the Well-Served, was particularly well counselled in this matter of army reform; the identity of his advisers, however, has remained obscured. Praise for this important work, so potent in the liberation of the kingdom, has been variously bestowed—usually on the Constable de Richemont, Dunois, or the Marshal de la Fayette. In general, the change was obnoxious to the nobles, who saw with jealous eyes provision made for raising troops without their intervention—cavalry independent of chivalry, foot-soldiery whose ranks were open to the commons, and artillery which nullified the strategic value of the mediæval castle.

We do not know the full part taken by Jacques Cœur in this programme; that he had some connection with it—at least to the extent of importing armor from Genoa—is shown by a paragraph in one of Campo Fregoso's letters to the Argentier. (143). Commines, the great war minister of the succeeding reign, whose

authority on such a subject is conclusive, states that
Charles VII's new army was "formed in imitation of
the princes of Italy." Certainly the brothers Bureau
did not hesitate to borrow ideas from abroad; they
availed themselves of the services of a Genoese cannoneer, one Louis Giribault or Guibaut, who, we are
told, had invented "a carriage for moving the guns
about," and who played an important rôle in the campaigns of Normandy and Guienne. The use of ord-
nance, at this period, had reached its highest development among the Turks, whose predominance in this
arm was shortly to accomplish the fall of Constantinople. These infidel practices were probably not generally known to the advisers of the King, whose ig-
norance of Ottoman fighting methods was soon to
be displayed in one of the charges brought against
Jacques Cœur.

It is, therefore, not unreasonable to suppose that
Charles VII's army reform was urged if not suggested
by the cosmopolite merchant who of all the royal counsellors best knew the outside world—perhaps supported
by his patrons the Princes of the House of Anjou, the
King's brothers-in-law, whose war for the crown of
Naples had familiarized them with the tactics of Italy.
(144).

The truce between England and France was not to
grow into a permanent peace, as many had hoped it
might. Normandy called loudly for deliverance, and
provocations growing out of the tardiness of the English in obeying the treaty provisions for the surrender
of Le Mans were seized upon by the French King as
pretexts for recommencing the war.

The campaign for the conquest of Normandy was of relatively short duration—from August, 1449, through the same month in the following year. The soldiers of Charles VII were hailed everywhere as liberators, and the comparatively small English garrisons, badly supported by their countrymen across the channel, found themselves foreign enemies in a hostile land. The French King took the field in person at the head of his reorganized and regularly paid troops; Jacques Cœur accompanied him throughout the entire campaign; royal chroniclers set the clocks of history ticking to record what could easily be foreseen would prove to be memorable events in the annals of France.

The city of Rouen was recaptured with the aid of a rising of its inhabitants. The English, besieged from without and attacked from within, yielded the ancient Norman capital under an honorable capitulation which permitted their retirement to Caen.

November 10, 1449, after ten days of preparation and rehearsals under the direction of the royal herald, during which numerous requisitions were doubtless drawn upon William de Varye's richly stocked storehouse at Tours, Charles VII made his ceremonial entrance into the city which had witnessed Jeanne d'Arc's martyrdom, and passed in procession through the midst of a rejoicing populace to its celebrated cathedral, there to offer up his thanks to God.

The cortege displayed a pomp and solemnity befitting an occasion so historic, and is minutely described by the chroniclers, both in poetry and prose. The King of France was mounted on a palfrey, with housing of azure velvet, spangled with golden *fleur-de-lis* and reaching to the ground. He was preceded by Poton de

Xaintrailles the royal equerry, by the Chancellor of France, the Archbishop of Rouen, and several bishops, abbés, and other churchmen. After the sovereign, an eye-witness tells us, came "Count of Dunois, Lieutenant-General, mounted on a charger covered with vermilion velvet [decorated] with a great white cross, himself clothed in a jacket of the same material, trimmed with fine sables, wearing on his head a hat of black velvet, and, at his side, a sword embellished with gold and precious stones, and carrying in its scabbard a ruby valued at 20,000 écus. In his company were the Seneschal of Poitu, Lord Jacques Cœur, Argentier, and the Lord of Gaucourt, mounted, caparisoned, and dressed like the said Count of Dunois——." (145).

The Seneschal of Poitu was Jacques Cœur's friend, the brilliant Pierre de Brézé, lately first minister of the Crown, now appointed captain of the regained city in token of his return to royal favor; Gaucourt, the Lord Chamberlain, was a martial personage who, like Dunois, had served in the campaigns of Jeanne d'Arc. The chroniclers stress the fact that Jacques Cœur, a man of the people, should be habited on this state occasion in the same manner as the King's cousin, the Lieutenant-General of the Kingdom, the great French military hero of the day.

> "Le dit Dunois estoit monté,
> Sur un cheval plaisant à l'euil,
> Enharnaché, bien appointé
> Et couvert de velours vermeil. . . .
>
> Après li le suyvoit de court
> Brézé, Jacques Cueur, l'argentier,
> Avec le sire de Gaucourt,

Tenant les rencs de leur quartier.
Ces trois estoient vestus de mesmes
De jacquettes et paravant,
Comme Dunois, et en tout esmes,
Sans différence aucunement. . . ." (146).

In the following spring the English sent over rein-
forcements. The overwhelming defeat of these new
troops in the open field of Formigny forecast the close
of the great epic of the One Hundred Years War. The
Duke of Somerset was besieged at Caen where the
superior French artillery, under that master cannoneer,
Jean Bureau, rapidly reduced the mediæval walls and
forced the surrender of the city.

During the progress of this siege occurred an incident which, although unfortunate in itself, proves the
high estimate placed upon Jacques Cœur's services to
the French cause, by his adversaries from across the
channel. The English succeeded in corrupting several
influential Scots, archers in the famous body-guard
which protected Charles VII. Yielding to the bribes
of the Duke of Somerset, these recreant members of a
troop renowned for its fidelity agreed to betray to the
enemy four of the principal leaders who were conducting the war for the King of France and whose removal
from the field, the English leader apparently believed,
would turn the tide of battle in the Normandy campaign. Those fixed upon for this attention were, in
the order named: the Count of Dunois, the Lord of
Villequier, Jacques Cœur, and the Master of Artillery,
Jean Bureau. The plot was discovered before it could
be carried out, and Robin Campbell, a Scottish archer,
paid the penalty with his life.

The choice of Villequier is puzzling. Although at this time beginning to enjoy a royal favor which surprised even his contemporaries, this individual's principal claim to eminence was to come a little later as the complaisant husband of a mistress of the King. In his other selections Somerset showed no little acumen. Dunois, Jacques Cœur, and Bureau, respectively the greatest soldier, organizer, and artillery genius of the times, constituted a trio the loss of which would have weakened any martial cause. (147).

All contemporary historians testify to the leading rôle played by Jacques Cœur in the deliverance of Normandy; he loaned to it his sword, his counsel, his wealth, and his credit. They freely admit that without this aid the army could not have been assembled in such force, or kept from disbanding later and that, but for him, the reconquest of France's fairest province might never have been achieved. We remember Thomas Basin's version of the matter—how Jacques Cœur alone had responded after the great nobles and war captains, enriched by the spoils of war, had hung back, pleaded poverty, and evaded the opportunity to serve their country's need. Now Basin himself had taken no unimportant part in the campaign. An influential Norman prelate, attached to Charles VII's headquarters and repeatedly employed as an intermediary between the King and his subjects in the disputed territory, his story of what transpired in the French camp may be relied upon, so far as it goes. The annalist de Coucy, or Escouchy, as he is sometimes called, relates what had happened at the very inception of the enterprise, before the troops were in

the field. The King and Jacques Cœur, he says, "found
themselves once in a secluded place, where were only
the sovereign and his minister, engaged in matters relating to the King's pleasure; in which spot the afore-
mentioned Jacques said to the King: 'Sire, under your
patronage I know that I have great profits and honors,
even in the lands of the infidels; for, because of your
glory, the Sultan has given safe-conduct to my galleys
and factors. *Sire, all that I have is yours.*' Whereupon
the King made the request of him to lend him money
to invade Normandy; in accordance with which request he consented to lend 200,000 écus, which he
did." Chastellain fixes the amount at double this
figure and specified its instalments. Jacques Cœur,
he says, "had loaned to his master 200,000 écus of
[original] loan and 200,000 more for the recovery of
Normandy." The facts of the matter seem to be that
the royal borrowings before the start of the expedition, described by de Coucy, were supplemented by
additional ones which became necessary during the
course of the campaign, as related by Basin, both of
which occasions are referred to by Chastellain. (148).

After the recapture of Caen, when the finances became completely exhausted, it was suggested that a
levy be made upon the property of the great prelates
and churchmen of the realm. Although there was an
ordinance permitting such a policy in time of public
stress, the suggestion was received with consternation,
almost horror, by the public opinion of the time. "To
demand a tribute from the members of the tribe of
Levi is to meddle with the apple of the eye of Jesus
Christ," writes the devout and patriotic Robert Blon-

del, the chaplain of the Queen. Nevertheless, Charles VII, pressed by the urgent need of paying and subsisting his troops, went so far in pursuit of this plan for relief as to petition Rome to consent to it; his appeal being denied, the proposal was allowed to drop.

The English at about this time had recourse to the pledge of their crown jewels to finance the defense of their possessions in France. The French King, in his extremity, turned to Jacques Cœur, whose patriotism was equal to any draft that could be drawn upon it, and whose wealth was consecrated to the liberation of the national soil. (149).

Now, even if we accept de Coucy's more moderate statement of 200,000 écus as measuring the entire amount of Jacques Cœur's loans, their metal value, expressed in present denominations, would equal nearly 2,500,000 francs. Money's purchasing power was then, as we know, many times greater than it is now; just what the true multiplier should be it is probably idle to attempt to calculate or conjecture in these days of unstable currencies and prices. An easier way to form a conception of Jacques Cœur's financial aid to his country, is to consider it in connection with the total annual revenues of the realm.

At the lower estimate of his advances Jacques Cœur loaned his sovereign more than one-fifth of the amount that ruler was then receiving in annual taxes from all of his other subjects. (150).

Even so rich a merchant could not produce so much ready money without the use of his credit. We need not be surprised, therefore, to learn from Jacques Cœur's testimony at his trial that he himself had borrowed from 100,000 to 125,000 écus to make his advances to the King. The evidence also shows that his aid was not confined to the Normandy campaign, but that he also helped to finance the later one for the reconquest of Guienne. [The records do not show that the royal borrowings were ever repaid in full; the sole exhibits that remain are two of the lender's receipts— one for 60,000 francs; the other for 40,000 écus, loaned for the recovery of Cherbourg. (151).

Thus Jacques Cœur, starting from a modest beginning, had arrived at the very pinnacle of fame and fortune. His favor with his sovereign was unbounded. Rich, powerful, ennobled, living at the court in intimacy with the royal family and great ones of the land; honored by all as one of his country's saviors; a patron of the arts, owning sumptuous palaces and châteaux throughout the realm; in relation with the rulers of the East and the great merchants of the world; distinguished and trusted by the Pope—the consideration which he enjoyed was only equalled by his wealth, so prodigious for the times in which he lived.

Honors and dignities accumulated both for himself and the members of his family.

His eldest son, Jean, shortly after receiving from the University of Paris the degree of Master of Arts, was appointed papal notary for France and canon of the ancient cathedral of Poitiers. In September, 1446, having first been named by the local chapter, a special dispensation from Rome authorized him to fulfil the offices of the Archbishopric of Bourges. This indulgence was rendered necessary because of his immaturity; he was then not quite twenty-three years of age, whereas the incumbent of the see was required to be at least thirty. The document recites the fact that the King had joined in the request for Jean's confirmation, and that the papal concession was made not only for the grantee's personal merit, but also in the hope that he would be able to repair the losses which the Bourges diocese had suffered "by reason of the wars and dissensions which had long and grievously afflicted the kingdom." It deferred his final consecration, however, until he should have reached the age of twenty-seven. Accordingly, it was not until September, 1450, that Jean Cœur, the merchant's son, attended by the great nobles of the duchy of Berry, and by the Bishops of Agde, Carcassonne and Nevers, passed in ceremonial procession through the streets of Bourges to its queenly cathedral, there formally to be inaugurated as its Archbishop and Metropolitan, Patriarch and Primate of Aquitania. (152).

The Argentier celebrated the occasion by giving a splendid feast in his newly erected palace, when, we are told by his steward, he exhibited to his guests "a great image of Mary Magdalen of solid gold or silver gilt." The chivalrous Charles of Orleans responded to the event by presenting Jacques Cœur with four pints of precious wine from the cellars of the Castle of Blois, and creating him a knight of the Order of the Hedgehog, which had been founded by Louis of France, the Poet-Duke's own father, in commemoration of his son's birth. (153).

Jacques Cœur's second son Henri was a Bachelor of Laws, a degree probably received from the University of Angers. He was likewise honored by being made papal notary, probably in succession to his brother when the latter became Archbishop. He seems to have been an especial favorite of Nicholas V, who, in 1448, appointed him canon and prebend of Narbonne, Lodève, and Viviers, and, two years later, canon of Bourges and Limoges. (154).

Of the younger sons Ravant and Geoffrey, then minors, the former has left us only his name, and the latter's eminence belongs to the following reign.

Perrette, the great merchant's only daughter, whose maiden name was the same as that of his niece, Jean de Village's wife, made an advantageous marriage. She was wedded to Jacquelin Trousseau, son of the Viscount of Bourges, and became the mistress of the châteaux of Saint-Palais, Nancié, and Tannenay. Her marriage contract, dated June 13, 1447, may still be seen in the National Library in Paris, drawn with faultless care, providing for a handsome *dot* from the bride's father, and that the instrument itself shall be interpreted "according to the customs of the nobility in the land of Berry." (155).

CHAPTER XXI

CHIVALRY

"CERVANTES smiled Spain's chivalry away," runs one of Byron's famous lines. The power of the great Spaniard's humor can only be heightened by correctly attributing the effect thus poetically claimed for it. No less a force than that of gunpowder blew away this knightly mediæval institution. The rapid fire of the accurate and disciplined English bowmen at Crécy, Poitiers, and Agincourt, opposed to a thirst for personal glory which awaited no concerted signal, had dealt the first great blow to the chivalric ideal in France. The establishment of Charles VII's regular army further reduced the military value of the individual unit. As in the days after Vercingetorix, the Roman conception of the ascendancy of the legion and the state began again to predominate over Gallic individualism. The French chevaliers who, in the earlier battles with their enemies from across the channel, had rushed unrestrainedly onto the field, flaunting their escutcheons and crying the names of their ladies fair, reluctantly gave place to disciplined soldiery, fighting under the banner of the King. The boom of cannon sounded the doom of personal physical prowess in the game of war.

Nevertheless chivalry, which, in dying, has left us its spirit to be reincarnated in the character of gentleman, did not entirely pass away during the life of the subject of our memoir. It continued to furnish spectacles at festivals and tournaments, before the days of other sports.

Although Jacques Cœur, in the decorations of his palace at Bourges, had poked fun at the extravagance of this mediæval institution, and laughed at its deviations from common sense, he was himself too chivalric, in the word's broader meaning, not to appreciate the fine qualities of honor, loyalty, courtesy, magnanimity, and justice for which it stood. The practical merchant well knew that knight-errantry could not police the realm; the King's wise counsellor favored cavalry as against chivalry. Yet the patron of Jean de Village and William Gimart, the leader of the dashing Finale expedition, could not be insensible to stirring scenes and heroic deeds. And so we find him entertaining Jacques de Lalain with a sumptuous hospitality that recalls the *Arabian Nights* and a ceremonious courtliness that outmatches even that of the young Burgundian paladin.

This young Sir Launcelot, *le Bon Chevalier*, as he is often styled, was the darling of his age. At an early age he had set out from his father's castle in search of romantic adventure, caitiff knights to unhorse, damsels fair to succor, princesses' praise to win. "Know," said his father to him on this occasion, "that few noblemen have arrived at a high degree of prowess and good renown, if they have no dame or damsel to whom they are devoted; but, my son, beware that it should not be a foolish love, for such will ever be to you a great villainy and reproach."

Messire Jacques de Lalain had now become a champion of great celebrity, known throughout Christen-

THE ARMY UNDER CHARLES VII.

Mounted man-at-arms of a Compagnie d'Ordonnance.

E. Lavisse, "Histoire de France." Librairie Hachette, Éditeur.

dom as the "flower of chivalry." He sought his adversaries even beyond the seas. The year after his visit
to Jacques Cœur he was to have a famous encounter
in a tournament in Scotland. Hearing of the prowess
of James Douglas, doubtless reported to him by some
of Charles VII's famous Scottish archers, he challenged
the border lord to a combat at arms, with lance, battle-
axe, sword, and dagger. His summons being accepted,
accompanied by his uncle Sanson or Simon de Lalain
and a Breton knight named Hervie de Meriadec, "all
of very haughty valor and desirous of practising the
very noble and renowned exercise of arms," Jacques
arrived at Stirling and, in the presence of the Scottish
King and a great concourse of people, the three did
battle with James and John Douglas and John Ross,
Lord of Hawkhead, "all of lofty lineage, powerful, and
well formed in limbs and body and highly celebrated
among the most valiant." The contest, which was a
bitter one, though highly creditable to the French side,
was stopped by James II before being attended with
fatal results. (156).

The young Burgundian knight was now on his way
back from the court of Aragon, where he had been
tilting with the Spanish cavaliers. His uncle we remember as having been one of la Brocquière's fellow
pilgrims, who became Jacques Cœur's shipmate on the
ill-fated return voyage from Beirut. We will allow
Jacques de Lalain's biographer, his contemporary,
Georges Chastellain, to describe the meeting of the
Argentier and *le Bon Chevalier*.

"And so rode Messire Jacques and his company
through the county of Roussillon, always bearing his

emprise, until he came to Perpignan, then to Narbonne, and carried on his journey until he arrived at
Montpellier; and so at about three o'clock he encountered one named Jacques Cœur, who was at that time
Argentier of France, and was on his way to install one
of his sons in the Archbishopric of Maguelonne. (157).

"At their mutual meeting the Argentier paid the
greatest respects and honors to Messire Jacques de
Lalain, saying to him: 'Messire Jacques, I would have
been greatly chagrined if you had not sought me; for
this long time have I eagerly awaited your arrival.'
Then Messire Jacques de Lalain responded and said:
'My Lord the Argentier, tell me what it pleases you
to command of me, for I am very much at your service and if there is anything possible for me to do for
you, providing it do not conflict with my honor, I will
do it most willingly.'

"When Jacques Cœur heard Messire de Lalain's
words, he was most joyous, and besought him very
insistently that it should meet with his pleasure to
sojourn several days at Montpellier, which request
Messire Jacques most freely accorded him and stayed
there from Friday evening until Monday after mass.
Sunday, my Lord the Argentier fêted him most grandly
at a very handsome dinner. After the dinner they had
several chats together.

"Among other things the Argentier took Messire
Jacques de Lalain by the hand and drew him apart,
and, accompanied by three or four gentlemen of his
[the Argentier's] household, led him into a counting-
house, where he had a vast quantity of gold, rich jewels,
and rings. Regarding Messire de Lalain with a smile,

he said to him: 'Messire Jacques, I am well aware
that you have been a long time away from your own
country at great expense and on an important mission;
for this reason, I pray you that you will do me the
honor to take all that you need and require; for, in
sooth, I would more freely do this for you than for
any knight that lives, as well out of honor and reverence to my very redoubted Lord, the Duke of Burgundy, as for your own person, of which I have a very
high opinion.'

"Then Messire Jacques de Lalain, seeing the honor
and courtesy which the Argentier of France intended
to do him, thus responded: 'My Lord the Argentier,
for the beautiful offer, which out of your courtesy and
good-will you make me, I thank you as much as I am
able. For what you have done I and my family will
always be greatly obliged to you. And if I knew anything which was possible to do and which would be
agreeable to you, I would do it with very good heart. I
will thank my very redoubted and sovereign Lord the
Duke for the good cheer which you have shown me in
his honor. But when, with his permission and license, I
parted from my very redoubted Lord, he provided me
with all that was necessary for me. My Lord the Argentier, I pray you that it may please you to excuse
me.'

"Then responded the Argentier and said: 'Messire
Jacques, if you have left any baggage in storage, as
sometimes happens in foreign travel, and especially in
such missions as yours which are noble and memorable
ones and worthy of great honor, there is hardly a kingdom or even a province where I do not have my bureaus

of exchange, and I will write very gladly and cheerfully, to have it forwarded to you, if you care to have me do so.' But Messire Jacques thanked him sufficiently for the occasion.

"I do not wish to recount to you at length," says the chronicler, who seems to have been personally present during the events which he so circumstantially records, "the feastings and good cheer which the Argentier provided or caused to be provided, the dames, damsels, towns-ladies, and young girls whom he invited, all as though [his guest] had been his son or brother, and not only for him but, out of regard for him, for his suite as well.

"Then, when Sunday came, after supper and after wine and spices had been partaken of, he took his leave of the Argentier, who urged him heartily to remain another day, even until after dinner. Of compliance with this request Messire Jacques prayed him earnestly that he might be excused. After having embraced each other he accompanied Messire Jacques to the latter's own lodging, where, having again embraced, they took their leave of each other.

"When on the following morning Messire Jacques had heard his mass, he took his departure from Montpellier."

This "gentle knight's" whole life seems allegorical, more abstraction than reality. He was not only chivalrous, he was Chivalry; not only mediæval, he personified the Middle Ages. Not much longer was he to play his dual rôle. Five years later Jacques de Lalain, last of the knights-errant, dressed in full steel armor, was slain by a cannon-ball while aiding his most redoubted Duke to repress the rising liberties of the Flemish burghers.

His death not only foreshadowed the passing of a great institution; it had a far deeper allegorical significance. Coming, as it did, only a few weeks after the fall of Constantinople, it serves as the epilogue of the great drama of the Middle Ages.

When next the curtain rises, after an *entr'acte*, it is to disclose the fresh scenery of a newly discovered world, and, with printed programmes, to begin the first act of Modern Times.

CHAPTER XXII

THE DAUPHIN. STATE TRIALS

ONE scans in vain the roster of the French princes, war captains, and heroes of the campaigns of Normandy and Guienne, for the name of the heir to the throne. The King himself had taken the field; the nominal command at Formigny had been intrusted to his son-in-law, John of Bourbon, but the scion of the royal house had borne no part in the glory of the ending of the One Hundred Years War. The Dauphin was not unskilled in arms; he had proven his leadership in the relief of Dieppe and in an expedition against the Swiss. Yet in the final work of the liberation of the kingdom, and in the triumphant entries of the French into Rouen, Caen, and Bordeaux, Louis of France was conspicuous by his absence.

A youth of unusual precocity, at the age of sixteen he had allowed himself to be made the head of a rebellion of the great nobles, jealous of their privileges and resentful of the encroachments of the Crown. Pardoned for this unfilial and disloyal act and rendered vain by his early military success, he had schemed for a share in the government of the kingdom which Brézé and the other royal ministers wisely withheld from him. Thwarted in his ambition for power in the direction of affairs, he had formed the most bitter hatred against his father's counsellors and officers. Some of the expressions of his animosity were childish; others, as we shall see, were more dangerous.

"In the year 1446," says a chronicler who has withheld his name, "it happened that the King, on returning from hearing mass, found on his bed a missive of which the following is the tenor:" then come twenty-nine verses of anonymous denunciation addressed to the King against his ministers, complaining especially of the administration of the finances and the imposition of the taxes, and threatening endless wars as a result. (158).

The death, that year, of the Dauphin's young wife, the poetical and soulful Margaret of Scotland, had severed the last tie between the heir to the throne and his royal sire. The daughter of James I, King of Scots, himself a brilliant poet, her lot in France had been a sad one. Although a great favorite with the other members of the royal family and the court, she had been treated by her husband with marked indifference and disdain.

Louis's rancor against Brézé had taken a more violent and definite turn. He had plotted to win over the Scottish guard, capture the stronghold of Coudray, assassinate the first Minister and carry off the King. Antoine de Chabannes, Count de Dammertin, famous ex-chieftain of *écorcheurs*, his confederate, had received 10,000 écus as the price of his adhesion, but had been dissuaded by his brother and compelled to return the sum. Later the attempt had been discovered, and Louis banished from the court.

The scene in the old castle of Chinon, when the young Prince was confronted by Chabannes, in judgment before the King, had been an intensely dramatic one.

"*King:* Louis, I know the plot which you have set on foot against the Grand Seneschal [Brézé] to cause him piteously to end his days, but I will prevent you from executing it.

"*Dauphin:* Your Majesty, I have been incited to it by the Count de Dammertin.

"*King:* By Saint John, I do not believe you. Count Dammertin, have you incited my son to cause the Grand Seneschal of Normandy to be assassinated?

"*Dammertin:* Sire, I received his commands to do it, but he knows that I have prayed him to excuse me from carrying them out.

"*Dauphin:* Saving the presence of His Majesty the King, you have lied.

"*Dammertin:* Your Royal Highness [the Dauphin] I would answer with my person against yours, if you were not the King's son. But if there is any gentleman of your suite who is willing to make this charge, I will cause him to retract it in personal combat.

"*King:* Louis, I banish you for four months from my kingdom; you shall leave for Dauphiny.

"And then," says the chronicler, "the Dauphin left the audience-chamber bareheaded, and uttered these words: 'By this head which has no covering, I will revenge myself on those who have cast me out of my house.'" (159).

Accepting his banishment as an indefinite one, he retired to Dauphiny and ruled that province as an independent sovereign, there trying out all the subtleties, indirections, and intrigues which he was afterward so artfully to display as Louis XI, King of France.

"As terrible in his hates as able in the concealment

of them, impious from his youth but early become superstitious by one knows not what foolish hope of deceiving Divine Providence as he deluded men, Louis was able fully to develop his faults and his vices in the solitude of his appanage of Dauphiny." (160).

He framed designs on Italy independent of the King's, and negotiated secret treaties which tended to frustrate the foreign policy of the Crown. When informed of the defeat of Brézé's and Jacques Cœur's project for the extension of French dominion over Genoa, "he was most joyous," and stated that "the King governed so badly it would be impossible to do worse." At almost the very moment when the banners of the *fleur-de-lis* were being raised for the liberation of Normandy and Jacques Cœur was pledging his fortune to the cause, Louis the Dauphin was signing a secret treaty with the Duke of Savoy directed against his "enemies, the ministers of the King." He cultivated intimate relations with his "*bel oncle*," the Duke of Burgundy, his father's bitter rival, whose hospitality he was eventually to seek when, after a decade of mischievous rule in Dauphiny, he was chased from his appanage by an angry sire. Fearful of disinheritance in favor of his younger brother Charles, he made presents to the Chancellor of France and maintained secret agents among the royal courtiers. (161).

Louis had been playing his rôle of King of Dauphiny about a year when a notarial secretary of Charles VII, named Mariette, was arrested, subjected to criminal process, and put to death charged with reporting to the Duke of Burgundy the doings of the court. The Dauphin, in whose jurisdiction the accused was recaptured after an escape, played a leading part in his prosecution, and subjected the prisoner to an ordeal of torture in order to sharpen his recollection and broaden his avowals.

Louis's zeal for justice applied itself as well to the pursuit of larger game. He denounced Pierre Brézé, Prime Minister of the Crown, and accused the Grand Seneschal of tacit acquiescence in Mariette's guilt, and of having sacrificed the King's interests for his own enrichment.

The chronicler Commines, who became one of Louis's counsellors after the latter's accession to the throne, in one of his reflective moods makes some shrewd comments on the dangers to which royal ministers were constantly exposed. "An idle apprehension or an extravagant report," says he, in referring to those who wear a crown, "disturbs them exceedingly; and this is the secret distemper that reigns in the courts of great princes, from whence many mischiefs arise to the sovereign, his ministers and subjects; . . . if they confronted the accused with the informer . . . nothing would be reported but what was true. But there are some princes so stupid as to promise and swear to the accuser they will never discover them; and these are they who are subject to those anguishes and torments of mind of which I speak, and who many times hate and injure the best ministers they have upon the bare reports and calumnies of evil-minded and designing people, by which means they occasion great mischiefs and sorrows to their subjects."

Charles, the Well-Served—the Ungrateful, if you like—lost no time in depriving the Grand Seneschal of his offices and appointments, and remanding him for trial before the Court of Parliament in Paris. The records of the process have escaped historical research, but from the letters of remission which Brézé in the end obtained we learn that he faced the ordeal boldly and succeeded in vindicating his probity and honor in time to take a leading part in the Normandy campaign, from which he emerged with new marks of royal favor, though not of equal royal trust.

Jean de Saincoins, or Xaincoins, the Treasurer-General, was not so fortunate. The conquest of Normandy had emptied the royal coffers "to such an extent that the King in his great need would not have been able to find the money to pay the soldiers in the conduct of the war for the recovery of his land of Guienne; but," significantly remarks the official annalist, "*it served his turn to discover other marvellous means of financing himself.*" Accused of peculation and falsification of public records, Saincoins was brought to trial before special commissioners appointed by the King. We have only the word of the complaisant royal chronicler, Jean Chartier, for the assertion that the defendant confessed the crimes which were imputed to him. On the other hand, the fact that he was not allowed to undergo the regular course of judicial procedure, but was judged by a "Bed of Justice," as it was colloquially called—the "habitual character of iniquitous and frequent political executions"—prevents his conviction from being pleaded in bar of the judgment of history. "If they want sufficient evidence to condemn a man," says the perspicuous Commines with reference to the rulers of this century, "they have ways of multiplying interrogations and falsifying the examinations of the witnesses, to weary the defendant, and destroy him with expenses, delaying his trial and by that means giving encouragement to any that will bring a fresh information against him. If that will not do, and answers not their intentions, they have a shorter method, by stating the case as they please themselves, and giving out it was necessary the culprit should be made an example of."

In any event, in June, 1451, Jean de Saincoins was condemned to suffer imprisonment and the confiscation of all of his property, and Bertrand de Beauvais, Lord of Precigny, was entrained in the same disaster.

Precigny, like his brother-in-law, Brézé, was high in the statecraft of the King. Both had been concerned in the affair of Genoa, and it was to them that Jacques Cœur had reported the course of his treaties with Campo Fregoso. As for Saincoins, official and friendly relations bound him to the Argentier, although incidentally we find the latter in a private memorandum finding fault with the Lord Treasurer's bookkeeping. (162).

In November, 1450, during the course of Saincoins's trial, which lasted for nearly a year, a mass was celebrated in the cathedral of Bourges, whose youthful Archbishop had been installed only a month before— a prayer for the safety of the Lord Argentier of France. At about this time, incantations were being performed in secret by William Gouffier, Charles VII's latest worthless favorite, and Otto Castellane, an Italian who had risen in the administration of the finances in the south of France and was ambitious for still higher honors—mystic rites with two wax images, procured, as was afterward disclosed, from Doctor Pierre Mignon, a professor of the black arts, "one to place the late Jacques Cœur, then our Argentier, in bad grace, and to make him lose his office; the other to cause the said Otto Castellane, William Gouffier, and their accomplices to be in good grace and affection" with the King. (163).

Truly these were perilous days for "the high and eminent who, in the bad times of confiscating princes . . . are the most exposed to jealousy, avarice, and envy."

CHAPTER XXIII

AGNES SOREL. HER DEATH. SUSPICIONS

"Here lies entom'd the fairest of the fair.
   To her rare beauty, greater praise be given
Than holy maids in cloister'd cells may share,
   Or hermits that in deserts live for Heaven;
For, by her charms, recover'd France arose,
Shook off her chains and triumph'd o'er her foes." (164).

So runs an English version of a famous epitaph in honor of Agnes Sorel, the original written by a royal hand, long after the death of the celebrated "Dame of Beauty." Condemned by moralists yet sung by poets, the name of the mistress of Charles VII has held a prominent place in the story of the deliverance of France. The credit of having inspired the King to take a resolute and personal part in the reconquest of Normandy, which tradition had already accorded her when Francis I composed his eulogistic lines, is confirmed by a chronicler of her times whose statement cannot be rejected. The author of the *Jouvencel*, from which we are about to quote, was himself a prominent actor in the events which he recounts.

"After dinner," he relates, in describing a scene in the castle of Chinon, before the opening of the Normandy campaign, "the King left the table; he retired into his apartments; there came into his presence the Queen and several dames and damsels, and made merry and engaged in many gay pastimes as was the custom.

"Among the rest, a most beautiful dame [Agnes Sorel] talked and said to the King: 'Sire, I have heard it said that you have good news; God's Mercy! Lead us to the war, and all your followers will thus gain greater fame. Our destiny will be more exalted than you dream.' To a facetious response of the King's the lady replied: 'Do not be utterly lacking in ambition; do you imagine that you can be a King without duties? Far from it! There have never been such. Great Kings have great deeds to perform. You will have sufficient time afterward in which to devote yourself to beautiful ladies. . . .'"

"If the nose of Cleopatra had been shorter, the whole face of the earth would have been changed," said a religious philosopher of the seventeenth century whose *Thoughts* we are surprised to find straying to these subjects. The transcendent beauty and charm of Agnes Sorel were the sensation of her day, and so great has been their subsequent acclaim that curiosity as to its cause has led, in comparatively modern days, to the violation of her tomb. (165).

The royal mistress was conscious all her life of the attaint which she brought to good order and morality; she finished her days remorseful and repentant. She sought to redeem her conduct by works of benevolence and charity; she had the merit, very rare in her class, of endeavoring to offset the evil of her example by employing her influence in the public good.

Her contemporary, Olivier de la Marche, who lived in the rival court of the Duke of Burgundy, says that about the year 1444, "the King had lately introduced an impoverished damsel, a gentlewoman, named Agnes Sorel, and placed her in such triumph and such power that her estate is comparable to that of the great princesses of the realm, and certainly she was one of the most beautiful women whom I have ever seen, and in her way did much good for the kingdom of France. She advanced in the favor of the King, young men-at-arms and noble companions, by whom the King was thenceforth well served."

"This King Charles," Jacques Du Clerq tells us, "before he made peace with the Duke of Burgundy, led the most pious life and said his canonical prayers; but after making peace with the said Duke he made the acquaintance of a young woman, come from a small place in the neighborhood of Tours, named Agnes, since called the Beautiful Agnes, who maintained a greater state than the Queen of France. And the said Queen Marie counted for little with the said King Charles, although she was a very good and humble dame, and, as was said, a most devout woman. This beautiful Agnes, according to general report, was one of the loveliest women in the kingdom. . . ."

The Crown then possessed a graceful château on the River Marne, near Paris, called Beaulté (Beauty); Charles VII presented it to his mistress. "In order that she might have some title," says a contemporary historian, "the King gave her during her life the lands and castle of Beauty, near the forest of Vincennes." "And," observes another author, "as among beautiful women she was considered the fairest, she was called

My Lady of Beauty, as much for this reason as because the King had given her the castle of Beauty near Paris." (166).

We are told by Chastellain, Jacques de Lalain's chronicler, who seems to have been a competent judge in matters of pomp and display, that Agnes "had her quarters in the palace of the King, better ordained and appointed than those of the Queen, more beautiful draperies for her bed, better tapestry, better linen and coverlets, better plate, better rings and jewels, better cuisine, and better everything."

Nevertheless, despite the general looseness of the times, her relations with the King did not escape censure. The citizen of Paris whose anonymous journal has given us such an insight into the life of the French capital during the first half of the fifteenth century, but who never lost his Burgundian partisanship, thus reports a visit of the fair Agnes to that city: "The last week in April, 1448, there came to Paris a damsel who was said to be loved publicly by the King of France, without faith and without law, and without honor for the good Queen whom he had espoused; and it was apparent that she maintained as great state as a countess or a duchess; she went about generally with the good Queen of France without regard for the scandal occasioned by her shame; on account of which the Queen had much sorrow in her heart; but it was proper for her to bear it for the time being. And the King, to flaunt his great sin and shame, gave her the castle of Beauty, the fairest and loveliest castle and the best placed in all the Isle-de-France. And she named herself and made others call her 'the Beautiful Agnes'; and because the people of Paris did not do her the great reverence demanded by her overweening pride, which she was not able to conceal, she said on departing that they were only rabble, and that, if she had only known that they would not do her greater honor, she would never have set her foot there, which would have been a misfortune, but a small one. Thus departed the 'Beautiful Agnes' the tenth day of May following, to take up her shame as before. Alas! what a pity when the head of the state gives such a bad example to his people!"

The story of Agnes's encounter with the citizens of the capital cannot be taken very seriously. The diarist, who is known as the "Bourgeois of Paris," had recorded untruths about Jeanne d'Arc in her day, and was given generally to allowing his prejudices and imagination to run away with him. Agnes was at this time on a pilgrimage to the shrine of Saint Geneviève, and, if she did not feel the humility of sincere worship, was bound to feign it because of the pious rôle which she had temporarily assumed. All of her correspondence that has been preserved proves her to have been a person of tender sympathies, considerate, benevolent, and charitable to those about her. (167).

Agnes bore the King four daughters; she died shortly after giving birth to the last one, who only survived her mother several months.

The last hours of the Dame of Beauty are full of pathos. The pomps and consolations of religion were marshalled at her bedside. De Monstrelet describes her death and the pious end she made: "The said

Agnes," he says, "was very charitable and generous in her donations to the poor and to the church. During her illness she shewed great contrition and repentance of her sins, remembering Mary Magdalen, who was also a sinner, and invoking God and the Virgin to aid her; after having received the sacraments she asked for her book of orisons to repeat therefrom Saint Bernard's prayers for the dying which she had written therein with her own hand; and afterward made many vows which were reduced to writing to be carried out by the executors of her testament, ordering certain alms to be given and sums paid to her servants, to the amount of 60,000 écus."

Feeling her end approach, she said to those around her that "life was a petty matter, impure and tainted with our frailty." Having been given absolution, by virtue of a special indulgence from the Pope, "lifting up her voice in appeal to God and invoking the blessed Virgin Mary, her soul parted from her body."

Following an age-old custom for the sepulture of great personages, her mortal remains were divided and separately entombed. Her body was buried in the collegiate church at Loches, which during her life-time she had richly endowed. In one of the towers of the beautiful Château Royal which graces the stern old castle of Loches, this tomb may still be seen, surmounted by a recumbent statue of Agnes, wearing the emblems of the title of duchess, posthumously granted her by the King. Her other sepulchre in the Abbey of Jumièges was destroyed a century later during the religious wars in France. It was adorned by a statue representing her kneeling in supplication to the Virgin to be reconciled with Heaven. On it was inscribed this epitaph:

> HERE LIES AGNES SOREL, NOBLE DAMOI-
> SELLE, IN HER LIFE–TIME LADY OF ROCQUE-
> CESIÈRE, OF BEAUTY, ISSOUDUN AND OF
> VERNON–SUR–SEINE; PITEOUS TOWARD ALL,
> WHO OF HER WEALTH GAVE LIBERALLY TO
> CHURCHES AND TO THE POOR; WHO DIED THE
> NINTH DAY OF FEBRUARY, IN THE YEAR OF
> GRACE, 1449. PRAY GOD FOR HER. (168).

Agnes chose for her executors in order to carry out her testamentary benevolence and charitable bequests: Robert Poitevin, the Queen's physician, who had attended the fair Magdalen in her last illness; Étienne Chevalier, one of the most distinguished officers of the court, the illustrations from whose prayer-book, the beautiful miniatures of Jean Fouquet, to-day figure among the art treasures of the Château of Chantilly; and Jacques Cœur, whom she thus defended in advance against the calumny which was to assail him. By her command, "the King alone, and for all" was to be placed above these three.

Although Charles VII's idolatry of Agnes survived her death, he gave no practical proofs of his honor for her memory. When her jewels were put on sale, some months after her decease, they were bought in by the royal lover, with funds borrowed from Jacques Cœur, and were bestowed upon his new favorite, Antoinette de Maignelais, Agnes's niece, who had begun even before the death of her aunt to supplant her in the royal favor. From this time on, the court became a seraglio "in which figured Marion, the work-girl, and Alison, the laundress." (169).

"After the beautiful Agnes died," writes Jacques Du Clerq, "the King introduced in her place the niece of the said beautiful Agnes, who was the titular wife of the Lord of Villequier; and her husband trailed about with her; and she was equally as lovely as her aunt, and there were also five or six of the most beautiful damsels of the kingdom, of humble birth, who followed the said King Charles wherever he went; and they were clothed and arrayed like queens, in the richest fashion possible; and they maintained the greatest and most dissolute estate, all at the King's expense. . . . The Dauphin was most displeased with this conduct, and for this reason had absented himself from court more than twelve whole years, retiring to the province of Dauphiny, during all which period he had never received any supplies from his father *nor from the kingdom*: therefore he was forced to live on the country."

Agnes Sorel's premature death caused a great sensation at the court. Regarded at first as a result of her accouchement, rumors of poisoning began to circulate —a diagnosis, which, as we know, laymen of the Middle Ages were not slow to advance in default of more exact pathological knowledge. Suspicion whispered the name of the heir to the throne in this connection. Burgundian chroniclers availed themselves of their greater freedom to commit this great scandal to writing. "She was hardly dead," wrote Du Clerq, "until they said that she had been poisoned. . . . And some also dared to assert that the said Dauphin had caused the death of a damsel, named the Beautiful Agnes, who was the loveliest woman in the kingdom and entirely in the affections of his father, the King." Monstrelet has recorded: "The hate of Charles VII against Louis XI came from the fact that this Prince had several times blamed and murmured against his father, because of . . . . the Beautiful Agnes—who was in the grace of the King much more than was the Queen, who was a very good and honorable dame—against whom the Dauphin had a great despite, and, because of his hatred, *he caused her death to be hastened.*"

This was, however, merely aimless rumor which after its brief season of general currency gave place to other gossip of the court. The progress of the Guienne campaign, the Treasurer-General Saincoins's striking fall, and the partition of his property among the courtiers—the grant of his noble house in Tours to the heroic Dunois, his landed estates to the sycophantic Gouffier—all were vivid topics in their turn. Report ran that an even loftier court figure was to topple, a more stupendous fortune to be divided. Jean Chartier, the royal historian, closed his report of Saincoins's fate with the significant comment that "*it is well to note this affair in order to give an example to others, and for additional reasons.*" The name of the Argentier of France was coupled with hostile criticisms.

"Thus," says his contemporary, de Coucy, "envy commenced to assail him, and it was said to the King that it was impossible that a man, come from such a small beginning, could have amassed so much wealth, to carry on the business which he did, to accomplish the great works, to acquire the lands and manors, and to keep up the great state which he did; for, throughout his great house one was served only off silver plate, from which envious and malevolent people judged that he must have derived these things from the revenues of the King, and it was said to the latter that he had sufficient other reasonable grounds to cause his imprisonment."

The distribution of largess from Saincoins's possessions whetted the appetites of the hungry courtiers already sharpened by feasting on the spoils of war. As was said of another era of forfeitures in a different realm: "The lion having sucked the blood of his prey, threw the offal carcass to the jackal in waiting. Having tasted once the food of confiscation, the favorites became fierce and ravenous."

To Jacques Cœur, nothing was impossible—nothing except the evasion of envy, hatred, and malice, against whose invisible and underground attacks no man can guard, and for deliverance from which we are taught to seek the aid of Heaven in our prayers.

PART V

ADVERSITY

"The King is not himself, but basely led
By flatterers; and what they will inform,
Merely in hate, 'gainst any of us all,
That will the King severely prosecute
'Gainst us, our lives, our children and our heirs."
(*Richard II*, Scene I, Act IV.)

"Flee with thy life if thou fearest oppression and leave the house to
tell its builder's fate,
Thou wilt find for the land that thou quittest, another; but no soul wilt
thou find to replace thine own."
("The First Royal Mendicant," *One Thousand and One Nights*.)

CHAPTER XXIV

ARREST AND CONFISCATION. POISON CHARGE

"Pretexts for confiscation are never to seek," says the astute Machiavelli, than whom no one has been better versed in the ways of autocratic princes. The reflective Commines, less than a generation after the events which we are reviewing and when their poignancy was still in the memories of living men, quoting Charles VII's son, Louis XI, gives us some further enlightenment on the conduct of princes, in a comment so pertinent to the subject of our memoir as almost certainly to have related to him. "I must insert," writes he, "two things which the King, my master, told me once about persons who had done great service (and he named the authority from which this information was derived), that to have served too well is sometimes the ruin of the agent; and that most often, great ingratitude is the reward of long and faithful services; usually upon account of the arrogance of those who have performed them, who, presuming too much upon their good fortune, behave themselves insolently toward their master or fellow subjects; so that princes are not always to be blamed, if their subjects are not rewarded according to their deserts. His Majesty told me further that he thought that person more happy in his preferments at court, whom his prince had advanced beyond his desert, whereby he remained a debtor to his prince, than he who by any signal service had put his prince under great obligation to him." (170).

On the subject of ingratitude, Louis XI had qualified himself to give expert opinion; as for his judgment of what constituted arrogance and insolence in an officer of the Crown, we cannot accept the standards of a ruler who showed his appreciation of proper courtly bearing by the rewards he heaped upon his barber, Olivier de Daim.

During the latter part of July, 1451, Jacques Cœur was at the castle of Taillebourg, where the King held court so as to be near the field of military operations of the Guienne campaign. Although conscious of the menaces around him, he went bravely about his business, executing the tasks incident to his multiple employs. On the 26th, he received what appeared to be a special mark of royal favor. The King accorded him a considerable sum "to aid me in the maintenance of my station and in making a more suitable appearance in his service," as the recipient expressed it in his neatly worded receipt for the money. (171). Reassured by this token of his apparent restoration to grace, Jacques Cœur wrote his wife from Taillebourg that his position with the King was as firm as it had ever been, "whatever may be said about it." Five days later, on the mandate of his sovereign, he was arrested and committed to prison without examination.

A woman of the court, Jeanne de Vendôme, and Jacques Colonna, an Italian who had established himself in France, had come forward boldly and laid information against the Argentier for the poisoning of

Agnes Sorel. Both Jeanne and her husband, François de Montberon, the Baron of Mortagne, were in Jacques Cœur's debt. This declaration, supported by the cabal of intriguing courtiers who were behind the woman, and who had bolstered the principal charge with others which afterward became counts in the indictment, had found instant credit with the King. (172). It had sufficed to obtain from Charles VII an order for the arrest of the Argentier and the seizure of his property.

Before the execution of this process Jacques Cœur voluntarily presented himself before the King and his Grand Council, and stated that several of his subordinates had been forcibly laid hold of by royal command, and that he had heard it reported that a "certain action" impended against him. Praying the King "to have regard for his business affairs and person and to hold terms of reason and justice," he offered to constitute himself a prisoner until it should please his sovereign to acquit him of the crimes of which he had been accused. (173).

The King enumerated the accusations against him and made the formal statement that if he should succeed in clearing himself of the poison charge, all others would be dropped. Jacques Cœur was thereupon remanded to the castle dungeon and his estate ordered to be seized, inventoried, and held in the custody of "good and safe" royal commissioners, to await the outcome of the trial. No sooner had the iron doors shut upon his fallen minister than the King, aided by his all too zealous courtiers, began his levy on the prisoner's property. Of the first receipts from these collections, the early fruit which had ripened so seasonably for the sovereign needs, the royal trustee applied 100,000 écus to the expenses of the Guienne campaign, and liberally rewarded his accomplices in the spoliation. (174).

Not satisfied with this appropriation of trust funds, in advance of the decision as to their ultimate disposal, Charles VII took steps to sustain it. Following "a contemptible abuse which soiled the justice of the fifteenth century," he formed a special court to try the late owner of the confiscated wealth. As members of this Royal Commission—"Bed of Justice," as it was colloquially called—he appointed Antoine· de Chabannes, Otto Castellane, and William Gouffier, all three debtors and denunciators of the accused, and the two former his "capital enemies." Chabannes, as we have seen, had been willing to commit murder for 10,000 écus; Gouffier and Castellane had invoked black arts of magic to accomplish the Argentier's fall. Jean Dauvet, the Attorney-General, and Jean Barbin, King's Advocate, "contrary to the law and custom" of the realm, became judges as well as prosecutors, and other Crown ministers became commissioners, with prospects of a share in the royal confiscations should they be upheld. (175).

The valiant-hearted prisoner did not allow himself to be daunted by his fate; on the very next day after his commitment we find him executing an agreement with William de Varye and one Hervé Paris for the creation of a new commercial enterprise to operate in Flanders. (176). Jacques Cœur was taken from prison to prison, following the movements of the court. He remained in the castle of Taillebourg for five weeks; from thence he was removed to that of Lusignan, since

BED OF JUSTICE HELD BY CHARLES VII AT VENDÔME IN 1458.
Miniature by J. Foucquet.   Munich Library.
E. Lavisse, "Histoire de France." Librairie Hachette, Éditeur.

destroyed; afterward he was incarcerated in the grim old fortress of Maillé, now known as Luynes, in the neighborhood of Tours and still shown to tourists visiting the beautiful and imposing châteaux of Touraine.

The trial of the case followed its course at Lusignan from the month of September, 1451, to June in the succeeding year. Meanwhile, "the vultures of the court" —to quote the historian La Thaumassière's vigorous expression, used two centuries later—flocked around seeking their share of the booty.

The first examinations were addressed to an investigation of the poison charge. This was speedily obliged to be abandoned by the prosecution. "For the said Sorel was never poisoned, as is a fact subject to proof and easy to prove, and that the truth was that the said woman had had a child before her death which lived six months, which is clear proof that she was never poisoned, all of which appears by the testimony of Doctor Robert Poitevin," as Archbishop Jean Cœur later said of this charge in discussing it with his lawyers. Convicted, almost from the start, of malicious prosecution, Jeanne de Vendôme and Jacques Colonna were committed to prison, later to receive their punishment on the same day as that on which it was meted out to Jacques Cœur.

The conviction of the informers was not allowed to work the acquittal of their victim, even of the charge which they were found guilty of having basely invented. The accusation was recognized as false, but the accused was not admitted to be innocent of it. This glaring inconsistency was as manifestly against the laws and approved practice of that period as it would be in any civilized court of justice of to-day. It absolved the King from redeeming his promised pardon of the other charges. Equally does it absolve us from the duty of associating ideals of justice with any part of this sham proceeding.

CHAPTER XXV

OTHER CHARGES

THE principal charge against the prisoner thus broke down. A pretense of its continued vitality, however, was maintained, somewhat half-heartedly, throughout the trial, apparently for its impression on the sovereign's mind and, perhaps also, to bar the legal effect of his anticipatory pardon of the other accusations.

These latter were originally three in number: of having presented armor to the Saracens, "the ancient enemies of the Christian faith"; of having been guilty, as a representative of the Crown, of divers extortions and exactions in Languedoc; and of having exported silver alloy from the country, in contravention of law. These counts in the information were from time to time altered and enlarged, and others were added to them. We will give them each our attention in the form and order in which they are recited in the final judgment. For the defense which was interposed to them we must draw on several sources.

Jacques Cœur was not only refused the privilege of having counsel; he was not allowed to summon witnesses in his defense; only his own testimony and documentary evidence were received on his behalf. (177).

We do not have the original minutes of Jacques Cœur's trial as we do for Jeanne d'Arc's prosecution. What we do have is a digest of the testimony, containing several extracts from it, all contemporary with the trial and in the script of the fifteenth century—what lawyers technically call a "case" or record on appeal —and, with the accompanying exhibits, doubtless used on review in the rehabilitation proceedings; the journal or minutes of the Attorney-General, Jean Dauvet; the remarkably clear and lucid statement and analysis of the "Very Reverend Father in God, Monsieur the Archbishop of Bourges and his brothers, sons of the said Jacques Cœur," sent to their counsel in Paris, on the subject of the appeal; the equally luminous and more learned opinions of these seven lawyers; and the record of the proceedings of the appeal itself, including especially the interlocutory decree of Louis XI authorizing the reopening of the case and its review by the Court of Parliament. (178).

It is from these records that we are enabled to reconstruct the defense which was made by the accused, and to form our opinion of its merits. They are entirely ample for the judgment of history on the matter at its bar. Perhaps only inveterate students of jurisprudence and scholars whose nerves are rendered uneasy by failure of complete knowledge on any subject, irrespective of the purpose served, will regret that the complete record has not come down to us, "which is contained in six huge books and several writings amounting almost to a horse-load, of which three-fourths do not count for anything *pro* or *contra*," as the appellants described it in the statement to their counsel.

Following, then, the order which we have named and omitting from our enumeration the alleged crime against Agnes Sorel:

1. The first charge with which Jacques Cœur was

faced was a revival of the twenty-year-old prosecution which he had undergone at the début of his career, when a subordinate in the Mint at Bourges. All of his subsequent magnificent achievement for the rectification of the coinage of the realm was ignored, and he was accused of the technical violation in his youth when, with the King as his accomplice, he had minted coins as false as the monarch's face they bore.

Jacques Cœur invoked the pardon which had been granted him at the time. He gave careful instructions where his copy of the instrument was to be found. Whether it was actually produced before judgment is of no moment to our inquiry; it can only bear on the unfairness of a trial whose prejudice cannot for an instant be denied. The instrument was a public record whose absence could easily have been supplied. However, the counsel who were consulted before the appeal, and who had before them substantially the complete record of the case, state that this document was in evidence at the trial and that it "was not contradicted by the Attorney-General nor any others of the said commissioners." Certainly it forms a part of the record of the *procès* as it has been handed down to us. Nevertheless, the King's pardon of 1429 was, as we shall see, of even less value than his money had been at that period, before the reform of his coinage by Jacques Cœur.

2. The next accusation was a more timely one, better calculated to catch the prevailing winds of popular disfavor. Constantinople was on the eve of falling, and all Christendom had been listening for the crash with bated breath and invectives against the "mis-

creant infidel." The evil had been temporarily averted by the death of the Ottoman Sultan. Meanwhile, the Pope preached a new crusade to stem the tide of Turkish aggression which menaced the countries of the Christian faith. In the midst of this situation Jean de Village's ambassadorial gifts to the Sultan of Egypt were recalled and used against the defendant. He was accused of having "sent and caused to be presented by his agents to the said Sarrazins, a certain quantity of coats of armor and habiliments of war . . . and, what was worse, had caused this armor to be given to the said Sultan in our [the King's] name, although not charged or commissioned so to do by us, and it was common renown that, by means of the said armor, thus transported to the said Sultan and Sarrazins, by the said Jacques Cœur, these Sarrazins had gained a battle over the Christians which we have been charged and blamed with having permitted, those who have thus censured us stating that it had been done with our permission and consent, although this was not so."

As for the battle in question, where the infidels were alleged to have donned these warlike garbs so foreign to their general tactics, it was not specified. It was perhaps just as well for the prosecution to leave it to "common renown" to describe it. The trial had been begun during a lull on the Turkish front incident to the succession of Mahomet II to the Ottoman throne; Charles VII's correspondence with the Egyptian Sultan at this time shows only trifling grievances in their relations. (179).

Another evil complained of as having flowed from Jacques Cœur's criminal courtesies to the Sultan—

and, incidentally, one which betrays the origin of the
entire charge—was that the gift had been made "in
order that his galleys should be better treated, and
that he might be able to bring two or three hundred
esportes of pepper from Alexandria, without paying the
Sultan's duty which would amount to fourteen or fifteen ducats per *esporte*." The interest of France in
upholding the operation of the Egyptian potentate's
revenue laws even against that ruler himself seems to
have been assumed.

The force and credit of this entire charge might have
been greater but for certain truths. One was that
Jacques Cœur *did* have his sovereign's permission for
de Village's embassy and the amenities which it had
involved; when reminded of it, his royal master did
not have the hardihood to deny this, although his
memory would not function further. Then, too, the
defendant had obtained for his transaction, in advance,
a special license from the Pope, whose canonical laws
governed it; Charles VII had accepted the Sultan's
presents granted in return; his kingdom had enjoyed
the benefits of the commercial treaty resulting from
this exchange of international courtesies. Also, it may
help us in forming our judgment in the matter to bear
in mind that the gifts were not made to enemies, but
to allies, whose own justly renowned link-armor Jacques
Cœur had been engaged in importing for the French
campaigns, and, lastly—that the real foes of the Christian faith *did not wear plate-armor in their wars.* (180).

3. The third count in the information against
Jacques Cœur was that of having exported, in the
form of coin, or otherwise, silver to the Levant and

gold to other lands, in contravention of his country's laws. The ban was one which was "more honored in the breach than the observance." The nobles exported French money to pay their ransoms to their English captors. Charles VII's extensive hiring of Scottish troops made his pieces the principal medium of exchange in Scotland. The collections of St. Peter's drew French coins to Rome. The prohibitory legislation had its origin when French commerce was in its infancy. Obviously, in an era which did not employ paper money, a literal compliance with the edict would restrict all trade to an impracticable barter of evenly matched values; there could be no adjustment of balances. Even the witnesses against Jacques Cœur expressed surprise at the enforcement of a statute so irrational. "Without the use of money," added one of them, "one can do no merchandising in the Levant."

Nevertheless, Jacques Cœur's testimony proved that he had endeavored to obey the law, unreasonable as it was. He maintained that it was not French money which he had sent to the Levant but pieces which he had obtained from Germany, Lorraine, and other countries. His statement is corroborated by the witnesses against him, who always speak of *ducats*, never of the currency of France. (181).

The testimony on this subject disclosed one of the secrets of Jacques Cœur's quickly established fortune. He had profited on a grand scale by the East's relatively greater fondness for the white metal as expressed in the comparative values of silver and gold. For each mark of the former which he had employed at Alexandria he had purchased a several times greater weight

of gold than the silver could have been exchanged for
in Montpellier or Marseilles. Thus his operations had,
on balance, increased the value of his country's store
of precious metals, irrespective of where his silver was
obtained.

4. The next charge was a revival of the story of the
slave whom, as we recall, Jacques Cœur had caused to
be returned to his Saracen master. It brought an hour
of triumph to Michael Teinturier, whose testimony
shows that he did not stint himself in quenching his
thirst for revenge against his former patron. Inasmuch
as Michael's brother, Pierre, Montpellier's mayor and
Otto Castellane's ally, was one of the judges, the discharged ship-captain's accusation was assured of a
sympathetic reception by the bench. One cannot but
suspect that the more favorable treatment which the
defendant's pepper received from the Sultan's customs' officers, had something to do with the Teinturier
family's indignation over the bondsman's fate. It is
perhaps not being too mistrustful even to conceive
that Michael's original hospitality to the fugitive may
have been extended in the hope that it might lead to
a correction in the inequality in the administration of
the Egyptian laws. That Jacques Cœur thought so is
evident from his conduct as described by the witness
Teinturier; he not only rebuked Michael but threatened to hold his father, Isaac or Yzarin, responsible
for the consequences. Isaac, we recall, was an unsuccessful Montpellier merchant, to whom Jacques Cœur's
transcendent prosperity was a constant reproach.

We remember Jacques Cœur's position in the matter
—his constructive and pacific relations with the Sultan

which were imperilled by his subordinate's action; the danger which it entailed to commerce, to the Knights of Rhodes, to the pilgrims to the Holy Sepulchre, even to the success of Christian arms against the Turk. We learn from Teinturier's testimony that there was involved the safety of hostages given to bind the treaty with the Sultan, which contained among its provisions one for the rendition of fugitive slaves. Teinturier's action threatened war at an unfavorable moment for the Christian banner, and it would indeed be an extreme follower of Wilberforce or Lincoln who, counselled by all of the advance in human morals in the intervening centuries, would have acted differently than did Jacques Cœur in the crisis with which he was confronted.

5. The evocation of the last three charges had not exhausted all of the potency of Otto Castellane's waxen images. There was still other gossip along Montpellier's rapidly receding water-front, which a zealous aspirant to the Argentier's rôle could marshal against the fallen incumbent of the office. How about Jacques Cœur's use of impressment to man his vessels with able-bodied rogues and vagabonds and persons following no useful calling? Surely there was material here to employ against him.

And so we find revived against the too successful merchant the old story of the German pilgrim who had thrown himself overboard rather than work his way to the Holy Land, the goal of the greatest of all earthly pilgrimages. Two bailiffs also were alleged to have become sailors against their will.

Jacques Cœur produced in justification certain letters patent granted by the King in 1443, entitled "*ad capiendum vagabondos,*" authorizing the owners of a merchant vessel then under construction to require "the embarkation of idlers, vagabonds, and other worthless persons, of which there was so great a multitude in the country of Languedoc." If there had been errors committed in following this precedent, Jacques Cœur cast the responsibility, where it belonged, on the King's officers who had used their discretion in the enforcement of the royal authorization.

6. The prisoner was also accused of having in his possession a duplicate of the royal seal. He replied that he had been authorized to employ it by the King in connection with the negotiations relating to Genoa; that it had remained in the custody of his fellow ambassadors, Jacques Jouvenal des Ursin, now the Archbishop of Poitiers, and Doctor Jean Thierry, and that he did not recall "ever having held it" himself.

7. The next charge was of having wrongfully retained and preserved an obligation of the Duke of Bourbon for 2,000 écus, given under the following circumstances: The Duke had sent the Lord de Canillac and the Marshal de la Fayette to the court to arrange a marriage between his son, the Count de Clermont, and the King's daughter, Princess Jeanne of France. Jacques Cœur, it was said, had advised the ambassadors to make a present to the King of 2,000 écus "to celebrate royally the Christmas holidays." He had loaned the money, taken the ambassadors' note, signed on behalf of their principal, and had tendered the gift to the King in the Duke's name. Charles VII, having refused the present, the Argentier had retained

both note and money, as was discovered when his papers were seized. The King considered the proposal as a reflection on the royal honor; "never would we have desired or deigned to think of such a thing," he caused to be inserted in the record.

The explanation was simple, though embarrassing. Jacques Cœur denied having suggested the transaction, admitted having loaned the money to the over-zealous agents, and stated that he had held the note as security for a large sum owed him by—the Duchess of Bourbon.

8. The defendant was accused of having profited unduly in his management of the "marques" of Genoa, Catalonia, Provence, and Avignon. These were special taxes levied against the nationals of those countries, resident in France or bringing their merchandise there, imposed by way of reprisal against the wrongful acts of their country or countrymen and to compensate Charles VII's subjects who had suffered therefrom. The marques were usually invoked to redress injuries to shipping. Representation of French claimants, at this time, naturally devolved upon Jacques Cœur as his country's ablest and largest merchant and ship-owner. The machinery was cumbersome and the proceedings usually were dragged out over a period of years. Commissioners from the opposing countries involved took testimony, and assessed the damages in favor of each party injured in the commercial venture. The total award having been thus arrived at, the collection of taxes to be accumulated to meet it was farmed out to the most favorable bidder. These steps were naturally hurtful to the commerce of the offend-

ing nation, which frequently endeavored at some stage to arrange a composition of the claims against it.

Jacques Cœur was accused of having favored himself as against the other claimants, of having collected undue sums to defray his expenses and those of the commissioners, and of having collected money from the judgment debtors to procure the King's remission of the proceedings, which funds he had not distributed.

This charge was another one of those which Otto Castellane's drag-net had fished up from the shallowing waters of Montpellier. Jacques Cœur stated that the French merchants involved had only indemnified him for his travelling and other expenses; that the distribution had not been entirely finished when he was hastily called away by the war in Guienne, but that "each [claimant] would receive what was coming to him." As for the marques which had been compromised and withdrawn, "he had done nothing which was not by the deliberation of the King and the people of his counsel, and that the money which had been received from the said marques had been distributed as the King had ordained, and that for his pains and the work involved in having purchased [from the several claimants] the release of the said marques, which had been for the good of the inhabitants of the said countries, he had been given certain sums which it had been lawful for him to receive."

The defendant's statement with regard to the remitted reprisals we find confirmed by his subsequent conduct with regard to one of them; he caused his son the Archbishop to write to the friendly authorities of Avignon to procure the settlement agreement, with the receipts of the claimants annexed—an action which might have been damaging, had there been anything to fear in what these papers might expose. Whether the documents were obtained in time to be introduced in evidence before the final judgment, we have no means of knowing. (182). If they were, the effect which they produced can be judged from the weight which was given to his other justifications known to have been duly submitted.

Jacques Cœur's sons did not fear this charge when it came to meeting it on appeal. In their private memorandum to their lawyers, wherein they had every motive for setting forth only what they were confident of being able to prove, they state that the prosecution's witnesses, Procide and Panois, were "two loose individuals from Montpellier, abandoned and corrupted, murderers provided with a couple of pardons, who now repent of having testified as they did." Indeed, the appellants give much the same description of most of the witnesses marshalled by Castellane, whatever charges they support. "The majority of the witnesses produced in these informations," they inform their counsel, "are irresponsible crooks, abandoned and infamous, of whom several have been bribed, and now are ready to admit it, if they be interrogated on the subject."

9. The ninth count in the information against the accused charged him with having participated in some of the farm-leases of taxes in Languedoc while an officer of the state.

Jacques Cœur pointed out that he was not a Crown officer nor connected with the executive administration of the realm; that as Argentier he was in the personal service of the King, who had himself known of the transactions and permitted them.

10. In answer to charges of having received "great and excessive sums, commonly called 'sweetmeats,'" while representing the King in Languedoc, and of having obtained other donations and exactions from that province, Jacques Cœur said that "he could not recall (without his books of account) ever having exacted any sum in gold or silver, of which he had not rendered, or obligated himself to render, good and loyal account; that it might be that the said country, in addition to the sums publicly voted him, had accorded him some small honorariums which he had received and applied to his own profit."

We can easily be drawn into giving too much consideration to this group of charges; we must not tilt against the customs of the age. The "sweetmeats" had been granted to the Royal Commissioners by the states of Languedoc, in open assembly, in accordance with traditional practice. These sums, which do not appear to be excessive, were distributed among the Commissioners by the King, or with his consent; there were in some years as many as seven of these royal representatives, and it does not appear that Jacques Cœur got the lion's share in the divisions. The petty honorariums were also in harmony with fifteenth-century conventions. In general, Jacques Cœur had served the people of Languedoc and Montpellier for ten years in a difficult rôle, not only without their protest or denunciation, but with their compliments and praise. The commendations of his conduct, formally expressed during his term of service, cannot, with either propriety or force, afterward be traversed.

11. The King, "basely led," speaks in the last charge. In so far as the royal meaning appears clear, his accusation is, that by the wrongful acts described in the other charges, "the said Jacques Cœur has caused financial loss to us, inasmuch as, at times when he had in his custody vast sums of our revenues, he repeatedly made us loans, as he called them, from these funds of ours; nevertheless, he imposed on us financial loss (interest) for the said loans."

Are we not now getting close to the secret of the King's wrath against his talented subject? The royal borrower found himself a debtor; he had emerged victoriously from the campaigns for the liberation of his country, to have his triumph chilled by the realization that he owed money, which he would be called upon to repay, together with money's hire for its use. His charge that Jacques Cœur could have provided for the national needs, or any substantial part of them, either out of surpluses in the household funds—or even from accumulations of his own honorariums—if honest, is absurd on its face.

Jacques Cœur's loans, at the lowest statement of them, amounted, as we have seen, to more than a fifth of the entire public income of the kingdom. This fraction represented also about the proportion of the total revenue which was annually allotted to the royal household. There is not the slightest intimation throughout the entire proceedings that Jacques Cœur did not administer this fund with rectitude; the only suggestion is that he did not promptly apply the surpluses. To suppose that at any one time the fund contained an excess above the royal needs equal or nearly equal to the entire amount by which the fund was annually replenished, imposes a strain upon credulity. (185).

The great discrepancy between the aggregate of Jacques Cœur's honorariums and the damages awarded against him because of them, was one of the appellants' strong points on the subsequent appeal of his case. Yet these particular damages were only half the lowest contemporary estimate of his advances to his King.

Jacques Cœur's loans to the Crown were not profitable to himself; they were made at a great personal sacrifice. The lender was primarily a merchant, not a banker. The interest—variously given at from fifteen to twenty per cent—could not compensate him for the withdrawal of the money from his business, where its normal employ in his Levantine commerce brought him far greater returns. (186).

Answering generally all of the charges of misconduct in office, Jacques Cœur protested, as his contemporary de Coucy informs us, "that he had all his life served King Charles with all his might, prudently and loyally, without having committed any dishonest act in the handling of his revenues; but, largely through the great favor which the King had shown him, he had advanced himself in business and established himself in merchandise, in which he had gained his fortune and success."

CHAPTER XXVI
TRIAL. TORTURE. JUDGMENT

Such were the apparent reasons for the sudden and striking downfall, degradation, and punishment of this valiant figure; such the defense, decisive and convincing, with which he met them. The elaboration of the charges had taken over a year, during which "the said Otto Castellane had diligently devoted himself," as a state document of the succeeding reign recites, "and had caused to be examined all those having hatred and malevolence against [the prisoner], both his varlet servitors and others, some bribed by money, some compelled by threats."

The obvious falseness of the accusations and the absolute unfairness of the trial focussed sympathy and interest upon Jacques Cœur at the time, and have since led to the rejection by history's tribunal of the judgment pronounced against him by Charles VII's "Bed of Justice"—death-bed of justice it might more fittingly be named.

The proceedings dragged on at great length. Apparently there was some embarrassment in convicting him on the evidence which had been produced; it was necessary to lay some basis before his justifications could be overruled. One year after his arrest the commissioners, formally assembled, made an interlocutory decree. This recited that "the matter was not yet in a condition for judgment"; ordered that the defendant

234

should be given two months to complete his defense; that after the expiration of this period he should be interrogated anew, "and if he did not speak the truth on the said charges, they would know it from his lips, by the extraordinary means of the question [torture]; thus they would find out what should rightfully be done."

Jacques Cœur was notified of this decision by certain of the commissioners, among them Antoine Chabannes, Otto Castellane, and Jean Barbin, the Advocate of the King. The report of this session is interesting as being one of the rare instances in which we are permitted to have Jacques Cœur's literal responses.

"*Question:* Do you desire a delay to enable you to show us your accounts?

"*Answer:* With regard to the financial matters, I am not given as much latitude as should be given and is usually given to others; I should have a counsel to reply for me. As for the adjournment, so long as they hold me in the condition that I am, I doubt whether I will be able to show the things which are demanded, nor indeed anything by way of my justification. As to the licenses from the Pope and all that which I have testified in my statements, I have spoken the truth and only the truth.

"*Q.:* When an officer is accused of anything touching his office, it is not the usage to allow him counsel. You must defend yourself.

"*A.:* I throw myself, for all of this, on the good grace of the King. Myself and all my property, all are the King's and at his disposal to do his good pleasure.

"*Q.:* Show us the bulls of the Pope of which you have spoken.

"*A.:* The license from Pope Eugenius can be obtained of My Lord the Bishop of Agde, who procured it; I do not know where it is but it can easily be found, for I had it as well as one from Pope Nicholas for the delivery of a suit of armor or so to the infidels."

These pontifical indulgences, of which Jacques Cœur had received duplicates, still form a part of the archives of the Vatican. (187).

"*Q.:* I submit to you a list of the justifications which are required of you.

"*A.:* I do not believe that, however long the delay that is given me, prisoner that I am, I can show so many things."

The Commissioners had announced that if these documents were not forthcoming in time, the charges to which they related would be deemed as admitted by the accused.

"*Q.:* You are permitted to talk to your people, to Thierry and to Jobert.

"*A.:* Thierry and Jobert do not understand financial matters. To talk to them or any of my other people would not profit me any. But since I am given this offer, if it is the good pleasure of the King, I would like to speak with the Lord Bishop of Agde; there is no man in the world who can counsel me better on this occasion.

"*Q.:* The Lord Bishop of Agde is not here to enable you to speak with him.

"*A.:* If I cannot talk with the Lord Bishop of Agde, if it should please the King to give a safe-conduct to William de Varye, I could better arrange this matter with him than with another.

"*Q.:* De Varye is not in the kingdom; you well know it.

"*A.:* If I cannot consult with the Bishop of Agde nor with the said de Varye, I ask that it should please the King that I be allowed to speak to my son the Archbishop of Bourges. My people, both factors and employees, will do more for the Archbishop than they will do for Thierry and Jobert.

"*Q.:* We cannot promise it now but will take it up with the King.

"*A.:* Then I ask to talk with Thierry and Jobert."

Jacques Cœur thereupon gave the following instructions to his two employees, in the presence and hearing of his judges:

"You will interview Gimart, de Village, and Gaillardet, who have commanded my galleys, about the letters from the Holy Father Eugenius and Pope Nicholas. They were placed on the galleys to show them to pilgrims and merchants; it can be learned from my Lord of Agde if they are at Rome. Jean de Village obtained them to give some arms to the Saracens. The letters of remission for that which has passed at the mint will be found at Pierre Godard's house or in the registry of the mint. You will bring all the receipts for the marques of Genoa and Catalonia. Those of the marque of Provence will be found in the chamber of accounts of the King of Sicily [René]. I hand you some letters for the Archbishop of Bourges, the Bishop of Agde, William Guimard [or Gimart], and Antoine Noir."

The task given to these faithful subordinates was indeed gigantic: to seek records within and without the kingdom, to interview factors who had fled the country, to find Antoine Noir's books which he had taken with him on his flight. Some evidence we know they were able to produce but, in all probability, in those days of slow travel, most of the documents which they sought could not be obtained in time to stay the process of the King. (188). Jacques Cœur's own records and those of William de Varye, relating to the Argenterie and the storehouse at Tours, were already in the hands of the Crown officers; their tenor has been handed down to us, and for good order and accuracy they are models for any age.

Meanwhile, Pope Nicholas V was making powerful interventions on the prisoner's behalf. The Cardinal d'Estouteville, who had left St. Peter's for his post in France two months after Jacques Cœur's arrest, was charged with the mission of interceding in his favor; a clerk of the Apostolic Chamber was sent from Rome with a special message for the King; the Pope issued a bull confirming to Jacques Cœur the indulgences of the previous papal grants and testifying to the Holy See's appreciation of his devotion to the Church.

At length, despairing of obtaining justice from the Commissioners, and doubtless at the suggestion of his clerical supporters, Jacques Cœur "avowed himself a clerk," and demanded to be judged in the ecclesiastical forum. He had, as we remember, in his early life obtained letters of tonsure which entitled him to claim the "benefit of clergy." The Bishop of Poitiers and the Archbishop of Tours demanded the custody of his person and the jurisdiction of his case; incidentally, the former of these two churchmen was the brother of the Lord Chancellor and himself had been the primate of the realm. Although the legal question presented was a close one, the plea was overruled. (189).

In March, 1453, a new commission presided over by Otto Castellane decreed that the prisoner should be put to the "question"—that favorite mediæval method of getting at the truth, which dared not be called by its real name and which was at a later day to extract from Galileo a denial of the motion of the earth.

According to a document of Louis XI's reign decreeing a review of Jacques Cœur's trial, the accused was brought before a committee of his judges who informed him that "he must consider well, for if he did not speak the truth they would proceed against him by *Gehenna* and torture." The following day he was led before the formidable instruments, their grim operators were summoned, and Jacques Cœur, the man who had created the maritime commerce of France, who had devoted his services and wealth to his country's cause, "was stripped and fastened hand and foot, ready to be *Gehennaed*." He declared that he was a clerk and had been arrested while wearing "the habit and tonsure of a clerk, that they were doing him a wrong and treating him with injustice, and that he appealed from the

Commissioners' procedure." Thereupon certain of the judges said to him that "if he carried on in this manner, the question would be all the more severely applied." (190).

The inquisition commenced, and, "because he did not respond sufficiently according to their taste, they led him to the place of torture, where they seated him on the culprit's seat [*sellette*], and interrogated him anew on several of the charges. And for the great displeasure which he had of having been detained so long a prisoner, and the fear which he had of the said question, intrusting himself to the grace of our late sovereign and sire [Charles VII], who as to all the charges, saving that of the poisoning, had pardoned and absolved him, he abided by the deposition of the witnesses who had testified against him, except as to the poisoning, although he said that he had not committed the said crimes, and that the witnesses were his malignant enemies." Thus was the way cleared for Otto Castellane to report exultantly to his fellow conspirators the "confessions" of Jacques Cœur!

The death of his wife came to add its poignancy to the sum of the prisoner's misfortunes. Macée de Léodépart, his companion since his youth, fell a victim to tortures more real than those inflicted on her husband. His brother, the Bishop of Luçon, passed away.

Meanwhile the Church continued to reclaim its former benefactor. The efforts of the Archbishop of Poitiers and the defendant's son, the Archbishop of Bourges, were untiring. Vainly, up to the moment of final judgment, they presented their protests and demands for a change of forum and afterward renewed them, to avert the humiliation of punishment.

JACQUES CŒUR MAKING THE *AMENDE HONORABLE*

before the Lord Chancellor, Guillaume des Ursins, in the Palace of Justice at Poitiers. He holds in his hands a lighted wax candle, weighing ten pounds. Photograph of a miniature contained in Monstrelet's *Chronicles*, Bibliothèque Nationale, Paris.

The final decree was pronounced in the name and presence of the King, at the Château of Lusignan, May 29, 1453, almost two years after the trial's commencement. Jacques Cœur was declared guilty of five of the eleven or twelve counts on which he was accused. His crimes were declared to involve *lèse-majesté* which carried "the forfeiture of his life and property. Nevertheless," the judgment states, "for certain services to us rendered by the said Jacques Cœur, and in contemplation and favor of our Holy Father the Pope, who has written and requested us on his behalf, and for other causes and considerations to us moving, we have remitted and do remit to the said Jacques Cœur the pain of death, and we have deprived him of and declared him forever disqualified for all offices, royal and public, and we have condemned and do condemn the said Jacques Cœur to make the *amende honorable* before our said Procureur-General, bareheaded, without hood or belt, on his knees, holding a lighted wax torch weighing ten pounds; confessing that he had wickedly, unlawfully, and without reason, sent and caused to be presented armor to the Sultan, enemy of the Christian faith; that he had restored the said youth to the Sarrazens, and had transmitted to them, and elsewhere beyond the kingdom, a great quantity of silver and gold, against the royal ordinances; that he had exacted, taken, collected, received, and retained several large sums of money, as well from us as from our said lands and subjects, to their great desolation and destruction; begging mercy and pardon of God, of us, and of justice.

"And also we have condemned and do condemn him to redeem from the hands of the Sarrazens the said youth and to cause him to be brought back and established in the city of Montpellier from whence he was taken, if possible so to do, and, if not, to redeem a Christian from the hands of the said Sarrazens and bring him to the said place of Montpellier; and we have declared and do declare the said note and obligation for the sum of 2,000 écus null and void, and to have been falsely and wickedly taken and exacted of the said Lords de Canillac and de la Fayette by the said Jacques Cœur.

"And further, we have condemned and do condemn this Jacques Cœur to render and restore—for the sums by him received and wrongfully retained, belonging to us and also for the sums extorted, taken, and improperly exacted from our lands and subjects—the sum of 100,-000 écus; and, in *amende profitable* to us, the sum of 300,000 écus, and to hold prison until the full satisfaction thereof. And besides, we have declared and do declare all the goods of the said Jacques Cœur confiscate to us, and we have banished and do banish this Jacques Cœur perpetually from our kingdom, subject to our good pleasure.

"And, with regard to the poisoning, inasmuch as that [branch of the] case is not for the present in a condition to be decided, we do not make any judgment concerning it and for reason."

Charles VII's judgment against his fallen minister was not the only historic event which signalized this fateful 29th of May. On the same day that this fickle, suspicious, and envious sovereign was filching the purse of a great merchant and devoted subject of a sum more than one-fifth the annual revenues of the realm, the

long-deferred and inevitable moment arrived for the
fall of Constantinople, "and the last of the Cæsars
folded round him the imperial mantle and remembered
the name which he represented in the dignity of heroic
death."

CHAPTER XXVII

IMPRISONMENT CONTINUED. ADMINISTRATION OF ESTATE

THE same day that Jacques Cœur underwent his ignominious ordeal in the great hall of the Palace of Justice at Poitiers, Jeanne de Vendôme, also, in similar fashion, and in the same place, made her *amende honorable* for having borne false witness in the principal charge of which he was accused; from which, nevertheless, his judges had refused to exonerate him and under color of which he continued to be detained. (191).

While Jacques Cœur was being requited in the manner in which we have described, steps were being taken to restore the memory of his saintly predecessor in the history of the deliverance of France. Jeanne d'Arc's rehabilitation began as her successor's influence ended, as though the mean heart of Charles VII was too narrow to entertain gratitude toward more than one benefactor at a time. Even this act of dilatory justice was not uninspired by thoughts of self; the memory of the Maid was only righted in clearing title to his crown. (192).

The Attorney-General, Jean Dauvet, was appointed by the King liquidator of Jacques Cœur's confiscated property. He has left us a journal of over 500 pages in which he has recorded in detail the performance of his gigantic and complicated task; it is from this document that we derive most of our information on the great merchant's vast estate. Never did officer perform similar duties more zealously, more vigorously, or with more meticulous observance of the formalities due. Jean Dauvet's able, energetic, and inflexible administration in the interests of the Crown must command our admiration, wherever our sympathies may stray. His official zeal knew no favoritism, shirked no controversy, omitted no duties, and he marshalled intricate and conflicting rights with sure and skilful touch. Up and down the kingdom rode the tireless conservator; even beyond it, to follow assets in Provence. In some of his quests he was, perhaps, aided by a favorable forum. He successfully contested the claim of Jacques Cœur's sons to the heritage of their mother, and was equally fortunate in compelling the Archbishop of Bourges, as executor of his uncle, the Bishop of Luçon, to relinquish the latter's estate to the receivers of the Crown.

His missions in Provence did not have so prosperous an issue. The local officers eluded him in his pursuit of Jacques Cœur's Marseilles real estate; the general forum he found less partial to his cause. In vain did he request King René to coerce the recalcitrant municipal authorities; equally futile was his formal application for the extradition of Jean de Village, and his attempts to lure Antoine Noir, with his precious books of account, within the jurisdiction of France.

Many of the incidents which mark the course of his activities are worth our brief attention. The artful yet dignified diplomacy of King René in denying the petitions of his royal brother-in-law; the learned arguments of Dauvet and René's Chancellor at their hearing; Jean de Village's own skill in his encounters with Charles VII's Attorney-General; the latter's compromise with the Marseilles authorities, whereby he accepted in lieu of the property a relatively small sum of cash, because, as he relates, "the said officers and inhabitants of this city are a most austere people and difficult to deal with"; the later development that the city fathers had but acted to protect the property's owner; the usurpation by the Duke of Bourbon of lands which he had previously sold to Jacques Cœur; the successful efforts of Perrette de Village and Jeanne Gimart to whisk away from the King's officers the furniture of their relative's Montpellier mansion; the thwarting of Otto Castellane's attempt to elude the payment to the confiscated estate of the joint debt of himself and William Gouffier; the controversy with the Archbishop of Bourges over the disappearance of six golden goblets, which resulted in the disclosure that they had been presented as a gift to the Cardinal d'Estouteville, *"an ambassador from our Holy Father the Pope to accomplish the deliverance of . . . Jacques Cœur"*—all are rich in human interest. (193).

Nothing, perhaps, but the sack of Constantinople produced the quantity of gold and silver vessels and ornaments, pearls and precious stones, furs, silk, and textiles which now were thrown upon the market, to find buyers among the merchants and moneyed class of France. Such a scurrying took place among the noble debtors of the fallen merchant for favorable terms in the acquittance of their obligations, now being administered by the peremptory Dauvet, or to beg their entire remission of the King, as almost to absorb the attentions of the court. Fawning courtiers, especially those who had advanced the issue, hungrily sought their share of the opulent spoils; rival royal mistresses vied with each other in this favorable moment to catch the sovereign's eye.

Auctions were held at Tours, at Bourges, at Paris, Lyons, and Poitiers, all previously advertised by trumpet and "public cry." The ships were sold at Montpellier "by an inch of candle," the method of exciting bidders in which Pepys was later to find such "good sport." (194). The sales effected at Bourges disposed of the famous rose-damask tapestries, "embroidered with the history of Nabugot-de-Nozor." The catalogue of this sale listed another asset which strikes with surprise our twentieth-century eyes. Jacques Cœur owned a three-quarters interest in two English prisoners, sharing the title with the Count de Dunois. Their names are given as the "Lords *Berquigny* and *Dormond.*" The latter has been identified by the historian Clément as having been probably the Earl of Ormonde, who, in 1449, had commanded Vernon for the English and had been forced to surrender it to Dunois after a bombardment; the former name is perhaps an early French corruption of that of Lord Berkeley. (195). The Crown's interest in *"Dormond"* was relinquished to Dunois; the right to collect *"Berquigny's"* ransom was offered to the highest bidder. The Attorney-General, after consultation with the King, in view of "the danger of death and other inconveniences and risks in guarding the said prisoner," decided to accept a bid of 24,000 écus, about one-fifth of the sum which the Duke of Orleans, as a prince of the French blood royal, had been required to pay for his redemption from his English captors. (196).

Charles VII, who had rejected the request of Jacques Cœur's children, addressed "to the grace, mercy, and benevolence of the King," that they be allowed to inherit the property of their mother, and who had relentlessly prevented them from benefiting by the testament of their uncle, nevertheless, showed some bounty toward one of them. Upon Ravant Cœur, the Argentier's third son, who swore to Dauvet that "he did not have the wherewithal to live," and that he had deserted his brothers in their efforts to reverse their father's judgment, the King bestowed 500 francs, paid out of the parental estate, as a reward for this apparent act of youthful weakness. A later application for a renewal of this benefaction found that the royal heart had hardened in the interval; this time the suitor received but 25 francs. Ravant's conduct should not be too severely judged; it may have had a deeper purpose than it disclosed. In any event, it was redeemed by subsequent deeds, as we shall find.

Henri and Geoffrey Cœur appealed their father's case to the Court of Parliament and strenuously resisted the sale of their family property. They complained on the grounds that the prisoner "had been confined so closely that no one had dared to speak with him, that he had not been allowed to have counsel, nor was he justly heard, that the crime of *lèse-majesté* had not been proven, that the sentence rendered in his absence was null"; they set up also his right to be judged by the ecclesiastical courts. This resistance only succeeded in irritating the prosecution, and Henri,

the notary of the Pope, canon of the archiepiscopal
churches of Bourges and Limoges, and the attorney
for Geoffrey, were both compelled to make an *amende
honorable* before the Attorney-General, to beg on their
knees mercy from the King and Royal Council and to
pay a substantial fine. Two notaries of Bourges who
had prepared the act of appeal suffered the same penalty.

Antoine de Chabannes, Count de Dammertin, had
been rewarded in advance for his leading part in prose-
cuting and judging Jacques Cœur. Immediately after
the latter's arrest, the magnificent baronial estate of
St. Fargeau and other vast domains of the great merchant had been turned over to this turbulent warrior and former *écorcheur*. Later, the donee's title to
these properties was formalized by his colorable purchase of them at auction; the price was 20,000 écus,
paid with money presented to him by the King before the sale. (197). One cannot but feel that, even at
this low valuation of Chabanne's emoluments, he was
being grossly overpaid. He had contracted to commit murder for only half of this amount.

William Gouffier was another one of the judges who
shared heavily in Jacques Cœur's noble landed properties. Agnes Sorel's successor as mistress of the King
became Macée Léodépart's successor as the mistress
of Menetou-Salon, one of the most beautiful estates
in Berry.

Otto Castellane became the Argentier of France;
two of his brothers were advanced to important offices
under the Crown.

Over three years had passed since Jacques Cœur's

arrest; nearly seventeen months since his sentence, during all of which time he had continued to be detained in prison within the kingdom from which he had been perpetually banished.

While the Pope was summoning Christendom to unite against the peril of Turkish invasion, which only Hungary now barred from western Europe, word ran through the realm of France that Jacques Cœur had broken his bonds and was a fugitive from the justice of his King.

CHAPTER XXVIII
ESCAPE

JEHAN, my good nephew, dear son:

Inasmuch as you have toward me an affectionate relationship, and as you have my life at heart, to you and to your diligence I recommend myself; and, for God, dear son, do not delay in coming to take me out of this refuge, in view of the fact that in five days they will drag me out of it themselves to put me to death or will murder me within its walls; I would already have come to such an end, had it not been for this good friar, Hugault, good brother that he is; and already have they sought to murder me with violence, a despatch sent by night from Otto having made known my presence, and I would have been killed if it had not been for a lead hammer which this good friar had given me, which put me in a posture of defense; and there having been a great stir in the convent because of this, they have introduced some poison, as I have been secretly informed, and would give me powders of realgar and arsenic in some wine; having failed in this design, yesterday at supper, they brought me a goblet in which were the said powders, which I pretended to drink, and so was able to throw it away and, since, pretend to be sick in languor, inasmuch as one should die from this [poison] within six days; and it is no longer possible that such a pretense should be kept up more than the said five days, after which they will kill me by force, seeing the failure of their said stratagem.

And, for God, dear son, hasten to come to my aid or you will not find me alive. And G. D. V. still holds my money $+ I \perp Z$ which he will certainly give you for this undertaking of rescue. As for myself, there remains to me sufficient cash for my needs, if it is to be had within [the value of] some jewels which I have in my belt, which the good friar has made me carry in [an illegible word]. And, for God, dear son, do not let me succumb insomuch as I am dear to you; and, treat royally this good friar in whom have all faith, as you would justly have in your good master and father,

J. C. (198).

Such was the letter which a Franciscan friar handed to Jean de Village in the city of Marseilles, on a certain day in February, 1455. Otto was, of course, the Italian Castellane; G. D. V. were the initials of William (Guillaume) de Varye; the amount of Jacques Cœur's money which the latter guarded is denoted by signs, doubtless well understood between the merchant and his factors.

The dashing young fleet captain was now high in royal favor in King René's pleasant realm, where he and Jacques Cœur's other shipmasters had found refuge after their master's fall. This sovereign, defending Jean against Charles VII's extradition, had informed the importunate Dauvet that "his said country of Provence was a maritime country, where the Catalonians, their enemies, might come any day as they had done in the past and, if there were not men of the sea to resist them, there might result the perdition or destruction of his said realm, for which cause he had need of maintaining the said Village and other people trained in maritime warfare." The Troubadour King's real reason may have been deeper-seated; his friendly relations with the fallen Argentier dated back to the days of Jeanne d'Arc.

Jean de Village had been aware for several months of his uncle's escape from prison; he and the other ship-captains had, doubtless, received the news with jubilation and 'were awaiting expectantly the issue of the event.

October 29, 1454, the King had advised his Attorney-General, then at Lyons, of the prisoner's flight and the zealous Dauvet had set up a hue and cry in an effort to intercept the fugitive. The manner of the escape is not known to us nor can we be certain of the prison from which it was made. The presumption is that it was from Poitiers, where the prisoner was last known to have been confined; in view of our present knowledge it is perhaps not too much to say that it was inspired and, perhaps, even aided by the same powerful and watchful agency which was to receive him at the end of his long flight and whose servants he and his family had ever been.

Like a homing bird the fugitive headed in the direction from whence he knew a welcome awaited him, halting on the way at various churches and convents which enjoyed the right of asylum from the process of the King. His first place of refuge is said to have been Montmarrillon; that he stopped at Limoges, where his son Henri was the cathedral's canon, we know from

the record of a subsequent proceeding to punish one
of the citizens of that community for aiding him to
make his way. (199). One would be surprised if he did
not seek the protection of the famous Christian stronghold of Le Puy or halt at Viviers, where Henri was
also an officer of the church, or at Avignon where his
factor, Antoine Noir, had been so hospitably received.
His son Ravant is known to have been at this latter
place at about this time and later to have joined his
father in Provence. For this reason Jean Dauvet suspected him of playing a leading part in the escape;
"wherefore it is to be believed and presumed that the
said Ravant has been the cause, means, and an accomplice of the escape of his said father," the alert Attorney-General entered in his comprehensive journal.
(200).

The friar had carried Jacques Cœur's letter overland a distance of fifty miles from a convent in Beaucaire, where, in his flight for freedom, the fugitive had
sought asylum from his enemies and the officers of the
Crown. His refuge had been discovered by Otto Castellane when he had already gained the frontier, in sight
of the land which was furnishing his subordinates with
hospitable shelter. Only the Rhone separated the
walled and turreted city of Beaucaire in Charles VII's
province of Languedoc and Tarascon in King René's
benevolent domain. Unfortunately for the fugitive,
the river here is wide and swift. His son had preceded
him in crossing it, doubtless to prepare the way, before the father's urgent danger, which had occasioned
his cry of distress to Jean de Village, had developed.

Jacques Cœur's peril from the machinations of the

KING RENÉ AND HIS WIFE JEANNE DE LAVAL.
Painting by Nicholas Frement, 1469. In the Louvre.

THE CHÂTEAU OF KING RENÉ AT TARASCON.
E. Lavisse, " Histoire de France." Librairie Hachette, Éditeur.

vindictive Italian was genuine indeed, as Jean de Village well knew; only a few months before Jean had told Dauvet that he himself "did not dare go to Montpellier nor elsewhere in France as a witness, for fear of Castellane, who had threatened his life and property, as had been reported to him." (201).

Jean de Village did not hesitate in this crisis nor did he desert the patron who had heaped favors upon him since his youth; he acted swiftly and surely, as became the man of action that he was. Later he found it convenient to seek King Charles's pardon for what he did on this occasion. It is from the recitals made by him in this document that we know the story of his deeds. Like all sailors Jean can tell a tale and we will allow him to relate the story in his quaint and mediæval phrase, without any other alteration than the transposition of his statement into the first person.

"The which letter, seen by me, considering that I was a relative and servitor of the said Jacques Cœur and bound to render him all service within my power, desiring to withdraw him from this danger, I left the said place of Marseilles and went to Tarascon and there placed myself in a convent of the Cordelier brotherhood, and sent word by a friar of this convent to the said Jacques Cœur, that I had come to aid him and to understand his situation and also to learn what it should please him to command me to do, and that if he had the desire to make his escape, I had the courage, with the aid of God, to rescue him. And then the said Jacques Cœur wrote on a tablet that he prayed me as his son and for God that I should pluck him out of there, for he greatly feared that they would murder him in the said asylum, without the King's knowledge, with other most piteous words which he wrote to me.

"The which letters having been read by me, moved with pity, I sent him word to comfort him that he should be of good cheer and that I would deliver him. And forthwith I left the said place of Tarascon and went to the said city of Marseilles, and talked to the said late William Gimart and to Gaillardet of Bourges [both of them former commanders of Jacques Cœur's vessels] and told them the things aforesaid and what I had undertaken to accomplish, at which the said Gimart and Gaillardet were jubilant and devoted themselves to the affair; and the said Gaillardet consented to go with me to execute the matter.

"And afterward, we left the said city of Marseilles to go to the said Tarascon, and took with us eighteen or twenty companions at arms who, at this time, were under my orders as a commander of ships of war [in King René's service] and when we arrived at the port of Tarascon, we took a bark to cross the Rhone at the hour of midnight or thereabouts, and went straight to the wall of the said city of Beaucaire in the neighborhood of an opening which was there, which one of the said marines named Yonnet had long well known of, and inasmuch as the said hole was not big enough, my men enlarged it, and we entered through it into the city and went straight to the church of the said Cordeliers, where was the said Jacques Cœur, who, after the matins were said, went outside as I had instructed him to do, and gladly accompanied us to pass through the said hole in the wall, and thence to the said boat to recross the said river.

"And afterward, I conducted the said Jacques Cœur
to the port of Bouc, and there placed him in a bark
which was his own and which I had caused to be
brought there for this purpose, and from thence I
sailed the said bark almost to Marseilles, and then I
landed him and conducted him [along that beautiful
azure coast!] as far as Nice; there I placed him on an
armed man-of-war on which I carried him as far as
Pisa, from whence he went overland to Rome.

"While the said Jacques Cœur was at Rome, I met
him there and settled with him for all the voyages and
administrations of the galleys and the businesses which
they had had, insomuch that we were satisfied the one
with the other."

It would seem that the encounter at the Beaucaire
monastery had not been quite as mild as the leader
of the rescue party portrays it. A record of the city
of Arles gives a much more sanguinary version of this
incident. This document recites that those who opposed Jean de Village and his band of marines were
"atrociously and mortally wounded." Had fatalities
actually resulted, it is unlikely that they would have
been omitted from the petitioner's prayer for pardon.

Nevertheless, Jean de Village's valiant party did not
go entirely scathless for their interferences with Charles
VII's justice. The King of France was sufficiently
powerful with his brother-in-law René to exact some
punitive measures against the hardy adventurers.
Three of the privates were arrested and underwent a
short imprisonment; in the end, like their leader, they
received a pardon; Kings could not at this epoch afford
to be too harsh to able-bodied seamen. Jean de Vil-

lage's wife and children were arrested at Marseilles; they were soon released, although their freedom was restricted to the city limits; thus they were held as hostages until the family head ultimately made his peace with the irate monarch, granted to him, as we have seen, because, as an expert navigator, "he may be of service to us [Charles VII] in future." (202).

Ravant Cœur accompanied his father on these latter stages of his flight to Rome.

CHAPTER XXIX

AT ROME. REAL REASON FOR HIS DOWNFALL

THUS Jacques Cœur arrived, safe and sane, at Rome and was welcomed by his friend and protector, the sovereign Pontiff Nicholas V. These were stirring days in the Eternal City. The Pope's generous welcome was also being extended to the scholars and artists of the East, like Jacques Cœur refugees, as a result of Constantinople's fate; the Vatican was being renovated to become a papal residence of surpassing splendor; its library was being enlarged and enriched by priceless legacies of classic culture, bequeathed to it by the fallen Byzantine capital; everywhere one talked the crusade which was to redeem Saint Sophia's from pollution by the Turk.

Jacques Cœur's own welcome was a most impressive one; the aged Pope, who neared life's journey's end, delivered a formal address in his honor before the consistory of the Cardinals. These pontifical utterances, by Nicholas's own order, were faithfully transcribed by a secretary of the Roman chancellery and, as they have a most important bearing on our story, will be examined in their place.

And now, having conducted Jacques Cœur to security and honor from danger and disgrace, perhaps we can safely leave him for a while to inquire into some of the deeper reasons of his sudden downfall.

Jacques Cœur's conviction seems mysterious and

strange. The feeble pretense of the continued validity
of the poison charge, after its complete exposure, the
weakness of all the other accusations, so competently
refuted, the employment of a form of judicial procedure
characteristic of a political execution and whose iniquity
was admitted by its abolition within the year, the re-
lentlessness which pursued the prisoner after his sentence—all indicate that his judges were animated by
what appeared to them as stronger reasons than were
set forth in the text of his indictment.

Envy and malice played their accustomed parts, we
know; the court itself was well described by one of its
members as "an assemblage of persons who, under
guise of the common good, meet together in order to
deceive each other"; nevertheless, one feels that back
of Jacques Cœur's case were motives of state which
were carefully guarded from the public record of his
trial.

It was easy enough with the poison charge to arouse
the morbid suspicions of a ruler who afterward was
to starve himself to death for fear of what might be
placed in his food by his own son. "When one of the
dogs of the palace," said the prelate, Thomas Basin,
"wished to destroy an honest man, he had only to
accuse him before the King of having spoken ill of the
'Beautiful Agnes.'" However, even in Charles VII's
tainted mind, lodgment would not have been found
for an indictment against a loyal and faithful servitor,
whom the very victim of the alleged crime had, in her
testament, defended against the charge, had there not
been some other powerful moving cause which had
previously stirred the anger and lost the confidence of

the King; nor, after the exposure of this silly accusation, could the prosecution have survived unless it had been sustained by some such potent influence, acting on the sovereign's will and reflected in the decisions of his specially chosen commissioners.

What is the answer to this enigma, and is it connected in any degree with the Treasurer-General Saincoins's fate, as Jean Cœur seems to have feared when celebrating the mass "for the Lord Argentier" which we have previously described?

And so we need not be surprised to find several of Jacques Cœur's biographers departing from the strict historical evidence, in order to advance their individual theories in explanation of their hero's fate.

The first of these seems to have been very tentatively put forth by Mézeray in his history of France, published nearly three hundred years ago. "Some think," said he, on the subject of our memoir, "that the King was prejudiced against him because he had loaned money to the Dauphin; others, that there was nothing of the kind but that the calumnies of courtiers served him this turn to gorge themselves with his goods." (203). The former of these alternatives has been expressed more boldly in modern times, but never, that we can find, has it been supported by any but the slenderest historical indications.

On its face, it has a certain plausibility. If true, it would account for the extraordinary favor which, as we shall see, Jacques Cœur's sons enjoyed during the ensuing reign, and for the royal edicts issued by Louis XI furthering the rehabilitation of their father's memory. In a recital of one of these latter documents this theory is even given some historical support by a phrase alluding to "the good and praiseworthy services to us rendered by the said Jacques Cœur."

On the other hand, we have hearsay evidence, as we remember, of the Dauphin's own unqualified admission that, during his ten years' exile in Dauphiny, he "never received any supplies from his father *or from the kingdom.*" Du Clerq, who relates this, was, as we know, a chronicler of the court of the Duke of Burgundy, where Louis lived for five years before his accession to the throne.

The very year of Jacques Cœur's arrest the Dauphin entered into an agreement for the purchase of the principality of Monaco from the Grimaldi family for 15,000 écus, *which he was not able to pay.* Had the coffers of the great merchant been already opened to this princeling, there would have been no reason for this humiliating default. (204).

The fugitive Jacques Cœur made no attempt to gain asylum in the Dauphin's domain, which, in view of its nearness, he would most likely have done had he any claim to protection there; at this time, we remember, Louis was openly arrayed against his father, eagerly seeking causes to balk the royal will.

As for the favors to Jacques Cœur's heirs, and the incidental honor to their father's memory, we believe that a much more mindful agency operated to produce them than the gratitude of Louis XI; this politic sovereign was more given to purchasing the influence of his enemies than to rewarding his friends. His recognition of Jacques Cœur's services to France and to its rulers, whose realm was thereby enlarged, is not nearly so strongly emphasized in his edicts as is his hatred of Chabannes.

No, it was a different cause, we shall find, than that of Jacques Cœur's relations with the Dauphin that reduced the King's estimation of his Argentier to the point where it could be infected by the charge of poison; it was another fever than rage on this account that totally destroyed the royal favor.

We have now examined all of the obtainable record of this celebrated case; we have even gone outside it to read counsel's confidential opinions prior to appeal. There is one source of possible information which as yet we have not tried. Surely the Pope must know something about a case in which he strove so strenuously, though unsuccessfully, to intervene. Just now we left the aged Pontiff addressing the Cardinals on the subject; let us listen carefully to what he has to say.

(*The Pope*). "As we have long known and we are now more immediately reminded by the arrival of the Argentier of France, who just recently has applied to be received in our city, his rivals and adversaries have attempted to place him in the bad grace and indignation of his Majesty [the King]; and among other reasons they have particularly calumniated him because of the things which he has done for us and for the Roman Church. He has received from us a large sum of money, amounting to 100,000 ducats and more, and he has procured for us some other things contrary to the wishes of [*contra*] the said Majesty, *on account of which* [*propter quod*] *he has suffered unjustly very grave and prolonged persecutions.* Considering ourselves, then, as upholders of the truth and always obligated to uplift good men, to you, venerable and very dear brothers, the Cardinals, it seems to us right and just to furnish the proof and testimony of the truth on this matter. Thus we will discharge our conscience and establish the integrity and good faith of this said Argentier in that he has always shown himself firm, loyal, and true toward us and toward the said Church.

"We bear witness then, before God and the world that this Argentier has been and is completely innocent of the crime with which they have wrongfully accused him; further that, inasmuch as he has worked with an indefatigable zeal for the good, for the unity, and for the aggrandizement of the Holy See, in which he has spared no labor or expense, we confess that we are all of us greatly in his debt. We attest most firmly that in our judgment all charges whatever that men have brought against him in money matters are false and far removed from any righteousness or truth.

"And inasmuch as we have always found and known this Argentier to be a most faithful and devoted servitor of his Majesty the King, that never in any act, sign, word, or deed has he departed from the true and faithful obedience required of such a servitor.

"Our paternal heart greatly affected by his calamities, we are impelled to compensate him for them, but, inasmuch as in the extremity in which we are placed we cannot conveniently provide for his necessities as we would like and are under obligation to do, we freely recommend him to you all to do for him what can be done. And we charge you to favor and justify his cause before the King and all other persons whatsoever, and

to further it in every way as we are bound and obligated to do; so that others, seeing this good man, who
has accomplished so many great works for the Church,
upheld in great favor and acclaim and uplifted in the
sight of men, should be prompted and animated diligently, solicitously, and faithfully to perform those
things which they know to be for the advantage and
honor of the Roman Church and the Sovereign Pontiff.

"Given at Saint Peter's, Rome, in the Apostolic
Palace in the Chamber of the aforesaid Pontiff, the
XVI of March, MCCCCLV since the birth of Christ.

"Read by me, Peter de Hoxero, in the presence of
the Sovereign Pontiff and the cardinals the XX of
March of the said year.

"(Signed) PETER DE HOXERO, *Secretary,*
Written with my own hand at the
Command of the Pope." (205).

Now we know the cause of Charles VII's wrath
against his Argentier; now we have unfolded to us the
secret count in the indictment which galvanized all of
the other feeble charges and gave them a vitality not
their own. The unceasing efforts of the Pope to intervene in the case, the Church's tireless attempts to
assert its jurisdiction, the final decree's significant recital of pontifical intercession on the defendant's behalf, the protection, carried to such unusual lengths,
accorded by the papal state of Avignon to the fallen
merchant's factors, the fugitive's own undeviating
flight toward Rome—all are now explained.

Jacques Cœur joins the vast army of those who have

suffered for conscience's sake on either side of the great controversies and conflicting beliefs and policies which have marked the path of religion's progress. Jeanne d'Arc's trust in her voices led her to the funeral pyre; though himself far from attaining her sublimity, Jacques Cœur's devotion to his faith brought upon him ignominy and disgrace.

The Pope was the principal defendant in this celebrated trial; almost with his dying breath he proclaimed his full responsibility and sought to right the injury which his service had entailed; five days after approving the transcription of his formal act of justice the aged Pontiff was no more. How faithfully his testamentary requests were carried out, under a succeeding reign in France, more favorable to ecclesiastical purposes, we shall see.

Jacques Cœur, a subject and officer of the King of France, was punished for his relations with the Head of his Church in the days when a universal religion exacted a loyalty superior to fidelity to state. We have the word of Nicholas V, almost a death-bed statement, that these relations comprised no "act, sign, word, or deed" of the Argentier's which conflicted with his duty as a faithful and devoted servitor of his royal master. As to just what they did require of him, sufficient to arouse the royal wrath, raises an inquiry which takes us into the field of historical reasoning.

The Pope stated that Jacques Cœur "had received from him a large sum of money up to 100,000 ducats, or more," and that for this and other reasons "he had unjustly suffered very grave and infinite persecutions,"

Now after the judgment against him and apparently with a view to establishing a legal basis for the sale of all his assets, Jean Dauvet and the Count de Chabannes visited Jacques Cœur in prison and interrogated him on his ability to meet the enormous fine imposed against him. To these inquiries Jacques Cœur responded "that he did not know what to say; that it would be impossible for him to pay nearly so great a sum, in view of the fact that *he owed already one hundred to one hundred and twenty thousand écus which he had borrowed from several persons for the affairs of the King*."

Is it not surprising that in all of the comprehensive and long-continued administration of his vast estate, the numerous reclamation proceedings of creditors, no one appears to claim this vast sum which Jacques Cœur admits he borrowed? True, a certain witness testifies that he had loaned the Argentier "6,000 florins for the conquest of Guienne which he [the witness] had borrowed at a loss [interest], for which loss he had not been reimbursed by the said Cœur"; it also appears from a letter of Jacques Cœur's to the Duchess of Burgundy, that he had obtained 4,000 livres from this noble lady which she was desirous of having repaid. (206). These, however, are petty sums, compared to the huge total of the Argentier's admitted borrowings. It is unlikely that his creditor or creditors utterly abandoned their loans. Failure to pursue them in the regularly appointed manner, presupposes that there was some other remedy available to the claimant, diplomatic channels which only sovereigns could employ. The only other ruler than the Pope from whom it was at all possible that Jacques Cœur could have borrowed such a sum was the Duke of Burgundy; Jacques Cœur's letter to the Duchess shows convincingly that the patriotic generosity of this noble house had been exhausted by the draft already drawn upon its female side.

The Papacy was at this time the sole Power which had a strong motive to place Charles VII in its obligation; it was the source of aid from which relief would be most bitterly resented. The King, by his Pragmatic Sanction of 1438, had committed his kingdom to a programme of greater independence of Rome in church affairs; he had reduced to a minimum the rights of the Holy See in matters of ecclesiastical benefices and judicial procedure. French bishops and abbés were thenceforth to be elected by the chapters and the convents; the papal forum on appeal was only to be availed of after all intermediate tribunals had been exhausted. On the other hand, the King had reserved to himself "and the princes of the kingdom," the right to interfere in the clerical elections "by benign and benevolent solicitations in favor of persons of merit, zealous for the good of state and kingdom." The patriotic French bishop, Jean Jouvenal des Ursins, although of the party favoring Gallican liberty, complained bitterly of the abuse of this royal privilege. Jean Dauvet was an especially ardent exponent of the anti-Roman side; most of the French prelates and court officials sustained the same opinions. (207).

We have seen the great commotion caused by the King's emergency proposal to tax the clergy to obtain funds for the Normandy campaign; how the Pope refused his permission and how the crisis was only averted by Jacques Cœur's stepping into the breach and providing the means. Part of this money we know he borrowed. Does it not seem likely that his principal lender was the power which benefited the most by the avoidance of the issue which his action entailed?

What other theory so naturally connects the Argentier's fall with that of the Treasurer-General Saincoins, the two so closely linked in contemporary opinion as to enable Jean Chartier, as we have seen, to predict the later event as the natural sequence of the prior one?

Is it not reasonable to believe that the Pope furnished Jacques Cœur with a large part of the money which the latter loaned his sovereign for the deliverance of Normandy; that, later, the Pontiff had occasion to recall his funds, probably in preparation for the relief of Constantinople; that the unexpected emptiness of the royal coffers occasioned by such repayment brought Charles VII's anger down upon his Treasurer-General, which later was visited upon his Argentier when the King ultimately learned to whom a part of his heavy obligations was due?

CHAPTER XXX

THE CRUSADE. DEATH

CALIXTUS III, the new Pope, continued the Vatican's favor to Jacques Cœur, and actively pushed the preparations for the crusade begun by his predecessor. Constantinople's fall, although long foreshadowed, had stricken all Christendom with consternation and compelled its realization of the fact that the age-old menace of Asia once more confronted the civilization of Europe. A congress of the Christian powers had been held at Frankfort, during Jacques Cœur's imprisonment, at which war was declared against the Turks. Æneas Sylvius, the papal emissary, had pointed out to the assembly that, "if Hungary be conquered or forced to join the Ottoman Empire, neither Italy nor Germany will be safe, nor will the Rhine render the French sufficiently secure." The Mediterranean, sea of civilization, was opened to the raids of Turkish corsairs; its eastern gates were closed to the commerce of the west. (208).

Meanwhile, the Pope and princes of the Occident were deluged with appeals for aid from their co-religionists in the east. Scanderbeg, the Albanian hero, who vied with the great Hungarian captain, Jean Hunyady, in leadership against the Ottomans, entreated the Western sovereigns "to consider more advisedly the imminent ruin which was threatened to the Christian liberty and religion; that they would at the last seek to redeem it from the miserable and

wretched yoke and servitude of the infidels and Mohammedans, otherwise they should be well assured that
the plague, which, by little and little, did grow within
their bowels, would in the end pierce into their hearts."

Mahomet himself is reported to have said of the
Christian powers of this period: "I know well that
they are distracted and troubled with private seditions
and continual partialities . . . so strange and divers
are their affections and so greatly do they differ among
themselves. . . . These Christians do dissemble one
with another notably, they are all of them exceedingly
ambitious, and immoderately covetous and they do
exercise immoderate hatreds and rancors each against
other." (209).

The Pope's efforts to enlist all Christendom to inter-
pose a united front against the Turk met with but
feeble response outside of his own dominion and the
regions immediately invaded; the flaming days of the
Crusades had passed.

Charles VII, although seconding the project loyally,
pointed out that he could spare "neither troops nor
money for the said banner" inasmuch as "he was always obliged to be on his guard against his ancient
enemies of England." These "ancient enemies" themselves were embroiled in internecine warfare. The
Venetians could not forego their constitutional rivalry
with Genoa. The Duke of Burgundy and Alfonso,
King of Naples, hailed with zeal and enthusiasm the
pronouncements at Frankfort.

The Duke's fervor for the cause manifested itself in
a series of magnificent banquets; these pompous so-
lemnities over, his ardor cooled.

Alfonso promised galleys to join those of the Pope; he even announced his intention of commanding them in person. His anger having been aroused, however, by some Genoese attempts to recover Corsica, he rejected with insult the republic's invitation to go against the Turks. "It is against you," the haughty Spaniard wrote to its Doge, "who are the true Turks of Europe, that we make it our duty to turn our first efforts; we will not halt until we have forced you with the aid of Christ to render yourselves suppliants at our feet. It is then only that we will achieve, and even in spite of you, this expedition against the Turks of Asia to which we have pledged ourselves." (210).

Jacques Cœur had been in Rome over a year when Mahomet II set forth from Constantinople with a great army, to complete his conquest of the world; the Grand Sultan marched through Servia to besiege Belgrade, taking with him numerous cannon of huge caliber, to batter down the walls of this strategic Danube fortress; a large fleet of Turkish boats sailed up the river to block its navigation above and below the city. An army of 40,000 men, raised by the Franciscan, Jean Capistrano, by preaching the crusade throughout Hungary, and commanded by the justly renowned Jean Hunyady, defended the place. Belgrade, although a Servian stronghold, had been ceded to Hungary, to prevent its capture by the Turks. (211).

It was planned at Rome to send a naval expedition to strengthen the garrison of Rhodes and other Christian outposts in the East, and to co-operate with the defenders of Belgrade by making a demonstration against Constantinople.

The Cardinal Scarampo, to whom the command of the papal troops was intrusted, wrote to Capistrano, April 26, 1456: "Already our triremes have been launched, and in great number completely equipped. . . . Our flag-ship, a magnificent quadrireme, marvellously furnished with everything necessary for combat and navigation, will be ready to sail in a few days. We pray you . . . to encourage the Princes of Hungary and Germany in this necessary and righteous war, that, forsaking ancient jealousies and old rancors, they should all unite to combat the common enemy and should be ready to sustain the battle by land, while we perform our duty on the sea."

About the 1st of June, the expedition sailed. It consisted, besides its flag-ship, of sixteen galleys and a number of smaller vessels, 1,000 sailors, 5,000 soldiers, and 300 cannon.

History has justly devoted many of its pages to chronicling the glorious deeds of Hunyady and Capistrano in hurling the Turk backward from the walls of Belgrade, driving Mahomet, wounded, in full retreat toward Constantinople, after a great battle which tended to fix the western limits of Islam in Europe. But little attention has been given to the auxiliary movement by the papal naval expedition which, in a minor degree, contributed to the fortunate result. The few descriptions of its exploits are more laudatory of the glory gained than informative of the facts. (212).

We learn that the fleet cannonaded Constantinople "by day and by night," and compelled the Sultan to withdraw from his operations before Belgrade "many of his troops and thoughts." It is suggested that the

vessels entered the Danube and that Cardinal Scarampo
shared in the laurels of the victory on land. What is
more certain is that the expedition strengthened the
kingdom of Cyprus, the island of Rhodes, and the
Genoese outpost at Chios and postponed their ultimate
submergence by the Turkish wave. At Rhodes the
fleet was joined by another division sent by the papal
state of Avignon; the Genoese took a prominent part
in the enterprise which only their own historians relate. That the island of Lemnos was regained from
the Ottomans we know from the fact that an order
of chivalry was established to commemorate the event.
The oath of the Knights of Our Mother of Bethlehem
bound them to take up their abode on the island and
to oppose the Turks in the Archipelago. "But shortly
after its creation," writes a historian of this institution,
"Lemnos was taken, and this beautiful design vanished." Even the decoration of the order remains unknown. (213).

This expedition bore two valiant hearts whose names
are not recorded in the story of Scarampo's deeds, two
valiant spirits which were to leave their bodies "in
glorious Christian field." Jacques Cœur, rich, famous,
and honored, threescore years of age and "toiled with
works of war," framed a soul which could not recline
while "the ensign of the Christian cross" was being
raised. His faithful ship-captain, William Gimart, for
the last time, in obedience to that familiar voice from
which he had taken sailing-orders since his youth, directed his vessel's prow "toward Jerusalem, the burial-
place of God."

This loyal subordinate, as we have already told,

met his fate in actual combat with the enemies of his faith. Jacques Cœur, possibly stricken by illness, but more probably as the result of wounds received in battle, fell, like so many noble knights before him, one of the last victims of "that superb, chivalric, and immortal epic, the Crusades."

"At the moment of death," writes his contemporary, Thomas Basin, "he protested by solemn oath, in the presence of many persons, that he was innocent of the crime of poisoning, and of all others of which he had been accused. At the same time he asked the King to forgive and he prayed God to pardon, as he did himself, his defamers, for the false charges which they had so wickedly brought against him."

He expired the 25th of November, 1456, on the island of Chios off the coast of Asia Minor, among strangers, far from the native land he had aided in saving, and was buried in the church of the Cordeliers, where, we are told, the Genoese "paid him the highest honors, as though to one of the great ones of Genoa." (214).

In Bourges's noble cathedral a tablet was erected to his memory acknowledging Saint Stephen's many benefits at his hands, and ordaining a solemn annual service on the anniversary of his death. On this monument there was inscribed as his sole epitaph:

LORD JACQUES CŒUR, SOLDIER, CAPTAIN OF THE CHURCH AGAINST THE INFIDELS

EPILOGUE

BEFORE his death, seeing his end approach, Jacques Cœur had written a last appeal to the King upon behalf of his children. This prayer, transmitted to Charles VII, doubtless through the agency of the Church, aroused commiseration even in that monarch's selfish bosom. Within a year after the death of his former Argentier, the King restored to Ravant and Geoffrey Cœur all of the real estate of their father which had not already been disposed of. The grant included the family mansion at Bourges, other houses and lands within and near that city, several houses at Lyons, and the mines in that vicinity. To them, jointly with William de Varye, were granted the uncollected obligations and claims due from Jacques Cœur's horde of noble debtors, and all unsold personal property of his estate, subject to the payment of its debts.

The explanation of this act of royal compassion, given in the preamble of the grant, recites that inasmuch as "the late Jacques Cœur, who during his detention escaped from our prisons, has recently passed from life to death, exposing his person against the enemies of the faith, and at the end of his days has recommended his children to us and prayed that it should be our pleasure to give them something so that those who are secular might live worthily without need . . . and in view of the fact that the said Cœur was in great authority with us and rich and abounding in this world's goods and ennobled in his posterity and line,

and, for this reason, they [his children] have commenced to live in a fashion befitting their station,
which they will not be able to keep up unless our grace
and liberality should be extended to them; it pleases
us to have pity on them. . . ."

The grantees were required to settle with the two
churchmen, Jean and Henri Cœur, and with "Perrette
Cœur, their sister, wife of Jacques Trousseau."

Four years later, Charles, the Well-Served, fell a victim to suspicions of the same nature as those which
he had entertained against Jacques Cœur; imprisoning
his chief physician in the Tower of Bourges and re-
fusing all nourishment for fear of poisoning by his own
son, he died of starvation in the castle in which he had
been proclaimed King of France. His reign, during
which a great war of national liberation was successfully concluded and many acts of constructive statesmanship were performed, is, perhaps, chiefly now remembered for its signal ingratitude to Jeanne d'Arc
and Jacques Cœur.

Louis XI's rule witnessed still further acts of justice
to the memory of the great French merchant and of
restitution to his heirs. The Archbishop of Bourges
and his brothers spared no pains or expense to right
their father's unjust condemnation. Fortified by the
favorable opinions of seven of the kingdom's leading
lawyers, they commenced, as we have seen, an appeal
to the Court of Parliament based upon the prisoner's
own objections to the tribunal by which he was tried.

On the appeal itself, argued almost entirely upon
intricate legal questions apart from the actual merits
of the case, no decision seems ever to have been handed

ing in the restored family property, seems thereafter
to have dropped from the records of his times. We
know he had accompanied his father on his flight to
Rome; it is possible that he may have preferred to
establish himself where the fugitives had been so hospitably received.

One of the first acts of Louis's reign was to restore
the Vatican's influence in his kingdom. We, who have
listened to the solemn testamentary requests of Nicholas V, need not be surprised at the magical return to
favor, under the new King, of the deceased Argentier's
relatives and friends.

William de Varye, like Jacques Cœur's two eldest
sons, takes his seat at the royal council board. Pierre
Jobert, whom, we remember, his master could not trust
in matters of figures, becomes Receiver-General of
Finances in Normandy.

The disgraced Saincoins is rehabilitated as Master
Extraordinary of the Chamber of Accounts; his fellow
sufferer, the Lord de Precigny, is named for high office
in the same department. (215).

Geoffrey Cœur was selected by the new monarch for
a special act of royal grace. The King restored to him
the baronial estate of St. Fargeau, taken by confiscation from Chabannes. Geoffrey's tenure of this property
was to be a troubled one, as we shall see.

Jean de Village, whom we left at Rome, did not sail
with his uncle and William Gimart in the naval expedition of Calixtus III; he was recalled to Marseilles
by the straits in which he found his family as the result of Charles VII's vindictive acts. His subsequent
career in that ancient seaport was particularly bril-

A STONE CARVING OF JACQUES CŒUR'S SERVANT AWAITING HIS
MASTER'S RETURN FROM HIS LONG VOYAGES.

liant. As King René's admiral he took part in the perennial attempts of the house of Anjou to regain the throne of Naples and, loaded with local honors, some of which became national on the annexation of Provence to France, he founded a noble house which still occupies its ancestral château de la Salle, acquired by his wife Perrette in 1454. His loyalty to his patron, as well as his own valiant spirit, were reflected in his armorial bearings, which featured a heart (*cœur*) with the Latin motto, *nec quisquam arripiet* (let no man seize). (216).

As for the villains in our story, the redoubtable Chabannes underwent an ordeal similar to that which he had taken such a leading part in inflicting on Jacques Cœur. Arrested and prosecuted on pretended charges, at the end of a trial during which he was confined for two years, he was sentenced to banishment and the loss of all his possessions. As had been the case with the Argentier, his sentence was arbitrarily converted into imprisonment and he was detained in the Bastille. Several years thereafter, making his escape during the confusion of a civil war, the indomitable old soldier enlisted under the banners of the rebellious nobles in arms against the King. Marching in the direction of St. Fargeau, he repossessed himself of this estate and of its new owner as well. One of the clauses of the treaty of peace which ended the hostilities of this "War for the Public Good," confirmed the Count in "all his honors, castles, territories, etc., as he and his wife . . . enjoyed them in the time of the late King." Geoffrey Cœur commenced a lawsuit for the recovery of the property from which his family had thus for a second time been ousted, which, after lasting thirty years, was compromised by the litigants' heirs. This settlement left the Chabannes family in full title and possession, subject to relatively small money payments to Geoffrey's descendants. (217).

Otto Castellane, the new Argentier, and William Gouffier, in their turn, succumbed to the intrigues of the court. Arrested on the bridge of Lyons, they were accused of carrying about with them "certain images through which, by diabolical arts, they sought to have the management of the King." Their trial dragged on for several years, during which they, like the victim of their plots, were transferred from prison to prison, following the movements of their judges.

After two years of such confinements, Gouffier was condemned to suffer banishment and the loss of all his goods; his sentence was, however, commuted to deprivation of honors and employs and exile from the court.

As for the wily Italian, his ultimate fate remains "unheard of and unknown, because he has had the misfortune to be transported from prison to prison," Jean Chartier records.

Michael Teinturier, after Jacques Cœur's fall, occupied himself with petitions to the King upon behalf of the city of Montpellier, seeking remission of its taxes and mourning its lost commercial greatness. "The said city," runs one of these memorials, "is so desolated that it is a pity to see, furthermore, a great part of the houses are closed and uninhabited; the artisans who occupied them have, some of them, gone to other lands, others have died, and foreign merchants no longer frequent it as in times past . . . the said city had formerly been well and numerously peopled and *had contained several great and noble merchants.*" (218).

Part of the desolation of this beautiful university town was due to pestilence and other causes; but the one whose magic touch had summoned to its aid the good genii of commercial prosperity slept at Chios across the seas.

The "Moon of Mahomet," which, until recently, had shone for nearly five hundred years on his tomb in that far-off Grecian isle, now is set:

"While, blazoned as on heaven's immortal noon,
    The Cross leads generations on."

NOTES

NOTES

1. The battle of Nicopolis was fought in 1396. The approximate date of Jacques Cœur's birth is deduced from that of his eldest son, Jean Cœur, whom a papal bull authentically shows to have been born in the autumn of 1423. (See Appendix II, No. 1.)

Jacques Cœur's birthplace is fixed at Bourges by the declaration of his sons in a reclamation proceeding to recover their mother's property after her death.

The facts regarding Pierre Cœur's origin and occupation are based upon local tradition adopted by early historians.

See Pierre Clément, *Jacques Cœur et Charles VII*, Paris, 1866, pp. 6–7.

2. See Note 5.

3. Nicholas Cœur's property became the subject of reclamation proceedings brought by Jacques Cœur's children after their uncle's death.

Bochetel afterward became Receiver-General of the Finances of the Queen.

Valet de Viriville, *Histoire de Charles VII*, Paris, 1865, III, p. 284, note.

Michel, *Les Ecossais en France*, I, p. 194, note.

4. Mathieu de Coucy describes Jacques as being "of small lineage"; Thomas Basin refers to him as "of a plebeian family." Although Basin was a churchman rather than a courtier, court events naturally absorbed most of the attention of all early chroniclers.

5. These houses are on the Rue des Armuriers, Bourges. Following the excellent authority of Maître Pierre Dubois, of that city, who has given the matter much study, the house which is pointed out to visitors as being the one in which Jacques Cœur was born, in reality belonged to his father-in-law, Leodépart. His own paternal home was opposite.

Pierre Dubois, *Le Procès de Jacques Cœur*, Bourges, 1913.

The Gentleman's Magazine, London, July, 1796, vol. 66, part II, p. 545, contains a description of "Dick" Whittington's London house with an engraving.

6. A. L. Masson, *Jean Gerson*, Lyons, 1894, p. 70.

7. *Ibid.*, p. 34.

8. See examples in the text of Jacques Cœur's own letters and those of Campo Fregoso to him in Latin in the Appendix.

9. Jean Chaumeau, *Histoire du Berry*, 1566. VI, chap. IX.

10. Masson, *Jean Gerson*, p. 34.

11. Burgundy remained neutral by secret agreement with Henry V. Hallam's *Middle Ages*, I, p. 74.

12. Cited in M. Geruzez' *Histoire de la Littérature*, etc., p. 107; also in Clément, p. 204.

13. Jean Chaumeau, *supra*.

14. The approximate date of the marriage is deduced from the date of the birth of their eldest child, Jean. The bull of Pope Eugenius IV, dated August 26, 1446, printed for the first time in our Appendix (in syllabus form), appointing Jean Cœur to fulfil the duties of the Archbishopric of Bourges, recites that he was then in his twenty-third year and suspends his consecration until he reach the age of twenty-seven. He was consecrated September 5, 1450, so that he was born some time between August 26 and September 5, 1423.

15. The most brilliant court in Europe at this time was undoubtedly that of the Duke of Burgundy. See *Memoirs of Philippe de Commines*, London, 1911 (Bohn Library), I, p. 341.

16. Valet de Viriville, I, pp. 174–184. For Louis XI's different version of the Bridge of Montereau affair, see Commines, I, pp. 273–274.

Barbezin antedated Bayard as the knight *sans reproche*.

17. Valet de Viriville, I, p. 184, citing *Mémoires de Burgogne* by du Tillet.

18. Valet de Viriville, I, pp. 359–360.

19. We are loath to call the Maid of Orleans either Joan of Arc or its French equivalent, *Jeanne d'Arc*. Every original document relating to the heroine, the letters of her ennoblement, the records of her trials, etc., give her name as Darc, without apostrophe. She was the daughter of *Jacques Darc, laboreur*, and in her life-time never employed the title or armorial bearings granted her by the King. Nevertheless, we yield to modern French usage in employing the apostrophe.

20. Gilles Bouvier, called Berry, *Chroniques sur les Règnes de Charles VI et Charles VII*, I, p. 54.

21. Valet de Viriville, II, p. 84.

22. The children are named in this order in Charles VII's decree restoring their patrimony. Clément, Pièce No. 12.

23. "J'ai quitté la Normandie où j'étais riche, quand les Anglais ont envahi le pays, et j'ai opté pour la France." Recited in Ledanois' Letters of Pardon for the affair of the Bourges Mint.

24. Gutenberg first printed the Bible in 1455.
Paper money came in with John Law of "Mississippi Bubble" fame.

25. Dante's *Paradise*, Canto XIX, l. 120.

26. Clément, p. 72.

27. Recitals in Ledanois' Pardon, dated Dec. 29, 1429, appearing in the *Procès Criminal de Jacques Cœur*. This latter is a partial record of the case, practically identical copies of which, made in the eighteenth century, are to be found in the Bibliothèque Nationale at Paris, the Bibliothèque Municipale of Bourges, and elsewhere. Hereinafter it will be referred to as the *Procès*.

28. Macaulay's Essays, *Machiavelli*.

29. The écu of Charles VII was a gold coin of the value of about 1.4 livres. The livre was a fictitious money unit used only in accounts. Its equivalent, the franc, then had a metal value about eight times that of the present gold franc.
Thus, 4 écus was worth about 5.6 livres (or francs), equivalent intrinsically to about 45 modern gold francs, or 9 dollars. However, the purchasing power of money was then much greater—five times as great as it was in 1865, according to Pierre Clément. Present-day derangement in prices and currencies makes it almost impossible to calculate the proper multiplier to use to place the money of the fifteenth century on a level with that of 1927.

30. Valet de Viriville, II, p. 104.

31. Albert Bigelow Paine, *Joan of Arc*, I, pp. 130–131.

32. *Ibid.*, II, p. 7.

33. *Travels of Bertrandon de la Brocquière*, put into modern French by M. Le Grand d'Aussy, translated into English by Thomas Johnes, Hafod Press, London, 1807.

34. "Ottobon Escot"; undoubtedly a corruption of the

French for "Otterburn the Scot," one of the numerous Scots then abroad.

35. Tarentum, or Tarento, a principality of the kingdom of Naples; its Prince was a member of the Orsini family. The Neapolitan throne, then occupied by Joanna II, was, on her death, shortly afterward, gained by Alfonso of Aragon, after a contest at arms with René, Count of Anjou and Provence. The injustice of the Sultan's proceeding is manifest.

36. *Travels of Bertrandon de la Brocquière*, p. 96, note by d'Aussy.

37. A gold ducat was of about the same value as an écu. (See note 29.)

38. L. Guiraud, *Recherches et conclusions nouvelles sur le prétendu rôle de Jacques Cœur*, Paris, 1900.

39. Masson, *Jean Gerson*, p. 69.

40. *Ibid.*, p. 53.

41. We have obtained much valuable information regarding fairs, highways, and riverways from Albert Malet's *Moyen Age;* on caravan traffic from the Guiraud work, cited above.

42. Sir Richard Venable. His deeds of banditry are described by Basin, Monstrelet, and Chartier, contemporary chroniclers.

43. Clément, p. 91.

44. *Ibid.*, 94.

45. The Trinitarians were instituted by Jean de Matha in 1197; they are often called Mathurins after their founder. The Order of Our Lady of Mercy was founded in Spain in 1258 by Pierro Nolasco. See E. L. Cutts, *Scenes and Characters of the Middle Ages*, London, 1922.

46. Guiraud, p. 44.

47. Samuel Lyson's *The Model Merchant of the Middle Ages* (*Whittington*), London, 1860, p. 40, citing Rotuli Normanniæ, 5 Henry V, 1417, naming twenty-five different *kinds* of Dutch vessels employed for this purpose, in addition to the English ships.

48. The Venetians had transported Saint Louis's crusading army of 10,000 men and 4,000 horses, with only fifteen vessels. Jules Lecomte, *Venise, etc.*, p. 458, cited by Clément, pp. 19–20, note. Guiraud, p. 35.

49. John Fiske, *Discovery of America*, I, p. 312.
50. Guiraud, p. 33.
51. Guiraud, p. 36.
52. Guiraud, p. 43.
53. Depping, *Histoire de Commerce entre le Levant et Europe*, etc., II, pp. 243–277, cited by Clément, p. 36.
54. Hallam, III, p. 339, note.
55. Short sales in Genoa. Depping, I, p. 213, cited by Clément, p. 26.
56. Valet de Viriville, I, p. 405.
57. Lyson, pp. 63–86.
58. Banishment of the Jews; namely, by Edward I in England, by Charles VI in France.
59. "In 1345 the Bardi at Florence, the greatest company in Italy, became bankrupt, Edward III owing them, in principal and interest, 900,000 gold florins. Another, the Peruzzi, failed at the same time, being creditors to Edward for 600,000 florins." The latter firm is more often called the Peruggi. Hallam, III, p. 340, citing Villani.
60. One of its oldest streets is named Jean Vidal, probably after the owner of the ill-starred "galley of Narbonne."
61. Capmany, I, p. 213, cited by Hallam, III, p. 340.
62. Hallam, III, p. 340; Clément, p. 21; Guiraud, p. 21.
63. Barcelona interest rate. Capmany, I, p. 209, cited by Hallam, III, 337, note.
64. Lavisse, *Histoire de France*, 4, II, p. 153.
65. At least two of the letters of Pliny the Younger discuss loans at interest—letter to Calvisius Rufus and one to Priscus.
66. Opinion of Gerson and Pierre d'Ailly to Pope Martin V on usury, Lavisse, 4, II, p. 154.
67. Clément, pp. 261–262.
68. Cited by Malet, pp. 215–216.
69. Mlle. Guiraud, in her work, herein so frequently cited, has shown that Yzarn Teinturier, of Montpellier, owned a ship in 1410, and has given a few scattering examples of other citizens of that place, having participations in cargoes. However, without organization, without foreign depots, adequate consular representation, and other facilities, it is very doubtful if these early French merchants, in their trade with the

Levant, did more than to act through their Italian and Catalan associates.

70. Cited by Malet, p. 214. Equal to about $1,000,000, present metal value; its twelfth-century purchasing power is probably incalculable.

70a. Fiske, I, pp. 262–263; 323.

71. Macaulay's Essays, *Lord Clive*.

72. Doge Mocenigo's speech. Reported by the Italian historian Sanuto, *Script. Rer. Ital.*, XXII, p. 958; also Daru, *Hist. de Venise*, II, p. 205. Cited by Hallam, III, p. 464, and by Clément, pp. 22, 23.

73. Rudolphe of Saxe, *De terra sancta et itinere Jheroso-limitano*, cited by Clément, p. 16.

74. Jacques Cœur's silk factory in Florence. Valet de Viriville, III, p. 291, note.

75. Clément, p. 25, citing Pardessus, *Tableau du Commerce antérieurement à la découverte d'Amérique*, part 2, p. cx, and Depping, I, p. 237.

76. Sale of public offices. See Samuel Pepys's arrangement with Thomas Barlow regarding the Clerkship of the Acts, *Diary*, July 17, 1660.

77. Commerce of Montpellier. We are indebted to Depping, Pardessus, and, above all, to Mlle. Guiraud's work for these particulars.

It is not improbable that Jacques Cœur's first commercial operations may have been directed from the ancient papal city of Avignon on the Rhone, which was a considerable commercial centre during the fifteenth century, and one with which his business relations were always close.

78. Clément, p. 146; Dubois, *loc. cit.*

79. See Letter of Charles VII to the Barcelona authorities in our Appendix (No. III).

80. Pasquier's version of this incident is not accurate. Jacques Cœur's factors and ship-captains did, however, as we shall find, account to him for the business and property remaining in their hands after the confiscation of his estate.

81. These were actual transactions taken from the lists of debtors and their obligations, set forth in an incomplete inventory of the papers of Jacques Cœur's estate and in Letters of Charles VII, dated August 5, 1457, effecting a partial restoration of Jacques Cœur's property to his sons and

William de Varye, being respectively Pièces Nos. 2 and 12, annexed to Pierre Clément's work cited above.

82. Valet de Viriville, III, p. 266, note.

83. Duhamel, *Un episode du procès de J. Cœur à Avignon.*

84. On jealousies in royal families, see Commines, II, pp. 254–255. "The dauphin was about three years old when he died, yet a very handsome and precocious child . . . for which reason his father (Charles VIII) was the sooner recovered from his sorrow, as being fearful lest he should have grown too fast, and lest, if his courage increased with his years, he would have entrenched upon his father's power and authority. . . . By this example we may see to what miseries great kings and princes, who grow jealous of their own children, are subject."

85. Marriage contract between Jean de Village and Perrette Cœur, in the notarial archives of Marseilles, 1447, reported through the kindness of M. Billioud of the Municipal Library of that city.

86. Letters of Grace in favor of Jean de Village. Pièce No. 9 in the collection of exhibits annexed to Clément's work above cited. Taken from the *Procès de Jacques Cœur, supra.*

87. *Viaggio de L. N. Frescobaldi in Egito é in Terra Santa,* Rome, 1818, cited by Depping and by Clément, pp. 14–15, from which latter work these facts are taken.

88. The Sultan's Letter, printed in Depping, II, p. 304. Originally taken from the *Mémoires de Mathieu de Coucy,* 1447.

Saint Catherine's shrine was on Mount Sinai, to which the pilgrimage was then made from Gaza by camels over the desert, then infested by fierce Arabs, la Brocquière tells us.

89. Jean Dauvet's *Journal,* p. 186, cited by Guiraud, p. 76. (Clément refers to this *Journal* as *Le Compte de la vente des biens de Jacques Cœur.*)

90. Guiraud, p. 76.

91. Letters of Remission in favor of Gimart's widow. Arch. Nat., sér. J. J., reg. 191, fo. 130, no. 242.

92. Frescobaldi, above cited, who visited Cairo in 1384, says that among the numerous Christians who inhabited the the city were Greeks, Nubians, Georgians, Ethiopians, and Armenians, but few Latins.

93. Slavery in Montpellier. Guiraud, p. 38; Lavisse, 4, II, p. 163.

94. Arab civilization. Malet, p. 63 *et seq.;* Fiske, I, p. 271. I have found the former work particularly helpful.

95. Repatriation of the Rhodian captives. February 8, 1446, the Grand Master of the Order enjoined his receivers in Provence to pay Jacques Cœur the expenses of the voyage of the peace embassy and for the transport of the Christian slaves back from Alexandria. Vertol, *Histoire de l'Ordre de Malta,* VI, cited by Clément, p. 118.

96. Witness Jacques Cœur's great desire to consult with the Bishop of Agde on the accounts of the merchant's estate, pp. 236–237 in the text.

Henri Cœur succeeded to the Bishop's former ecclesiastical charges at Narbonne and Lodève. See Appendix, bull of Nicholas V, dated August 1, 1448.

97. See in the Appendix syllabi of authenticated copies of these bulls obtained for this work from the private archives of the Vatican. The complete copies have been presented by the author to the Bibliothèque Municipale of Bourges.

99. Thus Rymer's *Fœdera* informs us that in 1428, 916 licenses were issued in England to make the pilgrimage to the shrine of Saint James at Campostella in Spain; 2,400 in 1434. On the continent the movement assumed much larger proportions.

100. Shakespeare's *Henry IV*, Part I, Act 1, Scene 1.

101. L. Guiraud, p. 81, cited and followed in Lavisse, *Hist. de France,* 4, II, p. 149.

102. Creditors of a state were at this time usually secured by being allowed to farm or administer its customs, a practice which still prevails. In 1329 the Bardi farmed all the customs in England for £20 a day. Hallam, III, p. 340, note.

In Jacques Cœur's trial there was no censure of his dealings as purveyor to the Court. True, Jean Jouvenal des Ursins, in a private letter to his brother, the Lord Chancellor, criticised Jacques Cœur's prices and the quality of his merchandise. The eminent prelate objected to the size of his profits, but not to the official channel through which they were partly gained.

103. Adapted from a list of Montpellier merchandise com-

piled from the notarial records of that city by Mlle. Guiraud, p. 42.

104. Pope Nicholas V approved the lease to Jacques Cœur and others of the mineral rights to certain monastic lands. See bull of that Pontiff in the Appendix, dated August 1, 1448.

105. Voltaire, *Letters on the English*.

106. "He had met with provocations both from the Regent and the Duke of Gloucester who . . . had endeavoured, by means of an invalid marriage . . . to obtain provinces in Hainault and Holland which Burgundy designed for himself." Hallam, I, p. 81.

107. Valet de Viriville, II, p. 322.

108. *Ibid.*, III, p. 289; Clément, p. 75.

108*a*. Jacques Cœur's letter regarding the counterfeiters. Reproduced from Clément, p. 173.

109. Jacques Cœur's armorial bearings are an example of what are called *allusive* or *canting* arms; thus the Pyne family bear three pineapples, etc. Allen, *Peeps at Heraldry*, London, 1912, pp. 6–7.

110. I have borrowed these extracts from Jacques Cœur's *Procès* from the above-cited address on the subject, by the distinguished Bourges lawyer, Maître Pierre Dubois.

As for *vair*, it was the skin of the wild boar. "These skins," says Mackenzie, "were used by ancient governors to line their pompous robes." . . . Cinderella's glass slipper, in the fairy-tale, was really a slipper of this kind of fur, the words *vaire* (old form) and *verre* having been originally confused in the English translation of this old French tale. Allen, p. 15.

111. Cannon at siege of Orleans. See illustration.

112. Valet de Viriville, II, pp. 451–452 and notes.

113. Digby MS., cited by Valet de Viriville, II, p. 454.

114. That he enjoyed this honor in 1442 is proven by Mlle. Guiraud, p. 18 of her work, herein so frequently cited.

115. England's economic relation to Flanders was then somewhat the same as that which Australia now bears to the mother country.

An interesting picture of the inducements held out to the Flemish weavers for their settlement in England appears in Fuller's *Church History*, quoted in Blomefield's *History of Norfolk* and cited by Hallam, III, p. 321, note. "Here they should feed on fat beef and mutton, till nothing but their fulness should stint their stomachs; their beds should be good and their bed-fellows better, seeing that the richest yeomen in England would not disdain to marry their daughters unto them. . . ."

116. Rouen and London. All of the indications point to the fact that the former was then the more populous city. As Cutts says in his recent work on the Middle Ages (p. 535) cited above: "The period of great commercial prosperity occurred in these (the continental) countries in the Middle Ages and their mediæval towns were in consequence much larger and handsomer than ours." Hume, in his *History of the House of Stuart*, estimates London's population at 150,000 as late as 1604. Rouen's population in the fifteenth century is estimated from contemporary sources by Clément, p. 123, at 250,000. London's population at this epoch was probably only a third of this figure. See Hallam, III, pp. 25 *et seq.*

117. La Brocquière describes the military equipment and tactics of the Turks very minutely. Thus, at page 292 of the Johnes translation above referred to, he says of the Turkish cavalry: "In their ordinary marches they only walk, but in these [surprise attacks] they always gallop; and, as they are besides lightly armed, they will thus advance further from evening to daybreak than in three other days—and this is the reason why they cannot wear such complete armor as the French and Italians."

And witness the oration of Æneas Sylvius before the diet of Frankfort in 1454 in contrasting the European and Turkish soldiery: "Vos nati ad arma, illi tracti. Vos armati, illi inermes; vos gladios versatis, illi cultris utuntur; vos balistas tenditis, illi arcus trahunt; vos loricæ thoracesque protegunt, illos culcitra tegit. . . ." Cited by Hallam, II, p. 135, note. And see Malet, p. 355.

118. The Cardinal Cæsarini seems to have been given to breaking treaties. In 1431, under warrant of a papal bull, he had commanded an army of 40,000 cavalry in an ill-fated expedition against the Hussites, with whom, as heretics, the existing truce had been annulled.

119. L. S. Costello, *Jacques Cœur*, London, 1847, pp. 203–204. The unanimity of Jacques Cœur's selection is not

mentioned elsewhere. See Clément, p. 117, citing *Histoire de l'Ordre de Malte* by Vertot, VI.

120. Eugenius IV's embitterment. His last words were stated to have been: "O Gabriello [for this was his name], how much better it would have been for the health of thy soul if thou hadst never been Pope nor Cardinal but hadst died a friar! . . ." *Vespasiano Memoirs*, London, 1926.

121. Amadeo Dambreville, *Histoire des Ordres de Chevalerie*, Paris, 1807, pp. 183 *et seq.*

Faire ripailles. All authors who have touched on the Duke's abdication seem to have been unable to refrain from this cynical jest.

122. Macaulay's Essay on Ranke's *History of the Popes.*

123. Schism. I have followed for the most part Clément and Valet de Viriville. The quotation last given is from the Latin of certain depositions in Jacques Cœur's favor, sent, at the time of his trial, to the court of France from that of Rome. Bibliothèque Nationale, MS., Fonds Saint Germain, No. 572; *Procès de Jacques Cœur*, cited by Clément, p. 141.

124. The terms of settlement are borrowed freely from Clément, p. 142, who in turn has depended on Daniel's *Histoire de France*, VII.

125. Letters of citizenship were granted to Jacques Cœur by the city of Marseilles, February 25, 1446. These gave him exemption from all taxes for a period of ten years, conditionally upon his erecting within two years, and maintaining, a home in the city. Original letters published in the *Bulletin du Comité des travaux historiques*, 1883, p. 286.

126. Although Fregoso was not a nobleman, the Dorias, who were attached to his party, were of aristocratic rank. "The Dorias are of the same party with the Campo Fregosos but cannot be Doges themselves because they are nobles; for no noble is capable of being Doge by their laws." Commines, II, p. 267.

127. It is interesting to find Charles VIII, Charles VII's grandson, following the same *ignis fatuus* in 1496, listening to Baptista Campo Fregoso, a descendant of Janus. See Commines, II, p. 268. Louis XII and François I yielded also to the lure of Italy. It remained for Napoleon to achieve French military glory in the peninsula.

128. These letters appear in the Appendix and have been obtained from the archives of Genoa especially for this work.

129. We have been greatly aided in framing the historical background of these negotiations regarding Genoa by G. Du Fresne de Beaucourt's admirable article, "Un chapitre d'histoire diplomatique au XV⁰ siècle," in *Revue des Questions Historiques*, 22ᵉ année, XLII, pp. 321–352.

130. Campo Fregoso's last two letters to the Argentier were dated respectively August 10 and September 25, 1448. Nicholas V wrote from Rome, August 8, in that year, describing the arrival of Jacques Cœur's embassy (see p. 147, *supra*).

131. Thus Jacques Cœur had built a chamber of commerce at Montpellier and guaranteed the expenses pending their reimbursement from local taxes ultimately appropriated to this purpose by the King. The squabble between its citizens and the Crown as confiscator of Jacques Cœur's estate was a protracted one.

132. *Diary of James Gallatin*, Heinemann, London, 1916.

133. Miss Costello in her work above cited, p. 125.

134. Michelet, *Hist. de la France*. The gifted author strains the facts somewhat to make his points. Jacques Cœur was not a parvenu; his ability in trade was only one of his many facets. The equestrian statue of the Argentier, mounted in the niche in the courtyard above the porte-cochère, was à-mule-back with the animal's shoes reversed. Even this allegory has remained a mystery. In the corresponding niche in the front of the house was a mounted statue of Charles VII. Both statues were destroyed at the time of the Revolution.

135. Valet de Viriville, III, pp. 277–278.

136. Testimony of Guillaume Trepant, *Procès;* reproduced as Pièce No. 1, "K," by Clément, p. 376.

137. Bourges is now (1927) building a new Palais de Justice, and it is hoped that this will free Jacques Cœur's house, so that it may become a complete museum of the sumptuous dwelling of the fifteenth century.

138. Crozet. *Les antiquitez chroniques et singularitez de Paris*, p. 143, cited by Clément, p. 164.

139. See Lavisse, 4, II, pp. 152 *et seq.*

140. Thus Nicholas Rolin, the Duke of Burgundy's chancellor, acquired more than forty seigneuries. *Ibid.*

141. Valet de Viriville, III, pp. 58 *et seq.*; Malet, p. 326.

142. Lavisse, p. 100.

143. See letter dated September 25, 1447, in the Appendix: *Quod autem de immunitate loricarum vestrarum*, etc.

144. Louis Giribault, see Lavisse, *loc. cit.*
The Turks of this epoch employed cannon of relatively enormous caliber. See Lavallée, *Hist. de la Turquie*, p. 246.
Jacques Cœur and Brézé seem always to have been of the Angevin court faction.

145. Gilles Bouvier (Berry), *Chronique de règne de Charles VII*, cited by Clément, p. 171.

146. Martial d'Auvergne, *Les vigiles de Charles VII*, cited by Clément, 171–172, note.

147. Valet de Viriville, III, p. 381.

148. See Basin, *ante*, p. 84 hereof. He gives the loan made in the field at only 100,000 écus, but Jean Chartier, who was also present, says that Jacques Cœur made many loans on this occasion. "This Jacques Cœur," writes he, "as it is said, has been the cause of the King's conquest of the Duchy of Normandy by reason of the great sums which he had loaned and advanced, and he had made to the said King *many loans*."

149. Valet de Viriville, III, pp. 192, note; 203, note.

150. The annual revenues, Commines tells us (I, p. 387), were 1,800,000 livres in the last year of Charles VII's reign. Lavisse, 4, II, p. 255, states that Normandy and Guienne produced 500,000 livres of this amount, leaving 1,300,000 livres as the receipts of the kingdom as it existed at the time of Jacques Cœur's loans. The minimum estimate of his advances, 200,000 écus, amounted to 280,000 livres—more than one-fifth the revenues.
In vol. II, p. 128, Commines speaks with awe of the several great loans of the Médicis to Edward IV of England, amounting in all to 120,000 écus.

151. Jacques Cœur's borrowings. *Procès*, cited by Clément, p. 282. His receipt for 60,000 francs is described in Valet de Viriville, III, pp. 264–265; another receipt for 40,000 écus, or approximately 55,000 francs, is found in the Bibliothèque Nationale, Paris, 20; 616; fol. 5. This latter docu-

ment shows that Thomas Gower, the captain of the English garrison, only evacuated Cherbourg on being paid by Jacques Cœur to do so.

152. These particulars regarding Jean Cœur are, for the most part, derived from the aforesaid bull of Pope Eugenius IV, dated August 27, 1446, appointing the merchant's son to the Archbishopric of Bourges. A syllabus of the bull appears in the Appendix.

153. Present of wine from the Duke of Orleans. A. Champollion, *Louis et Charles*, p. 366, cited by Valet de Viriville, III, p. 266.

Order of the Hedgehog—Dambreville, *supra*, p. 167.

154. See papal bulls appointing Henri Cœur to Church offices. Syllabi of these bulls appear in the Appendix.

155. Marriage Contract. Pièce No. 4 annexed to Clément's work.

156. Michel, *Les Ecossais en France*, I, p. 207, and authorities there cited, particularly *Chroniques de Coucy*, chap. XXVIII, 1448.

Also on Lalain, see Note "E" in Scott's *Count Robert of Paris*, and Lavisse, 4, II, pp. 171–172.

James II of Scotland was no friend of the Douglas, as this King's murder of his formidable subject afterward (1452) proved.

157. Georges Chastellaine, *Chroniques du bon chevalier, Messire Jacques de Lalain*. Cited by Guiraud, pp. 63–65. The chronicler has been supposed by Guiraud to have been in error in referring to Jacques Cœur's errand to attend the installation of his son in the Archbishopric of Maguelonne. We now know that he was substantially correct; the Argentier was on his way to the neighboring city of Narbonne, where Henri Cœur had been appointed Canon. See bull of Nicholas V, dated August 1, 1448, in the Appendix.

158. Valet de Viriville, III, p. 110.

159. Louis and Chabannes. *Chronique martienne*, H. Baude in Chartier, III, p. 129; *Les Ecossais en France*, I, p. 195; address of Maître Dubois above cited.

160. de Lettenhove, *Hist. de Flandre*, 1854, IV, p. 11.

161. Lavisse, 4, II, p. 291.

162. Thus in the inventory of Jacques Cœur's papers, above referred to, was found a receipt of Saincoins's for cer-

tain money claimed to have been given him by the King, with a note, apparently in Jacques Cœur's writing, to the effect that the grant, not being found in the rolls, the sum must be debited against Saincoins.

163. Mass for the Argentier. Cited by Valet de Viriville, III, p. 269, note. The Normandy campaign was then over: that of Guienne did not begin until the following spring.

Wax images, Valet de Viriville, III, p. 291; also cited by Michelet, *Hist. de la France*, chapter on Jacques Cœur, note 9. Taken from letters of remission granted to Maître Pierre Mignon in 1459 for making false seals and magical charms and practising sorcery.

164. Epitaph attributed to François I; translation by Miss Costello in her work on Jacques Cœur, above cited.

165. Agnes Sorel's body was exhumed in 1777 by virtue of an order of Louis XVI; this act was repeated several times thereafter.

166. Clément, p. 252, citing Nicolle Gilles and Monstrelet.

167. Agnes' pilgrimage to Saint Geneviève. See Valet de Viriville, III, p. 140.

Her solicitude for the lowly. See her letters cited by Clément, pp. 241 *et seq.*

168. February 9, 1449, old style; same day, 1450, new style.

169. Lavisse, 4, II, p. 229.

170. Commines, I, p. 231. We have changed the parenthetical clause slightly, to accord with what we conceive to be its correct translation.

171. We are greatly impressed by the tenor of all of the instruments to which Jacques Cœur set his hand and those received by him or his factors in their business affairs. For clarity and particularity of statement, they are models of their kind.

172. The poison charge was undoubtedly the principal one, but other charges seem to have been joined to it from the first. Otherwise there would be no meaning in the King's declaration, made at the time of Jacques Cœur's arraignment, that if the poison charge should be disproved, the others would be dropped. In their memorandum to their counsel on appeal (hereinafter called the "Consultation"), Jacques Cœur's children state hypothetically that the poison

charge was the sole one on which their father was held. This was repeated as a fact in Louis XI's order permitting the appeal. However, it appears clear that the former statement, which influenced the later one, was intended only as a conclusion of law. Poisoning was the sole charge in the sense that, by the King's ruling, the others would stand or fall with it.

173. These facts are taken from the recitals of the judgment decree of May 29, 1453.

174. The application of the 100,000 écus held in trust is from the Consultation: "It will be clearly proven that the late King gave a pardon to their [the appellants'] said father of all the crimes of which he was charged, reserving the said count as to the poisoning. But, notwithstanding this, hardly was the said property seized and placed in the hands of the late King, when he incontinently took 100,000 francs for the conduct of his wars and gave all the rest to the Count de Dammertin and others." The Consultation forms Pièce No. 10 annexed to Clément's work.

175. That Dauvet and Barbin were judges see the Opinion of Counsel on Appeal (hereinafter called the "Opinion"), given in reply to the Consultation. "That there was manifest error in the said trial . . . in that the Procurer and Advocate of the King, who were required to be parties *promoventes ex officio*, were judges and commissioners in the said trial and gave their vote against the said Cœur, *praesertim* in view of the fact that there was involved in the issue, the confiscations [in favor] of the said commissioners."

176. This enterprise was to sell spices in that country. The contract and its date are cited by Valet de Viriville, III, p. 226, note.

177. See Jacques Cœur's protest against the refusal to allow him counsel, p. 235 hereof. That he was not allowed to summon witnesses on his behalf appears from the Opinion: "*et tamen fuit sibi denegata facultas probandi per testes.*"

178. *Procès* (see note 181); Dauvet's Journal (see note 89); the Consultation, Opinion, and Louis XI's decree are annexed to Clément's work. Valuable extracts from the appeal record appear in Maître Dubois's printed address, above cited. We have also borrowed from him the order in which the different charges are discussed.

179. Charles VII's relations with Egypt. See Valet de Viriville, III, p. 219, note.

180. See note 117, *supra;* as to Jacques Cœur's importation of Moorish armor, see Valet de Viriville, III, p. 267.

181. *Procès*, p. 439. Thus one of the witnesses testifies that on each outgoing voyage his galleys carried from 16,000 to 20,000 *ducats*. The defendant was accused of having minted silver bullion and reminted coin at Rhodes, marking the new money with a fleur-de-lis with which he had deceived the money-changers of Alexandria. Jean de Village says (in the recitals of his Pardon) that the new coin was stamped with a clover-leaf, the mark of a certain Rhodian silversmith. In passing, it may be noted that the money-changers of Egypt at this epoch were probably the most skilful precious-metal experts in the world, and were not accustomed to accept coin at its face value. Owing to the many changes in their weight and alloy, Charles VII's pieces, although reformed at this date, because of their past history would probably be subjected to especially careful tests.

182. See in the Appendix, No. IV, Letter of Jean Cœur to the authorities of Avignon, specially obtained for this work from the archives of that city.

185. For the amount of the annual allotment to the household, see Clément, pp. 312, 313, note, fixing it at 240,000 livres.

186. "If under all these obstacles . . . the merchants of different countries became so opulent as almost to rival the ancient nobility, it must be ascribed to the greatness of their commercial profits." Hallam, III, p. 337.

187. Authenticated copies of these two bulls were obtained from the archives of the Vatican in preparation for this work. Syllabi of their contents appear in the Appendix.

188. It appears that they produced at least the royal decree permitting impressment.

189. The lawyers consulted on the appeal give their opinion in favor of the jurisdiction of the ecclesiastical courts, at least, preliminarily, to determine the question of clericature. Bonamy, in a memorandum, cited by Clément, p. 274, note, points out, however, that the laws of the times remitted a *clerc marié*, though tonsured, to the judgment of the lay

courts, if, at the time of his arrest, he were engaged in lay affairs, such as merchandising, etc.

190. The item regarding this threat is from the *Mémoires* by Bonamy, 1745, cited by Clément, p. 272.

191. Decree of Louis XI permitting the appeal.

192. Thus William Bouillé, the doctor of theology to whom Charles VII intrusted the preliminaries of Jeanne d'Arc's rehabilitation, entitled his memorandum on the subject: *"For the exaltation of the King of France and of the House of France."* In its preamble the treatise refers to the "iniquitous judgment, scandalous and dishonoring for the royal crown. . . . How the royal throne would be soiled, if our adversaries should persuade posterity, that the King of France had received into his army a heretic, an invocatrice of the Devil." Lavisse, 4, II, p. 112.

193. Journal of Jean Dauvet, KK No. 328, *Archives Nationales.* Several extracts from it are annexed to Clément's work, in which it was first published, under the title: *Vente des biens de Jacques Cœur.*

194. *Diary of Samuel Pepys*, February 28, 1661, ". . . and there made sale of many old stores by the candle and good sport it was. . . ."

195. *Les Ecossais en France*, above cited, gives many curious instances of French spelling of British names at this period.

196. Clément, pp. 284–285.

197. Recited in Louis XI's decree permitting the appeal.

198. This letter is reported in Clément, pp. 294–295.

199. I am indebted for this item to Maître Dubois in his work herein frequently cited.

200. Guiraud, p. 112.

201. Jean Dauvet's *Journal.*

202. The quotation is from the recitals of Jean de Village's pardon.

203. Mézeray, *Hist. de la France*, 1646, II, p. 70, cited by Clément in his preface.

204. Dauphin's contract to purchase Monaco. Lavisse, 4, II, pp. 291–292.

205. See, among our illustrations, facsimile of the old parchment manuscript in Latin, of which this is the translation. The manuscript itself is found in the Collection

Dupuy, MS. 760, folio 12, Bibliothèque Nationale, Paris. It is cited by Valet de Viriville, *loc. cit.*, III, p. 298, note, and by several subsequent authors, all of whom, however, in so far as we can find, seem to have rested content with reporting it and stating that its effect was to proclaim Jacques Cœur's innocence. As we have seen, its true significance is far greater; it is the key to the mystery of Jacques Cœur's persecution.

206. Jacques Cœur's letter to the Duchess of Burgundy, dated March 10, 1450, is cited by G. Fresne de Beaucourt in *Le Procès de Jacques Cœur*, above referred to. It is also mentioned by Prutz, *Jacques Cœur von Bourges*, Berlin, 1911.

207. Lavisse, 4, II, pp. 269, 273.

208. Æneas Sylvius: "Sive vincitur Hungaria, sive coacta jungitur Turcis, neque Italia neque Germania tuta erit, neque satis Rhenus Gallos securos reddet." Æn. Sylv., p. 678, cited by Hallam, II, p. 134, note.

209. These two extracts are from *The Historie of George Castriot, surnamed Scanderbeg*, translated from the French by I. Z. Gentleman and published in London in 1596. The French work, printed long before that date, is for the most part a translation of an earlier Latin work by Marin Barletius, a priest of Scutari in Epirus, written at a time when "no man can denie these things being so fresh and late in memorie, and whereof it little wanteth, but that our fathers might with their eyes have been witnesses." Although we do not claim the credibility of documentary records for these extracts, they at least reflect the spirit of the times better than present-day versions of these matters.

210. Alfonso's letter to the Genoese is taken from Sigismondi's *Hist. des républiques Italiennes*, 6, p. 309.

211. Lavallée, *Hist. de la Turquie*, p. 259. Belgrade's cession to Hungary is reported by la Brocquière.

212. For the history of the papal naval expedition, our main dependence is Gugliemotti, *Storia della marina pontificia*, Florence, 1871, II, pp. 266–277.

213. Dambreville, *Hist. des Ordres de Chevalerie*, pp. 191–192.

214. We depend upon Maître Dubois for this item. In his address above cited he reports that the registers of criminal causes before the Court of Parliament, at its session Febru-

ary 14, 1470, record the foregoing statement as having been
made in the pleadings of certain Genoese merchants who
had been reproached with being the enemies of French commerce.

215.　G. Fresne de Beaucourt, *Procès de Jacques Cœur.*
216.　Guiraud, p. 75.
217.　Clément, pp. 341–342.
218.　Guiraud, *Pièces justicatives*, No. II, 5.

APPENDIX

APPENDIX

I

CAMPO FREGOSO'S LETTERS

THE following six letters from Janus Campo Fregoso to Jacques Cœur have been copied from the counterparts of the originals in the archives of the state of Genoa. I am enabled to reproduce the tenor of these documents through the courtesy of Professor Edouard Chichizola of the *Civica Biblioteca Berio*, Genoa. The letter, dated September 25, 1447, being No. 4 in our list, is cited in Clément's *Jacques Cœur et Charles VII*, Paris, 1866, p. 135. In so far as I can ascertain, the other letters are here published for the first time.

Long and minute searches made by Professor Chichizola in these archives have failed to disclose any of Jacques Cœur's letters to the Doge or any original records of Genoa's part in Calixtus III's naval expedition in which the subject of our memoir met his death.

LETTER No. 1

Genova, Archivio di Stato. *Litterarum Communis Januae*, vol. 13, 1789. Littera No. 1038.

Magnifico et preclaro viro amico carissimo Domino Jacobo Cordi regio Argentario.

Audivimus Magnifice et preclare vir amice noster carissime; Alverium parisium iuvenem vestrum et qui ille rettullit plane intelleximus omnia. Itaque cras mane mittemus unum ex nostris Terdonem; existimantes quod in ea urbe invenire possit Magnificentiam vestram; cui si forsitan non obviabit Terdone; transibit usque Placentiam; ut sic vel Placentie vel in via occurrat Vestre Magnificentie; in cuius amplitudinem nos et nostra deferimus ex animo parato.

Data XXVIII Augusti (1447).

JANUS, DUX.

LETTER No. 2

Genova, Archivio de Stato. *Litterarum Communis Januae,*
vol. 13, 1789. Littera No. 1063.

Magnifico et ordinatissimo viro Domino Jacobo Cordi regio
consiliario et argentario, amico nostro carissimo.

Jocunda et gratissima fuerunt nobis magnifice et ornatissime vir amice noster carissime; consilia vestra et quicquid
vir egregius Franciscus Cavallus nobis vestro nomine rettullit libenter audivimus. Cum itaque eum ad nos remittamus;
magnificam amicitiam vestram rogamus ut in iis que referet
nomine nostro; habeat sibi indubitatam fidem velut nobis
paratis omni tempore in amplitudine et commoda vestra.

Data V Septembris (1447). JANUS, DUX.

LETTER No. 3

Genova, Archivio de Stato. *Litterarum Communis Januae,*
vol. 13, 1789. Littera No. 1064.

Eidem Domino Argentario.

Cum audissemus magnifice et ornatissime vir amice carissime; egregium virum Franciscum Cavallum ad nos rever-
sum; et eaque rettulit plane intelleximus placuerunt maxime
nobis consilia vestra. Ex quo statumus eum remittere ad
magnificentiam vestram cum plena rerum omnium instruc-
tione.

Superest autem amicitiam vestram rogare; ut ei salvum
conductum mittat ac provideat ut possit tutus accedere ac
redire.

In omnem autem vestram amplitudinem sumus semper
cupide parata.

Data V Septembris (1447). JANUS, DUX.

LETTER No. 4

Genova, Archivio di Stato. *Litterarum Communis Januae,*
vol. 13, 1789. Littera No. 585.

Magnifico et preclaro viro Jacobi Cordi regio argentario
amico nostro singularissimo.

Grate jucundeque fuerunt nobis magnifice et preclare

amice noster singularissime littere vestre hisce diebus nobis
reddite que ut verum fateamur summam in nos benevolen-
tiam ac studium vestrum omni ex parte redolent; ut profecto
vero esse experiamur ex que de virtutibus vestris constanti
omnium ore predicantur, habemus autem vobis ingentes
gratias quod de universo illius nobilissimi regni statu de
reditu dominorum legatorum ex Anglia ac plerisque eiusmodi
nobis ita prescripsistis ut non fuerit opus nobis harum co-
gnitionem aliunde desiderare.

Quod autem nos adhortatur prudentia vestra circum-
spicere quantum hoc tempore possimus amplitudini regie
maiestatis inservire; etiam cum dignitate et ingenti com-
modo nostro, nos quidem hec monita vestra in optimam
partem accipimus; utque non dubitamus a vero amore et
animi sinceritate proficisci.

Quo circa dicemus fuisse nobis semper inter vota precipua,
nobis occasionem dari, qua possemus illi preclarissimo regi
gratificari proque eius dignitate et amplitudine laborare.
Quam quidem cupititatem nostram ac studium, si quando se
occasio prebuit, re ipsa atque opere declaravimus. Neque
nunc quod alia nobis mens est. Verum si magnificentia vestra
et rei naturam et temporum condictiones consideret, intelliget
hec et eiusmodi litteris confici non solere. Ardua enim et
magna quibus semper fore difficultas admixta est; aliter
quam litteris transigi solent, hoc unum in summa dicimus,
nominem ut arbitramur inveniri posse quem vera animi
sinceritate ac studio ad regiam maiestatem, nobis preferen-
dum putemus, hec hactenus. Quod autem de immunitate
loricarum vestrarum promissa vobis sunt curabimus ut
omnino fiant, quicquid sine difficultate fieri non soleant.

Quod de reliquum est, rogamus ut sibi amicitia vestra
persuadeat hunc statum et nostra omnia sua esse, nosque
vehementer cupere pro vestra dignitate et commodis laborare.
Id si tentabitis experiemini nos a vobis in benevolentia et
officio non superari. Remque nobis gratissimam efficetis, si
sepe litteras et quidem prolixas ad nos dederitis.

Data XXV Septembris (1447).   Janus, Dux.

Letter No. 5

Genova, Archivio di Stato. *Litterarum Communis Januae*, vol. 14, 1790. Littera No. 1468.

Magnifico ac claro militi Domino Jacobo Cordis servantissimo [?] ac excellentissimo Domini regis Franchorum argentario et legato amico nostro carissimo.

Magnifice miles amice noster carissime, et si non multum expediret mittimus vobis salvum conductum his annexum quem M. V. a nobis postularit. Ceteris partibus litterarum vestrarum respondere non curamus quam quidem presentes speramus multa simul libere amiceque coloqui posse, parati in omnibus semper vobis gratis.

Datum die X Augusti (1448). JANUS.

Letter No. 6

Genova, Archivio di Stato. *Litterarum Communis Januae*, vol. 14, 1790. Littera No. 1468.

Magnifico ac claro militi Domino Jacobo Cordi regio argentario amico nostro carissimo et consiliario.

Magnifice et 'clare miles amice noster carissime, recursus ad nos egregius civis noster Franciscus Cavalus pleraque renuntiavit nobis vestri partis que superveniente nobis quadem egritudine non bene decernere intelligereque potuimus. Quare ipse Franciscus nonnulla superinde vobis respondebit, quibus contentamur fidem adhiberi parati ex animo in omnia Magnificentie Vestre grata semper.

Datum Janue die XXV Septembris, 1448. JANUS, D.

II

PAPAL BULLS IN FAVOR OF JACQUES CŒUR AND HIS SONS

IN preparation for this work authenticated copies of eight bulls of Popes Eugenius IV and Nicholas V in favor of Jacques Cœur and his two eldest sons, Jean and Henri Cœur, have been obtained from the archives of the Vatican through the kindly courtesy of Monseigneur Angelo Mercati, *Prefetto dell' Archivio Vaticano*. On completing this work these documents have been presented to the Bibliothèque Municipale of Bourges, and brief syllabi of their contents are given

below for the sake of future reference to them. Bull No. 1
has been cited by Clément in his work above referred to
and has been reported in full in H. Prutz's *Jacques Cœur
von Bourges*, Berlin, 1911. In so far as I can learn, the other
pontifical instruments are herein referred to for the first
time.

No. 1

Eugenius papa IV ad supplicationem Caroli VII Francorum regis et canonicorum ecclesiae Bituricen., mag. Johanni
Cordis, decano ecclesiae Pictaven., dispensationem concedit
super defectu aetatis, si de persona sua dictae ecclesiae Bituricen. per pontificem provideri contigerit. An. 1446 VI
kal. septembris. Reg. Vatic. Eugenii IV vol. 378 fol. 277.

No. 2

Johanni Cordis, electo Bituricen. Eugenius papa IV concedit quod ecclesias et coemeteria suarum civitatis et diocesis
per effusionem sanguinis, etc., violata, per idoneum sacer-
dotem reconciliare valeat. An. 1446 XVII kal. octobris
Reg. Vatic. Eug. IV vol. 378 fol. 277.

No. 3

Eidem Johanni Cordis electo Bituricen. con editur, ut
una cum ecclesia Bituricen. retinere valeat de anatum ec-
clesie Pictaven. donec et quousque cessaverit pensio 600
scutorum assignata super fructibus mensae archiepiscopalis
Bituricen. An. 1446 IV nonas septemb. Reg. Vatic. Eug.
IV vol. 378 fol. 278.

No. 4

Henrico Cordis clerico bituricen., nobilis viri Jacobi Cordis, Caroli Francorum regis consiliarii, argentarii et oratoris
nato, conceduntur canonicatus et praebenda Narbonensis et
Lodovensis ecclesiarum, resignatione Stephani electi Aga-
then. vacantes. An. 1448 XIV kal. augusti. Reg. Vatic.
Nicolai V vol. 407 fol. 213.

No. 5

Nicolaus papa V pro parte abbatis et conventus mona-
sterii de Savignano O. S. B. Lugdunen. dioecesis, approbat
et confirmat translationem et concessionem per eosdem et

conventum factas, certorum territoriorum et mineriarum cuprisitarum [sic] in paroecia seu mandamento de Chissiaco dictae dioec. de Charimiyne [sic] et Genenrey ac de Lavernie nuncupatis, una cum omnibus suis pertinentiis, in nob. virum Jacobum Cordis, consiliarium et argentarium Caroli VII Francorum regis, et certos mercatores lugdunenses. An. 1448 kal. augusti. Reg. Vatᶜ. Nicolai V vol. 387 fol. 120.

No. 6

Nobili viro Jacobo Cordis, Caroli VII Francorum regis consiliario et argentario, confirmatur a Nicolao V indultum alias per Eugenium IV ei concessum, ut quaecumque naves per mare, merces et quorumcumque mercimoniorum genera, etiam cum infidelibus, cuiuscumque conditionis forent, salvis a iure prohibitis, traducere seu traduci facere, et cum infidelibus eisdem per se vel alios loqui, mercatari et conversari posset, etc. An. 1449 VIII kal. octobris. Reg. Vatic. Nicolai V vol. 410 fol. 209.

No. 7

Mag. Henrico Cordis clerico bituricen., licent. in legibus et notario papae, conceditur confirmatio decanatus ecclesiae Bituricensis. An. 1450 V idus iulii. Reg. Vatic. Nicolai V vol. 416 fol. 50.

No. 8

Eidem Henrico Cordis conceditur decanatus ecclesiae Lemovicen., qui inibi dignitas maior post pontificalem existit, et quem quondam Johannes Richonis dum viveret obtinebat. An. 1450 V idus iulii. Reg. Vatic. Nicolai V vol. 416 fol. 254.

III

Letter of Charles VII to the Council and Deputies of Barcelona, 17 October, 1451

The following letter of Charles VII to the municipal authorities of Barcelona, seeking to recover certain ships and merchandise of Jacques Cœur's in that port, has been called to my attention by Monsieur Pierre Virenque, Sous-Bibliothécaire of the Bibliothèque Municipale of Montpellier.

notre dits seigneur ordonner nous employer, pour la part de son dit argentier, ou dit procès, avons baillé procuracion, ou non de moy Arcevesque de Bourges, qui suis son filz, au dessus dits seigneurs Thierri et Jobert, pour eulx employer en ceste matière. Si vous prions, tant que plus povons, que, en revérance de Dieu et de justice, il vous plaise bailler ou faire bailler ausdits Thierri et Jobert vidimus auctentique des lettres des dessus dits et autres que pourroient servir à ceste matière et dont ilz vous pourront parler. En nos faisant savoir, se chose vous plaist, que faire puissons pour l'acomplir de tout notre povoir.

Au plaisir de Dieu, lequel, très chers et especialaux seigneurs et amis, vous donne très bonne vie.

Escript à Bourges, le XVII jour de juillet.

Les tous votre l'Arcevesque de Bourges et l'Evesque d'Agde.

[*Au dos*]: A noz très chiers et especiaulx seigneurs et amis, les Sindicz et autres conseillers de la ville et cité d'Avignon.

[Copié conformé sur l'original du 17 juillet, 1453, conservé aux Archives Municipales d'Avignon, cote AA, 37.]

INDEX

INDEX

12/12/55